Extending the Macintosh® Toolbox

Extending the Macintosh® Toolbox
Programming Menus, Windows, Dialogs, and More

John C. May

Judy B. Whittle

Addison-Wesley Publishing Company, Inc.
Reading, Massachusetts • Menlo Park, California • New York
Don Mills, Ontario • Wokingham, England • Amsterdam
Bonn • Sydney • Singapore • Tokyo • Madrid • San Juan
Paris • Seoul • Milan • Mexico City • Taipei

Many of the designations used by manufacturers and sellers to distinguish their products are claimed as trademarks. Where those designations appear in this book and Addison-Wesley was aware of a trademark claim, the designations have been printed in initial capital letters.

```
Library of Congress Cataloging-in-Publication Data

May, John C.
   Extending the Macintosh toolbox : programming menus,
 windows, dialogs and more / John C. May, Judy B. Whittle.
      p.  cm. -- (Macintosh inside out)
   Includes bibliographical references and index.
   ISBN 0-201-57722-4
   1. Macintosh (Computer)--Programming.  2. Macintosh Toolbox
 (Computer programs)  I. Whittle, Judy B.  II. Title. III. Series.
 QA76.8.M3M3765  1991                                    91-14461
 005.265--dc20                                               CIP
```

Copyright © 1991 by John C. May and Judy B. Whittle

All rights reserved. No part of this publication may be reproduced, stored in a retrieval system, or transmitted, in any form or by any means, electronic, mechanical, photocopying, recording, or otherwise, without the prior written permission of the publisher. Printed in the United States of America. Published simultaneously in Canada.

The authors and publishers have taken care in preparation of this book, but make no express or implied warranty of any kind and assume no responsibility for errors or omissions. No liability is assumed for incidental or consequential damages in connection with or arising out of the use of the information or programs contained herein.

Sponsoring Editor: Carole McClendon
Project Editor: Elizabeth Rogalin
Cover design: Ronn Campisi
Set in 10.5-point Palatino by Don Huntington

1 2 3 4 5 6 7 8 9 -MW- 9594939291
First printing, August 1991

This book is dedicated to Pat Whittle.

Contents

Foreword by Scott Knaster xvii

Preface xix

Acknowledgments xxi

1. **Introduction** 1
    Is This Book for You? 1
    How the Book Is Organized 1
    Conventions Used 2
      Data Are or Data Is? 2
      Punctuation with Code 2
      Capital Letters in Source Code 2
      Monospace Font for Code 3
    Using the Routines in This Book 3

2. **Programming Language** 5
    Programming Language Used in This Book 5
    C Programming Standards 5
      Case (Switch) Statements 5
      Brace Rule 1 (separate lines) 6
      Brace Rule 2 (if and else) 7
      Parentheses Rule 1 (statements) 8
      Parentheses Rule 2 (functions) 8

Arithmetic Operators Rule 9
Commas Rule 9
Semicolon Rule 10
Capitalization Rule 1 (functions) 10
Capitalization Rule 2 (variables) 10
Useful Macros 11
Handling Errors 12
The Way Apple Prefers You to Program 12

3. Initializing the Toolbox 15

Setting Up Your Program with Init ToolBox.c 15
Summary 19

4. Menus 21

Overview of Menus 21
Building Menus 21
  InitMenu.c 22
The Apple Menu 23
  DoAppleMenu.c 23
Routines Involving Menu Items 24
  DablMenuItem.c 24
  EablMenuItem.c 25
  DAllMenuItems.c 25
  EAllMenuItems.c 26
  MarkMenuItem.c 27
Testing the Keyboard 28
  CommandIsDown.c 29
  CapsLockIsDown.c 30
  ControlIsDown.c 31
  OptionIsDown.c 31
  ShiftIsDown.c 32
Using an 'MBAR' Resource 32
  DrawMBar.c 33
A Simple Menu Example 34
  MenuExample.c 34
  MenuExample.R 35
Summary 36
Recommended Reading 36

5. **Cursors** 37
   Overview of Cursors 37
   Using Black-and-White and Color Cursors 37
   FetchCursor.c 38
   A Simple Cursor Example 41
   CursorExample.c 41
   CursorExample.R 43
   Summary 48
   Recommended Reading 48

6. **Windows and Dialogs** 49
   Overview of Windows and Dialogs 49
   Dialog Records 50
   Creating Dialogs 51
   OpenDialog.c 51
   Dialog Positioning 52
   CenterDialog.c 52
   Window Positioning 54
   CenterWindow.c 54
   Window Stacking 56
   StackWindow.c 56
   Writing Your Own Modal Dialog Routine 58
   MyModalDialog.c 59
   Changing the Default Dialog Font 66
   SetDFont.c 66
   Creating a General-Purpose About Dialog Routine 67
   AboutDialog.c 68
   The About Example 70
   AboutExample.c 70
   AboutExample.R 72
   Creating a General-Purpose Copyright Routine 73
   CopyrightDialog.c 73
   Summary 76
   Recommended Reading 76

7. **Alerts** 77

   Overview of Alerts 77
   A General-Purpose Alert Routine 78
   NoteAlert.c 78
   CautionAlert.c 79
   StopAlert.c 80
   A Standard Confirmation Alert Routine 81
   Confirmation.c 81
   The Alert Example 83
   AlertExample.c 83
   AlertExample.R 85
   Summary 86
   Recommended Reading 86

8. **Resources** 87

   Overview of Resources 87
   Resource Compilers 92
   Resource Editors 92
   Special-Purpose Editors and Builders 93
   Resource Decompiler 93
   RMaker Program Syntax 93
   RadioButton.R 95
   Resource File Merging and Overwriting 98
   Summary 99
   Recommended Reading 99

9. **Buttons** 101

   Overview of Buttons 101
   Routine to Draw the Outline of a Default Button 101
   FrmDefItem.c 102
   A Simple Button Example 105
   ButtonExample.c 106
   ButtonExample.R 107
   Summary 108
   Recommended Reading 108

10. Check Boxes   109

   Overview of Check Boxes   109
   Getting and Setting the Check Box State   109
      PutCheckBox.c   110
      GetCheckBox.c   111
   Toggling the Check Box State   112
      ToggleCheckBox.c   112
   A Simple Check Box Example   113
      CheckBoxExample.c   113
      CheckBoxExample.R   115
   Summary   117

11. Radio Buttons   119

   Overview of Radio Buttons   119
   Setting the Radio Button State   119
      GetRadioButton.c   120
      PutRadioButton.c   121
   Grouping Radio Buttons   123
      PushRadioButton.c   123
   A Simple Radio Button Example   125
      RadioButtonExample.c   125
      RadioButtonExample.R   126
   Summary   128

12. Icons   129

   Overview of Icons   129
   Using Icons as Control Buttons   130
      GetButtonIcon.c   130
      DoButtonIcon.c   133
      DispButtonIcon.c   136
   Using Icons as Toggle Switches   136
      GetToggleIcon.c   137
      DoToggleIcon.c   138
      DispToggleIcon.c   140
      IconOff.c   141
      IconOn.c   142
   A Simple Icon Example   143
      IconExample.c   143
      IconExample.R   145
   Summary   147

13. **Pictures** 149

   Overview of Pictures 149
   Drawing a Picture 149
   DrawPict.c 150
   A Simple Picture Example 151
   PictExample.c 151
   PictExample.R 154
   Summary 161
   Recommended Reading 161

14. **Static Text** 163

   Overview of Static Text 163
   Active and Inactive Static Text 163
   ActiveStatic.c 163
   InactiveStatic.c 164
   A Simple Static Text Example 165
   StaticTextExample.c 166
   StaticTextExample.R 167
   Summary 168
   Recommended Reading 168

15. **Edit Text** 169

   Overview of Edit Text 169
   Active Edit Text Fields 170
   GetActiveEditText.c 170
   SetActiveEditText.c 171
   Input and Output Routines for Integers 173
   InputShort.c 174
   InputLong.c 178
   InputHexShort.c 179
   InputHexLong.c 181
   OutputShort.c 183
   OutputLong.c 186
   OutputHexShort.c 187
   OutputHexLong.c 188
   Input and Output Routines for Floating-Point Numbers 190

  InputFloat.c 192
  OutputFloat.c 199
 Get and Put Routines for Edit Text 206
  GetEditShort.c 207
  PutEditShort.c 208
  GetEditLong.c 210
  PutEditLong.c 210
  GetEditFloat.c 211
  PutEditFloat.c 212
 Displaying Strings 213
  GetEditString.c 213
  PutEditString.c 214
 Text Edit Routines 215
  TECopy.c 216
  TECut.c 218
  TEPaste.c 218
  TESelectAll.c 219
 Lowercase, Uppercase, Capitalize, and Change Case 220
  TELower.c 220
  TEUpper.c 221
  TECapitalize.c 222
  TEChgCase.c 223
 A Simple Edit Text Example 224
  EditTextExample.c 224
  EditTextExample.R 226
 Summary 228
 Recommended Reading 229

16. Lines 231

 Overview of Lines 231
 Drawing Dotted and Solid Lines 231
  DrawDottedLine.c 231
  DrawLine.c 233
 A Simple Line Example 235
  LineExample.c 235
  LineExample.R 238
 Summary 242

17. **Rectangles** 243

    Overview of Rectangles 243
    Drawing Rectangles in Various Styles 243
      PlainFrame.c 244
      ThickFrame.c 246
      DoubleFrame.c 247
      ShadowFrame.c 248
    A Simple Rectangle Example 249
      RectExample.c 249
      RectExample.R 251
    Summary 253
    Recommended Reading 253

18. **Scrolling Lists** 255

    Overview of Scrolling Lists 255
    Drawing a Scrolling List 257
      DrawScrollList.c 257
    Handling the Scrolling List 259
      DoScrollList.c 260
    Updating a Scrolling List 261
      UpScrollList.c 261
    Setting the Cells of the Scrolling List 262
      AddCell.c 262
      SetCell.c 263
    Getting the Cells of the Scrolling List 264
      GetCell.c 264
      GetListString.c 265
    Selecting and Unselecting Cells in a Scrolling List 266
      SelectCell.c 266
      UnselectCell.c 267
    Setting the Cells of the Scrolling List 267
      GetStringList.c 268
    A Simple Scrolling List Example 270
      ScrollingListExample.c 270
      ScrollingListExample.R 272
    Summary 273
    Recommended Reading 273

19. **Pop-up Menus** 275
   Overview of Pop-up Menus 275
   Drawing a Pop-up Menu 275
   DrawPopUp.c 276
   Handling a Pop-up Menu 280
   DoPopUp.c 280
   Updating a Pop-up Menu 286
   UpPopUp.c 286
   A Simple Pop-up Menu Example 289
   PopUpExample.c 289
   PopUpExample.R 290
   Summary 292

20. **Putting It All Together** 293
   A Comprehensive Example 293
   Kit and Caboodle.c 293
   Kit and Caboodle.R 297

   Appendix A   Glossary 305

   Appendix B   Modules Developed in This Book 309

   Bibliography 313

   Index 317

Foreword by Scott Knaster

When any new computer system appears, its designers do their best to figure out how the world will receive and use their creation. Sometimes they get it right, and sometimes they get surprised. When the original Macintosh was being designed, lots of folks thought that its main advantage for application programmers was that they could safely ignore the human interface, since it was being done for them.

Of course, that isn't exactly what happened. Because the Macintosh Toolbox provided unprecedented power and flexibility to the user interface, application programmers were especially careful in their interface work. Building great interfaces, it turned out, became more important than ever, but it still required lots of hard work.

Although the Toolbox does much of the tough work for interface programming, it's up to application programmers to put it all together. This task includes designing the interface from the standard elements provided, figuring out how to use everything in the right situations, and knowing when to tweak the standard way of doing things just a little.

Inside Macintosh in its many beloved volumes has instructed programmers for years on the right incantations to use to summon up the nifty stuff that's in the Macintosh ROM and system, but it's not the job of *Inside Macintosh* to discuss user interface strategy and tactics in any great detail. This book will help you with that task.

As the Macintosh has matured over the years, the programming community has figured out sensible ways of using the user interface tools provided by Apple's system programmers. In this book, John May and Judy Whittle present a treasure chest of user interface programming code chunks and strategies for you to use.

This is not a book of theory or lectures. Instead, it's extremely practical, loaded with real-live working examples that you can use to make your own programs come to life. In the text, the authors explain just what's going on, so you can learn from what they've done in case what you'd really like to do is just a little bit different from what they've presented here.

The Macintosh Toolbox is a great place to begin writing any application. Now, with this book, you can jumpstart your programming with the great techniques and examples provided by John and Judy.

Scott Knaster
Macintosh Inside Out Series Editor

Preface

This book is the brainchild of John May and Pat Whittle. John became an enthusiastic Macintosh programmer in 1986 after years of developing programs for super computers through work stations. When he discovered that the Macintosh Toolbox presented a major stumbling block in designing software for the Macintosh, John began developing routines in accordance with Apple's Human Interface Guidelines that would assist programmers in overcoming the Toolbox obstacle. He approached Pat, a writer with many technical books and articles under his belt, and the two came up with a unique idea: a book full of ready-to-use, compiled, and tested routines that any programmer could add to an application—routines that would take over the task of providing the desktop interfaces at the appropriate time and in the appropriate format.

Pat died unexpectedly in January 1991, after he was well into the project. It was his fervent wish that the book be completed, so his wife Judy picked up where he left off and, with unending help from John and Elizabeth Rogalin of Addison-Wesley, fulfilled the wish. With appreciation for all of Pat's contributions, we dedicate this book to his memory.

We have tried where possible and applicable to include color attributes for the routines, keeping in mind that the Toolbox has undergone enormous changes with the advent of color machines. It is a certainty that the Toolbox will experience even more changes in the next few years. We're so enthusiastic about that we already have another book bursting its restraints on the drawing board.

John C. May
Judy B. Whittle
Danville, California
June 1991

Acknowledgments

We'd like to thank the following people for helping us with this book:

Mary and **Shawn May** and **Pat (Jr.)** and **Paul Whittle** for their encouragement, support and patience, without which we might have fallen by the wayside.

Stacey Reineccius and **Scott Knaster** for their detailed technical review of the manuscript and their excellent suggestions.

Carole McClendon and **Rachel Guichard**, the Addison-Wesley folks in Berkeley who got the book going and encouraged us throughout the project.

Lori Renn, copy editor supreme, who fashioned a silk purse out of a sow's ear and was nice to us in the process.

Mary Cavaliere, Diane Freed and the other Addison-Wesley production staff who kept the project on schedule.

Most of all, huge thanks to **Elizabeth Grose Rogalin**, Project Editor, without whose help, understanding, cajoling, encouragement, and a little nagging this book would not have been possible. She took on the project at a difficult time, gave us every kind of support we needed to get the job done, and brought joy to the effort. It's been a great experience!

1 ▶ Introduction

This book is a compendium of instructions and advice on how to construct graphic interfaces for the Macintosh using a combination of Toolbox routines, our original routines, and THINK C programming. With the techniques in this book, you can learn faster, easier ways to develop applications distinguished by professional quality and pleasing appearance, and you can concentrate on development without the distractions of coping with the technicalities of the Macintosh desktop interface.

▶ Is This Book for You?

If you are interested in software development for the Macintosh, this book is for you. This is not a primer, so you should be familiar with Apple's Human Interface Guidelines and have some programming experience with Symantec's THINK C. If you have not programmed in C, you should at least understand data structures, variables, and subroutines. Most of all, you need to understand the concept of resources as they are used in the Macintosh environment.

▶ How the Book Is Organized

We've organized this book into twenty chapters, most of which contain routines or functions that can be grouped around a central user interface theme: menus, dialogs, cursors, and so on. In Chapter 2, you'll find a summary of C programming standards, complete with code examples.

Chapter 3 introduces you to the Toolbox and the routine InitToolBox.c, which you must call for all of our other routines.

The remaining chapters cover more than one hundred routines and examples. First, we present an overview of the chapter's theme. Then, at the beginning of each routine, comes a brief description of its purpose, followed by the numbered lines of code. After the code listing, we review in detail exactly what happens in each line or section of the routine. At the end of most chapters is a recommended reading list of briefs, articles, and books that deal specifically with the subject of that chapter's routines.

▶ Conventions Used

Any book, whether a technical treatise or the great American novel, needs to be consistent. The following paragraphs explain the use of certain expressions, punctuation, and type faces.

▶ Data Are or Data Is?

What about data are or data is? We've standardized on regarding data as a collective noun in the singular; hence, data is.

▶ Punctuation with Code

Punctuation can get tricky when code is mixed with the straight text. If, for instance, a period at the end of a sentence could be misinterpreted as a code period, we leave it out. The same goes for colons and semicolons, which are especially tricky because a semicolon marks the end of a statement in the C programming language.

▶ Capital Letters in Source Code

A popular convention with C programmers that we have also adopted is to start the first word of a variable's name with a lowercase letter but to capitalize the first letter of each subsequent word, as in *screenRect*. (Also, the convention in this series is to italicize variables in the text.) Functions are treated differently, with an initial capital letter for each word in the function's name, as in CenterDialog.

▶ **Monospace Font for Code**

Code listings appear in Courier font, which is probably the most widely used of the monospace (or sometimes called "typewriter") fonts. Each character in Courier is of the same width, or uniformly spaced, so the characters line up neatly by column. In contrast, most fonts used in book, magazine, and newspaper text are proportionally spaced: that is, a *w* takes up more room than an *i*. Portions of code mentioned in the text are not set in Courier because the mix of type styles fragments the text and can confuse the eye.

▶ **Using the Routines in This Book**

The essence of this book is the routines, more properly called functions in C. You can keyboard the routines or load their files from the disk available by returning the coupon in the back of the book. Doing either is quite possible with little or no knowledge of programming; but the better you understand the steps, the easier it will be to get the quality you want in your application and to adapt and customize it. For this reason, we explain every line or section of the routine FrmDefItem.c in Chapter 9. (This routine puts a double frame around the default button in a dialog box.)

You'll find that certain functions, such as InitToolBox and FrmDefItem, crop up throughout the routines. In fact, InitToolBox is essential as the first function in every program in this book. Therefore, we devote Chapter 3 to InitToolBox, and we give detailed descriptions of every statement.

To include our routines in your own applications, you can keyboard them into your Include statements in a THINK C Project file. Or you can click on the Add item in the Project menu and then select the names of the routines you want from the C module file.

If you send the coupon to obtain the floppy disk, you will have everything you need to run the routines immediately. The disk includes all of the C routines, which are in a folder. It also includes all examples along with their resource files, source code, project files, RMaker-compiled resource files and the applications themselves.

2 ▶ Programming Language

▶ Programming Language Used in This Book

Routines in this book are written in THINK C. For readers who have not had much experience with C, we devote this chapter to a discussion of C programming standards, complete with examples of the hierarchical levels of the code. Although C is a popular language (developed in the UNIX environment), it is terse, and C programmers must follow prescribed conventions.

▶ C Programming Standards

One C convention is that if you can execute an if-test in one line, you don't need to enclose it within a pair of curly braces. This can be confusing, so it's a good idea always to use the braces. In the following paragraphs, you'll find other examples of C programming conventions.

▶ Case (Switch) Statements

"Case" is the name given to a type of statement that chooses one condition from a list of several. Imagine your mouth is watering for a sweet, crisp, fragrant apple. You go to the produce section of a market. You know what varieties please your palate most, but they may not all be available. Going through your mind is a case-statement that might amount to: "Get golden Delicious, my favorite. In case there are no golden Delicious, get red Delicious. In case they're out of red Delicious, get Winesap." You might add a default statement: "If I can't get any of my favorites, I'll grumble but take whatever variety they have."

The following shows a typical case-statement written in C.

```
switch (theVar)
{
  case (1):

    do stuff here

    break;

  case (2):

    do more stuff here

    break;

  default

    do default stuff here

    break;
}
```

In this example, note the "break" at the end of each "case." The break is a useful precaution. Say you have two cases, as shown. Later you add a third case, after the second. If it were not for the break, case 2 would run into case 3 and mess up your program.

▶ Brace Rule 1 (separate lines)

This is a convention we use to avoid misunderstandings and oversights. In the example of a for-loop, we prefer to put the brace on a separate line. C will let you keep the brace on the same line, but it can be confusing visually.

One good thing about indenting code is that it sets events apart and makes the code more comprehensible. The bad thing about indenting code is that a programmer tends to look at a particular level of indention and assume that every operation on that level is going on simultaneously, which is not necessarily true. C knows nothing about indenting; C uses braces, not indentions, to determine what actions will take place. That is one reason for making the braces stand out, as shown in the following example.

This:

```
for (i = 1; i <= 10; i++)
{
   do stuff here
}
```

Not This:

```
for (i = 1; i <= 10; i++){
   do stuff here
}
```

▶ Brace Rule 2 (if and else)

You need to follow this rule closely. If you don't, you can easily make mistakes that can be disastrous to your program. C allows you to do an if-statement with an else-statement without braces—if there is only one line of code after the if-statement and only one line of code after the else-statement. If you do not use braces (braces are shown in the first example), you stand a good chance of making the kind of mistake that you see under "Styles."

This:

```
if (i < 0)
{
   do one line
}
else
{
   do another line
}
```

Not This:

```
if (i < 0)
   do one line
else
   do another line
```

Styles:

```
if (a = b)       OK (bad form)
  c = d;
if (a = b);      Wrong (error)
  c = d;
```

You must not put a semicolon after "if (a = b)" in the preceding example. It is remarkably easy to make that mistake because in C almost every line of code has a semicolon after it. The statement here should say, "If *a* equals *b*, then *c* equals *d*." Instead, the "wrong" example says, "If *a* equals *b*, then do nothing and always set *c* equal to *d*." The best way to avoid this type of error is to use braces, shown below as the "best" style.

```
if (a = b)   Best
{
  c = d;
}
```

In this case, if you inadvertently put a semicolon after the "if (a = b)" expression, the brace on the following line will automatically flag the error.

▶ Parentheses Rule 1 (statements)

Inserting a space in front of the left parenthesis in the following statement separates that statement from a function that is not built into C.

This:

```
for (i = 1; i <= 10; i++)
```

Not This:

```
for(i = 1; i <= 10; i++)
```

▶ Parentheses Rule 2 (functions)

Here you do not insert a space in front of the left parenthesis. No space indicates that this is a function you have written that will be called and executed from your program.

This:

```
MyFunction(variable)
```

Not This:

```
MyFunction (variable)
```

▶ Arithmetic Operators Rule

The nasty statement below says: "*a* is equal to *i* plus *j* plus 1, times the value pointed to by *k*. After that assignment to *j*, increment *i* by 1." The only way to comprehend this statement is with the spaces around the operators. For example, two plus signs together (++) indicate a single variable operator, and one plus sign (+) signifies addition, requiring two variables. A star or asterisk (*) can mean multiplication, but it can also mean "object pointed to by." To differentiate, you put spaces before and after the binary operators that require two arguments. If they are not binary operators, you put no spaces around them. The spaces do not change the order of operation; single operations will be performed first, and binary operations will be performed second.

This:

```
a = i++ + ++j * *k;
```

Not This:

```
a=i+++++j**k; (Huh?)
```

▶ Commas Rule

This rule is mainly for esthetics, but it helps for clarity as well. A space after every comma inside a function call makes it clear that you are passing in discrete variables, in this case three variables. That fact is not as readily comprehensible in the second example.

This:

```
MyFunction(theVar1, theVar2, theVar3)
```

Not This:

```
MyFunction(theVar1,theVar2,theVar3)
```

▶ **Semicolon Rule**

The convention here is to put a space after every semicolon in the for-loop. This helps prevent the accidental omission of a variable. If you forget to insert one of the required variables, the for-loop may loop forever.

This:

```
for (i = 1; i <= 10; i++)
```

Not This:

```
for (i = 1;i <= 10;i++)
```

▶ **Capitalization Rule 1 (functions)**

In the name of a function, subroutine, or routine, you capitalize the first letter of each significant word within the function name (including the first). That helps you recognize it as a function and not as a variable.

This:

```
MyFunction(theVar)
```

Not This:

```
myFunction(theVar)
```

Not This:

```
myfunction(theVar)
```

Not This:

```
MYFUNCTION(theVar)
```

The last three examples are not written in valid code.

▶ **Capitalization Rule 2 (variables)**

Begin the first word of a variable's name with a lowercase letter, but capitalize the first letter of each significant word that follows. This convention helps you distinguish a variable from a function.

This:

```
short    eventRecord;
```

Not This:

```
short    EventRecord;
```

▶ Useful Macros

Many routines in this book include macros to save time and space. Following the list of macros, you'll find an explanation of how each is used. Note that each macro begins with a "#define" statement. A macro always appears in the declarations section at the beginning of a routine.

Listing 2-1. Nine useful macros

```
1:  #define SetRGBColor(rgb,r,g,b) {(rgb)->red = (r);(rgb)->green =
              (g); (rgb)->blue = (b);}
2:  #define SetRect(rect,l,t,r,b) {(rect)->top = (t);(rect)->left =
              (l); (rect)->bottom = (b); (rect)->right = (r);}
3:  #define SetPt(Pt,hor,vert)  {(Pt)->h = (hor); (Pt)->v = (vert);}
4:  #define abs(a)     ((a)<0?-(a):(a))     /*Absolute macro function */
5:  #define min(a,b)   ((a)<(b)?(a):(b))    /*Minimum macro function */
6:  #define max(a,b)   ((a)<(b)?(b):(a)     /*Maximum macro function */
7:  #define false  0                                       /*Logicals */
8:  #define true   1
9:  #define NIL    (0L)                                 /*NIL pointer */
```

The first macro, SetRGBColor, is not found in the Toolbox, although it probably should be. Here you define an RGB color and then define the separate colors.

Important ▶ We show this macro on two lines because the code would not fit on one line in this book. However, C does not allow you to have a carriage return within a macro. (The same is true for macro 2.)

SetRect is a Toolbox routine that we've replaced here with macro 2. As stated in the *THINK C User's Manual*, it takes more time to use the Toolbox's SetRect than it does to set up the coordinates yourself because of the overhead required by the Macintosh trap dispatcher. If you set the coordinates, it will take four lines to do so. This macro replaces the *rect, l*, *t*, *r*, and *b* with four lines. All you will see before you compile the code is the one line of the macro.

SetPt is another Toolbox routine we replaced with a macro for the same reason we replaced SetRect. This macro sets a point equal to the horizontal and vertical coordinates.

Macros 4, 5, and 6 are functions that are not normally found in the compiler. They are essentially low-level numerical routines. Macro 4 takes an absolute value of some number; macro 5 takes the minimum value between two numbers; and macro 6 takes the maximum value. The awful looking code in these statements is necessary to defend against precedence problems. It's a good idea to enclose each parameter in parentheses and then to enclose the entire result expression in parentheses to keep the macro out of a larger expression. In each macro the question mark and colon have special meaning. In macro 4 the question mark says, "If *a* is less than 0, then we take the negative of *a*." The colon says, "Otherwise, take *a*."

Macro 7 defines false as 0; macro 8 defines true as 1; and macro 9 defines NIL as 0 long.

▶ Handling Errors

Our philosophy in handling errors is not to go overboard in setting up error checks. We did not include a test for errors if an error could not possibly have been created by the user. Unless the user physically altered the program, the user could not create an error. Therefore, we elected to let the system handle errors such as running out of memory.

For the few routines in this book in which a user could originate an error, we built in tests for errors. An example is OutputFloat.c in Chapter 15.

▶ The Way Apple Prefers You to Program

The folks at Apple have established a hierarchical approach they would like Macintosh programmers to follow. Their approach minimizes the chance of incompatibility when new versions of the Macintosh operating system are introduced. The hierarchy, slightly dramatized, goes something like this:

Using the Toolbox—best of all
Assigning low-memory global variables—nowhere near as good
Changing a value in or getting a value from a record—the pits

If you change or get a value, Apple won't guarantee the procedure will work right. Consider what might happen if Apple decided to stick a new entry into the dialog record. They could put it ahead of the edit text field, and your application would return garbage. Such a change would be uncharacteristic of Apple, although they reserve the right to make it. What they almost assuredly would do is to append the new entry to the end of the record so as not to cause trouble for developers.

If you stick to Toolbox routines throughout your application, that application has the best chance of running properly with an updated operating system. Conformity may, however, cramp your style. The more innovative your programming, the more you'll tend to break the rules. Sound recording is one example; animation and screen savers are others. A good rule is to use Toolbox calls when they're available and when they will do the job.

3 ▶ Initializing the Toolbox

▶ Setting Up Your Program with Init ToolBox.c

You will need to call the InitToolBox.c routine in every application you write. It initializes the Macintosh Toolbox, setting up everything your program needs.

Listing 3-1. Initializing the Toolbox

```
PROCEDURE InitToolBox();

 1:     /***************************************************/
 2:     void InitToolBox()              /* Initialization routine */
 3:     /***************************************************/
 4:     {
 5:         InitGraf(&thePort);         /* Initialize Toolbox Managers */
 6:         InitFonts();
 7:         InitWindows();
 8:         InitMenus();
 9:         TEInit();
10:         InitDialogs(0L);
11:         InitCursor();               /* Set cursor to arrow */
12:         MaxApplZone();              /* Fix up memory */
13:         MoreMasters();
14:         MoreMasters();
15:         MoreMasters();
16:         MoreMasters();
```

```
17:     MoreMasters();
18:     MoreMasters();
19:     MoreMasters();
20:     MoreMasters();
21:     MoreMasters();
22:     MoreMasters();
23:     MoreMasters();
24:     MoreMasters();
25:     MoreMasters();
26:     MoreMasters();
27:     MoreMasters();
28:     FlushEvents(everyEvent,0);              /* Clean up events */
29: }
```

On line 2 of the listing the "void" statement informs the Macintosh that there is no value to return for this function—that's what "void" signifies in C—and tells it to get on with the initialization. The pair of parentheses with nothing between them () always means that there is no value to pass in. As you can see, most calls in this routine have the empty parentheses.

Note that "void" has to be lowercase. To capitalize any or all of its letters would earn you a good scolding, expressed by the compiler as a syntax error. Another syntax requirement in C is that every line has to be followed by a curly brace or a semicolon.

On line 4 is a left curly brace. Down on line 29 is a right curly brace. The pair signifies that everything between them is executable code.

The first few lines call several routines that initialize the various managers of the Toolbox. Apple specifies the order in which the calls are to be made. Departing from the proper sequence is sure to cause problems. As an example, the routine to initialize the fonts makes use of several QuickDraw routines, and if QuickDraw has not been initialized, the Macintosh is likely to crash.

Although we've put the several statements on separate lines for clarity, you could just as easily combine them into longer lines, with each statement ended by a semicolon. For that matter, you could merge all the lines in the program into one huge block if each statement ended with a semicolon. That illustrates one flexible feature of C. Another is that you can indent lines to make them more readable. The decision is yours, guided by your instincts for organizing the code and making it look better. You are also at liberty to insert any comments, delimiting each by a forward slash and a star (/*) at the beginning and a star and a forward slash (*/) at the end. The comments can go anywhere you like, but they would be likely to cause confusion if inserted in the middle of a statement.

The statement on line 5 initializes QuickDraw. The ampersand (&) is a symbol telling the C compiler that you want to pass the address of the variable, *thePort*, to this routine because the routine is going to change the value of the variable. One of the rules of Toolbox programming is that you need to pass the address of a variable whenever you call a Toolbox routine that is going to change a variable. If you don't pass the address, the routine will change the variable, but when you return to your routine, you won't get a value there.

> **By the Way** ▶
>
> A way to know whether you need to use the ampersand (&) is to note that when you want to change a variable in Pascal you have to declare the variable as a var.
>
> Another rule to keep in mind is that a variable greater than 4 bytes is a var, so it requires the ampersand to pass it in. A rectangle, for instance, is a var because it is 8 bytes long.

The statement on line 6 has no variables to be passed in, hence the empty pair of parentheses. It initializes the Font Manager, executing several useful functions. One is to read into memory the system font, Chicago, which is the standard font used to draw the menu items and the window titles. Other functions are hidden in Apple proprietary code.

The statement on line 7 initializes global variables and private variables for the Window Manager. It sets up a window to draw in. It also draws the desktop for the Finder; however, it leaves the old desktop there if the machine is running under MultiFinder.

Line 8 initializes the Menu Manager. As to exactly what it does, one can only guess because its workings are Apple's proprietary information.

Line 9 initializes the Text Edit Manager, which handles static text and all other kinds of text that are drawn into the window. Among this manager's functions is to set up TextEdit scrap, or TEScrap in brief. Any text you cut or copy goes into this private scrap on its way to the Clipboard or Scrapbook.

The statement on line 10 passes in the variable *0L* and initializes the Dialog Manager. The *L* denotes a long variable, meaning that it is 4 bytes long. A *0* by itself simply will not do, because it is only 2 bytes long and the Toolbox requires 4 bytes here. Notice that although the several previous initialization commands do not pass in variables, this one does. What it expects is a ResumeProc, an instruction to resume a program that bombs; however, programmers rarely make provision to resume a program if it crashes. Most avoid putting in a ResumeProc, preferring instead to restart rather than run the risk of damaging the memory or even the disk. That's why the Resume button more often than not is dimmed in bomb alerts.

Line 11 sets the cursor to the default arrow. If the cursor is invisible, it is made visible. Of all the initialization routines, this is the only one you can call at various times in the program.

MaxApplZone on line 12 is the abbreviation for maximum application zone. Memory in the Macintosh is segmented. At the upper end of memory is the stack; at the bottom is the application heap. Each call in a programmer's routines creates data that is put onto the stack, which grows downward toward the heap. Apple's Toolbox routines create data that goes onto the heap, which you can visualize as piling up toward the stack. Obviously, the space between the sinking bits in the stack and the rising bits on the heap gets smaller and smaller. Without some way to restrict this process, the two leading edges could meet and the bits get scrambled. Catastrophe!

Apple fortunately has provided protection that, if properly invoked, can prevent this disaster. The protection takes the form of a limit you can set on the heap so that it won't invade the stack. You can specify the amount of memory you want allocated to your heap, up to a maximum built in by Apple. In this routine, MaxApplZone() allocates all the heap memory that the Macintosh is capable of allowing. This protection is particularly welcome when your program gobbles up big chunks of memory. Color programs, especially those with lots of windows and menus, are profligate in memory consumption.

Although you can put a cap on your heap, the Macintosh provides no means of restraining the growth of the stack. This deficiency is of little consequence, however, because the compiler will warn you if the heap gets too close to the stack.

The MoreMasters() statements on lines 13–27 refer to master pointers, each of which is a location in memory.

| Important ▶ | Master pointers are locked in place because a handle—which is a pointer to a master pointer—expects to find its master pointer exactly where it looks. If the master pointer were to get moved, the handle would point to the wrong location and it would find garbage. |

Whenever you bring in a resource or create a window or a control, the Macintosh is going to need one or more master pointers. At the start of a program, the Macintosh automatically allocates space for sixty-four master pointers at the low end of the heap. This number is adequate for smallish programs, but big programs, especially color ones, can quickly use up all sixty-four. In the meantime, the Macintosh has been busy stuffing data into adjacent memory locations. It places additional master pointers here and there throughout the memory, fragmenting the large chunks of contiguous memory needed for big programs. Then, when the Memory Manager looks for a big enough chunk and can't find one, you get a system error.

This routine guards against this annoyance by including no fewer than sixteen MoreMasters() calls. You can be pretty sure your application won't encounter the fragmentation gremlin. The sixteen calls work their magic by expanding the default total of sixty-four master pointers to 16 x 64 = 1,024 master pointers in memory. Each master pointer takes up only 4 bytes, so this large number of master pointers occupies only 4,096 bytes of RAM. Because this small block is tucked neatly into the bottom of the heap, you can safely write large color programs and other byte-hungry applications that will find plenty of room in RAM. If, instead, you write a small program, you won't miss a measly 4,096 bytes of memory, even on a 500K machine.

The last subroutine call, on line 28, refers to the event queue.

> **By the Way** ▶ Macintoshes are event-driven machines. Events are mouse-down, mouse-up, key-down, and so forth. FlushEvents performs a useful function by cleaning out the event queue before the application starts. This function gets rid of such user events as clicking the mouse three times instead of the prescribed two, or inadvertently brushing a key. These events can interfere with proper running of the application, so it's a good idea to flush them out.

FlushEvents passes in a couple of variables. The variable *everyEvent* tells the machine not to leave any events in the queue. The variable *0* refers to a stop mask, not used in this program.

▶ Summary

This chapter presented the source code for and a discussion of InitToolBox.c, which is the first routine to call in every application you write.

4 ▶ MENUS

▶ Overview of Menus

Menus are paramount in Apple's human interface philosophy. They allow you to execute an operation on an item you have selected in a window or on the desktop. They also display the full range of activities that can be performed, so you don't have to remember a long list of commands. You can see quickly what actions are available in the menu bar of any application.

Menus come in four types: pull-down, pop-up, hierarchical, and tear-off. The most common menu is the pull-down, which we deal with in this chapter. Chapter 19 covers pop-up menus. We separate the two types of menus because the functions of and the routines to produce each type differ widely. This book will not cover hierarchical or tear-off menus.

▶ Building Menus

You can build new menus for your applications in a variety of ways, many of which are complex and tedious. In this chapter, we show you two ways to build menus with as few calls to the Toolbox and Menu Manager as possible.

The first routine we discuss is InitMenu.c. Toward the end of the chapter you'll find DrawMBar.c, which uses an 'MBAR' resource.

▶ InitMenu.c

This routine sets up all your menus and draws them. InitMenu.c requires that you pass in only the ID numbers of the first and last menus. Suppose you've given your first menu the ID of 300, the second menu 301, and the last menu 305. You pass in 300 and 305. The routine takes care of all menus with ID numbers between the first and last numbers. You need to deal only with mouse-down events.

Listing 4-1. Creating a menu

```
PROCEDURE InitMenu(firstMenu: INTEGER, lastMenu: INTEGER);

 1: /*************************************************************/
 2: void InitMenu(short firstMenu, short lastMenu)
 3: /*************************************************************/
 4: {
 5:    #define Apple    1
 6:    short            menu;
 7:    MenuHandle       hMenu;
 8:    hMenu = GetMenu(Apple);
 9:    InsertMenu(hMenu, 0);
10:    AddResMenu(hMenu, "DRVR");
11:    for (menu = firstMenu; menu <= lastMenu; menu++)
12:    {
13:       hMenu = GetMenu(menu);
14:       InsertMenu(hMenu, 0);
15:    }
16:    DrawMenuBar();
17: }
```

Line 2 of InitMenu.c requires you to pass in the IDs of the first and last menus.

After declarations on lines 5–7, the first real code begins on line 8. You need a handle to the Apple menu to insert it into the menu bar. The statement on line 8 calls GetMenu from the Toolbox and passes it a constant called Apple, which is equivalent to the number 1 in the resource file. The number 1 is a constant that tells GetMenu to return a handle to a 'MENU' resource with an ID of 1. By convention, the Apple menu always has an ID of 1.

Line 9 uses the Toolbox routine InsertMenu to insert the handle to the Apple menu into the Macintosh's built-in menu list.

At this point, the Apple menu in the resource file is empty because you don't know what desk accessories users of your application may have installed. Line 10 calls the routine AddResMenu to find those accessories and add them to the Apple menu. This single call to the Menu Manager asks it to search all open resource files and look for the type of accessories you specified—in this case 'DRVR', which is the resource type for desk accessories. The Menu Manager then inserts them as items in the Apple menu.

Lines 11–15 do a for-loop to get the rest of your menus. This for-loop states that if you have a variable equal to the ID of the first menu, you want to get the handle to it and insert it into the menu bar. The loop continues, incrementing by 1 each time, until it reaches the ID of the last menu.

Line 16 calls the Toolbox routine DrawMenuBar to redraw (or update) your menu according to the new menu list.

▶ The Apple Menu

Desk accessories installed on a user's system are always available through the Apple menu. The list of accessories may expand or diminish or simply change in character depending on what application is running. For example, you would have a spelling checker in the Apple menu only if you were running a word processing program.

▶ DoAppleMenu.c

The purpose of the DoAppleMenu routine is to find out what function is performed when a user selects an item from the Apple menu. You call this routine from your program's main event loop when a mouse-down event occurs in the Apple menu.

Listing 4-2. Handling the selection of an item from the Apple menu

```
PROCEDURE DoAppleMenu(appleitem:   INTEGER);

 1:   /***************************************************/
 2:   void DoAppleMenu(short appleItem)
 3:   /***************************************************/
 4:   {
 5:      #define (Apple = 1)
 6:      MenuHandle    hMenu;
 7:      long          refNum;
 8:      Str255        name;
 9:      hMenu = GetMenu(Apple);
10:      GetItem(hMenu, appleItem, name);
11:      refNum = OpenDskAcc(name);
12:   }
```

This is a short but useful routine. On line 2 of DoAppleMenu.c, you pass in an item number in sequential order from the top. Remember that the void-statement means that nothing will be returned. Also, remember that all menu items, including dividing lines, have an item number.

In the routine, you skip down four lines of declarations (lines 5–8) to the first real code on line 9. Here you get a handle to the Apple menu with the statement hMenu = GetMenu(Apple).

On line 10 you pass in the number of the menu item that was selected. The statement then returns the name of the Apple menu item, such as "Chooser."

To open the desk accessory, the statement on line 11 passes in its name. The routine returns the 'DRVR' reference number if it can open the desk accessory; otherwise, it returns a 0.

▶ Routines Involving Menu Items

The following five routines deal with specific menu items. They disable (or gray out) a menu item; enable (or brighten) a menu item; disable all items in a menu; enable all items in a menu; and check mark or unmark an item through a toggling routine.

▶ DablMenuItem.c

DablMenuItem.c disables (or grays out) an item or items in a menu.

Listing 4-3. Disabling a menu item

```
PROCEDURE DablMenuItem(theMenuID: INTEGER, theItemNumber: INTEGER);

1:  /***********************************************************/
2:  void DablMenuItem(short theMenuID, short theItemNumber)
3:  /***********************************************************/
4:  {
5:     MenuHandle    hMenu;
6:     hMenu = GetMenu(theMenuID);
7:     DisableItem(hMenu, theItemNumber);
8:  }
```

On line 2 you pass in the resource ID of the menu and the number of the menu item that you want to disable.

On line 6, the first line of real code, you call the Toolbox routine GetMenu, which returns a handle to the menu when you pass it the resource ID.

▶ Routines Involving Menu Items

With another Toolbox routine on line 7, you disable the item that you identified on line 2. That's all there is to it.

▶ EablMenuItem.c

EablMenuItem.c enables (or brightens) an item or items in a menu.

Listing 4-4. Enabling a menu item

```
PROCEDURE EablMenuItem(theMenuID: INTEGER, theItemNumber: INTEGER);

1:  /*************************************************************/
2:  void EablMenuItem(short theMenuID, short theItemNumber)
3:  /*************************************************************/
4:  {
5:     MenuHandle    hMenu;
6:     hMenu = GetMenu(theMenuID);
7:     EnableItem(hMenu, theItemNumber);
8:  }
```

EablMenuItem.c does the reverse of DablMenuItem.c. In every other aspect, the routines are identical.

▶ DAllMenuItems.c

DAllMenuItems.c disables (or grays out) all of the items in a menu.

Listing 4-5. Disabling all menu items

```
PROCEDURE DAllMenuItems(theMenuID: INTEGER);

1:   /*************************************************************/
2:   void DAllMenuItems(short theMenuID)
3:   /*************************************************************/
4:   {
5:      Str255        theString;
6:      MenuHandle    hMenu;
7:      short         itemCount;
8:      short         i;
9:      hMenu = GetMenu(theMenuID);
10:     itemCount = CountMItems(hMenu);
11:     for (i = 1; i <= itemCount; i++)
12:     {
13:        GetItem(hMenu, i, theString);
```

```
14:        if (theString != -)
15:        {
16:           DisableItem(hMenu, i);
17:        }
18:     }
19: }
```

In the function declaration on line 2, you pass in the resource ID of the menu. After declarations on lines 5–8, you reach the first real code on line 9. This statement passes in the GetMenu routine and returns a handle to the menu.

On line 10 you get the number of items in the menu through itemCount. CountMItems requires that you pass it the menu handle; it returns the number of items.

Lines 11–15 comprise a for-loop, which starts at the first item and increments by 1 until the number is equal to the last item. On line 13 you pass a handle to the item, and it returns a string. Line 14 states that if the string is equal to a minus sign, a menu dividing line (separating groups of items) resides there. The routine will not disable the line because it is already disabled. If the string does not contain a minus sign, the routine will disable the item.

▶ EAllMenuItems.c

EAllMenuItems.c enables or brightens all items in a menu.

Listing 4-6. Enabling all menu items

PROCEDURE EAllMenuItems(theMenuID: INTEGER);

```
1:  /*************************************************************/
2:  void EAllMenuItems(short theMenuID)
3:  /*************************************************************/
4:  {
5:     Str255        theString;
6:     MenuHandle    hMenu;
7:     short         itemCount;
8:     short         i;
9:     hMenu = GetMenu(theMenuID);
10:    itemCount = CountMItems(hMenu);
11:    for (i = 1; i <= itemCount; i++)
12:    {
13:       GetItem(hMenu, i, theString);
14:       if (TheString != "-")
```

```
15:      {
16:          EnableItem(hMenu, i);
17:      }
18:  }
19: }
```

This routine works exactly the reverse of DAllMenuItems. The statement on line 14 is identical in both routines. Here it ensures that a dividing line in a menu will not be enabled. To enable a menu dividing line and have it selected would likely cause your program to crash.

▶ MarkMenuItem.c

MarkMenuItem.c puts a check mark to the left of an item or items in a menu. If a check mark is already next to the item, this routine will remove it.

Listing 4-7. Checkmarking or unmarking a menu item

```
PROCEDURE MarkMenuItem(theMenuID: INTEGER, theItemNumber: INTEGER);

1:  /*************************************************************/
2:  void MarkMenuItem(short theMenuID, short theItemNumber)
3:  /*************************************************************/
4:  {
5:      char        oldMark;
6:      char        newMark;
7:      MenuHandle  hMenu;
8:      hMenu = GetMenu(theMenuID);
9:      GetItemMark(hMenu, theItemNumber, &oldMark);
10:     if (oldMark == 0x12)
11:     {
12:         newMark = 0x20;
13:     }
14:     else
15:     {
16:         newMark = 0x12;
17:     }
18:     SetItemMark(hMenu, theItemNumber, newMark);
19: }
```

To begin MarkMenuItem on line 2, you pass in the resource ID of the menu and the item number to check.

Line 8, the first real code, returns a handle to the menu when you pass in the menu resource ID.

On line 9, GetItemMark returns the check character and leads to an if-test on lines 10–13. This test makes the statement, "If the old mark is equal to the hex number 0x12, then set it to 0x20." In Chicago font (the system font), the hex 12 is a check mark, and the hex 20 is a blank space.

The else-statement on lines 14–17 says that if the old mark was not a hex 12, then make it a hex 12, completing the toggling aspect of the routine.

Line 18 calls the Toolbox routine SetItemMark. This passes a handle to Mark and sets the new mark—either a check mark or a blank space—next to the item.

▶ Testing the Keyboard

The names of all five routines available for testing the keyboard end in the words "is down": CommandIsDown.c, CapsLockIsDown.c, ControlIsDown.c, OptionIsDown.c, and ShiftIsDown.c.

Think of how often you have to hold down the Command key while clicking the mouse or hold down the Command and Shift keys while pressing another key. You can use these routines whenever you want to know whether the user is pressing a modifier key. The routines were designed with two criteria in mind. They work with any of the Macintosh keyboards, so you don't run into problems if you switch from a Macintosh Plus keyboard to an extended keyboard. They also tell you which key is pressed without your having to go into the modifier field of the event record.

Whenever an event takes place, an event record is created. A bit is set in the modifier flag: 1 if the key is down; 0 if it isn't. The flag is a short number representing each of the modifier keys.

The five is-down routines avoid your having to wait for a notification that a key has been pressed. You simply go in and ask for that information. The routines provide you with a "back door" into a program. The back door works something like this: You can write your application so that the user has to hold down a certain set of keys while double-clicking on the program icon. This modification will make the program enter, for example, a debug or diagnostics mode that the user doesn't know about—except that the menu bar may show some extra items for the debug or diagnostics procedure.

One of the first things you do in a program is to call InitToolBox to set up the starting conditions for the routine. Among its effects is to flush the event queue and make it ready for new events. If at this time your application wanted to know whether the user was holding down a set of keys for the back door, those events would be gone and confusion would reign. The five is-down routines prevent that from happening by denying access to the modifier flag.

CommandIsDown.c

CommandIsDown.c returns the answer to the question, "Is the Command key (⌘) pressed?" (The Command key is also called the Apple key.)

Listing 4-8. Finding out if the Command key is pressed

FUNCTION CommandIsDown(): BOOLEAN;

```
 1:   /**********************************************************/
 2:   char    CommandIsDown()
 3:   /**********************************************************/
 4:   {
 5:     char status;
 6:     KeyMap theMap;
 7:     GetKeys(&theMap);
 8:     status = (char)BitTst(&theMap, 48);
 9:     return(status);
10:   }
```

CommandIsDown.c is declared as a character function in conformance with popular conventions for C programming. Whereas Pascal has Booleans (meaning TRUE or FALSE, or yes or no), the C language has a character data type, which can be a short or a long. This routine uses a character data type as a Boolean. It requires no variables to be passed in. You say, "If the Command key is down, then perform a function."

The statement on line 7 calls the GetKeys Toolbox routine and passes it theMap, which is an array of 16 bytes, each comprising 8 bits. Every bit inside that map corresponds to one of the keys on the keyboard. When a key is pressed, some bit in the map is going to be set to 1, or TRUE, while all the other bits remain 0, or FALSE. GetKeys returns the status of the keymap, telling you which key is down.

Line 8 forms an if-test that calls another Toolbox routine called BitTst. You pass BitTst a pointer to the keymap, and you pass the bit representing a particular key. In this example, 48 is the Command key. Counting from the beginning of the string, BitTst tests the bits the way they are stored in memory, from the most significant bit down to the least significant. Apple, however, counts them from the least significant bit up to the most significant, as shown in Table 4-1. If bit 48 has been set, the status is set to TRUE and is returned as such. If bit 48 is set to FALSE, the FALSE status is returned instead.

Table 4-1. Correspondence between Keymap Array and Keys for the Apple Extended Keyboard

Array Index	Bit Number							
	7	6	5	4	3	2	1	0
0	X	Z	G	H	F	D	S	A
1	R	E	W	Q	B		V	C
2	5	6	4	3	2	1	T	Y
3	O	]	0	8	-	7	9	=
4	"	J	L	return	P	I	[	U
5	.	M	N	/	,	\	;	K
6	⌘		esc		delete	`	space	tab
7		cntl	option	shift	cntl	option	caps	shift
8	clear		+		*		.	
9		-		enter	/			
10	5	4	3	2	1	0	=	
11				9	8		7	6
12	F11		F9	F8	F3	F7	F6	F5
13	F12		F10		F14		F13	
14	end	F4	del. x>	pg up	home	help	F15	
15	reset	up	down	right	left	F1	pg dn	F2

▶ CapsLockIsDown.c

CapsLockIsDown.c answers the question, "Is the Caps Lock key pressed?"

Listing 4-9. Finding out if the Caps Lock key is pressed

FUNCTION CapsLockIsDown(): BOOLEAN;

```
 1:  /*******************************************************/
 2:  char    CapsLockIsDown()
 3:  /*******************************************************/
 4:  {
 5:     char status;
 6:     KeyMap theMap;
 7:     GetKeys(&theMap);
 8:     Status = (char)BitTst(&theMap, 62);
 9:     return(status);
10:  }
```

CapsLockIsDown.c is identical to CommandIsDown.c except that the keymap bit is 62, corresponding to the Caps Lock key.

▶ ControlIsDown.c

ControlIsDown.c tells you whether the Control key is pressed.

Listing 4-10. Finding out if the Control key is pressed

FUNCTION ControlIsDown(): BOOLEAN;

```
 1:   /*************************************************************/
 2:   char    ControlIsDown()
 3:   /*************************************************************/
 4:   {
 5:     char status;
 6:     KeyMap theMap;
 7:     GetKeys(&theMap);
 8:     Status = (char)BitTst(&theMap, 60);
 9:     return(status);
10:   }
```

ControlIsDown.c is identical to CommandIsDown.c except that the keymap bit is 60, corresponding to the Control key.

▶ OptionIsDown.c

OptionIsDown.c returns the answer to the question, "Is the Option key pressed?"

Listing 4-11. Finding out if the Option key is pressed

FUNCTION OptionIsDown(): BOOLEAN;

```
 1:   /*************************************************************/
 2:   char    OptionIsDown()
 3:   /*************************************************************/
 4:   {
 5:     char status;
 6:     KeyMap theMap;
 7:     GetKeys(&theMap);
 8:     Status = (char) BitTst(&theMap, 61);
 9:     return(status);
10:   }
```

ControlIsDown.c is identical to CommandIsDown.c except that the keymap bit is 61, corresponding to the Option key.

▶ ShiftIsDown.c

ShiftIsDown.c returns the answer to the question, "Is the Shift key pressed?"

Listing 4-12. Finding out if the Shift key is pressed

```
FUNCTION ShiftIsDown(): BOOLEAN;
```

```
 1:  /***********************************************************/
 2:  char    ShiftIsDown()
 3:  /***********************************************************/
 4:  {
 5:    char status;
 6:    KeyMap theMap;
 7:    GetKeys(&theMap);
 8:    Status = (char)BitTst(&theMap, 63);
 9:    return(status);
10:  }
```

ShiftIsDown.c is identical to CommandIsDown.c except that the keymap bit is 63, corresponding to the Shift key.

> **Note ▶** See MyModalDialog in Chapter 6 for an example of how these "is-down" routines are used.

▶ Using an 'MBAR' Resource

Drawing the menu bar at the top of the screen can be done two ways: through a program or through a resource file. Most common with Macintosh programmers is to make half a dozen calls to the Menu Manager. One call gets the handle of the menu from the resource. Another Toolbox call takes that menu and inserts it into the current menu list. Having made two calls for every menu they want to include, the programmers then call the DrawMenuBar routine to redraw the menu bar containing the new menus. Later, if they want to change any items in a menu, the programmers have to go through their program and then recompile it.

Apple gives us a more convenient method for redrawing the menu bar. It offers a way to change a menu from a resource file without the chore of recompiling your program. You use a resource editor instead. Trouble is, you have to make five Toolbox calls because Apple doesn't combine them into a single routine that would draw the menu bar and the menu items. You also have to make an explicit call to the AddResourceMenu routine to add the Apple menu, which contains the desk accessories.

The following procedure, DrawMBar.c, eliminates the need to make a number of calls to the Toolbox and also draws the Apple menu for you. If you check even the most popular Macintosh applications, you'll find that very few have a menu bar resource. Now you know why.

▶ DrawMBar.c

This routine calls the Toolbox DrawMenuBar routine and passes it the menu bar ID. QuickDraw automatically draws the menu bar at the top of the screen, complete with the various menu items.

Listing 4-13. Drawing a menu bar

```
PROCEDURE DrawMBar(mBarID: INTEGER);

 1:   /***************************************************/
 2:   void DrawMBar(short mBarID)
 3:   /***************************************************/
 4:   {
 5:     Handle hMBar;                          /* Menu bar handle   */
 6:     MenuHandle hMenu;                      /* Menu handle       */
 7:     #define Apple 1                        /* Apple menu ID     */
 8:     hMBar = GetNewMBar(mBarID);            /* Handle to menu bar */
 9:     SetMenuBar(hMBar);                     /* Make present menu bar */
10:     hMenu = GetMHandle(Apple);             /* Add desk accessories  */
11:     if (hMenu)
12:     {
13:       AddResMenu(hMenu, 'DRVR');
14:     }
15:     DrawMenuBar();                         /* Draw the whole thing */
16:   }
```

The statement on line 7, #define Apple 1, uses the precompiler to replace every occurrence of the word "Apple" by the digit 1, which is the ID of the Apple menu. You'll see in a moment why that's important.

The active code statements on lines 8–10 go out to the resources and pass in the menu bar ID. As a result, a temporary area of memory called a *menu list* is created. In it are all the items in the menu bar and the menus themselves. You then get the handle to the Apple menu, the one containing the Chooser, the Control Panel, and so on. Here's where the digit 1 comes into play. Some applications don't have the Apple menu, so the handle then is 0. If the application uses the Apple menu, as this one does, the handle is 1, and you call the AddResMenu routine with the statement on line 13. Pass it the handle and the 'DRVR' string that gets all the opened resources of type 'DRVR.' It is more than a happy coincidence that all resources of type 'DRVR' are desk accessories. The upshot is that whichever desk accessories are open are loaded into the Apple menu. Neat!

By this time, you've created the entire menu, and the moment has arrived for line 15 to draw it to the screen.

▶ A Simple Menu Example

This section contains a pair of source code listings that demonstrate the DrawMBar routine. The pair consists of one file with the extension .c and another file, containing the resources, with the extension .R. The two types of files always go together to make up an application.

▶ MenuExample.c

The following example tests the DrawMBar.c routine, and Figure 4-1 shows the result.

Figure 4-1. Menus created with DrawMBar.c routine

Listing 4-14. Example of a menu created with the DrawMBar.c routine

```
1:  /****************************************************************/
2:  void    main()                          /* Routine to test DrawMBar */
3:  /****************************************************************/
4:  {
```

A Simple Menu Example

```
5:    InitToolBox();
6:    OpenResources("\pMenuExample.rsrc");    /* For devel. */
7:    DrawMBar(300);
8:  }
```

▶ MenuExample.R

This section contains the resource file for the DrawMBar.c example.

Listing 4-15. Resource file for a menu example

```
MenuExample.rsrc
rsrcRSED

Type MBAR=GNRL
Menu Example,200
.I
3                       ;; Number of menus
1                       ;; Apple Menu
200                     ;; File Menu
201                     ;; Edit Menu

Type MENU

Apple,1                 ;; Apple Menu
    \14
About Menus...
Help...
(-

File,200                ;; File Menu
    File
Open.../O
Close/W
Save/S
Save As...
Delete...
(-
Quit/Q

Edit,201                ;; Edit Menu
    Edit
(Undo/Z
(-
Cut/X
```

```
Copy/C
Paste/V
Clear
(-
Select All/A
```

▶ Summary

This chapter presented thirteen routines for

- Creating menus
- Dealing with the Apple menu
- Marking, enabling, and disabling menu items
- Testing the keyboard to see if modifier keys are being pressed during an application
- Using the 'MBAR' resource

In addition, you have seen a sample menu routine and the resource file for the sample menu.

▶ Recommended Reading

Gordon, Bob. "Menus and Windows in LightSpeed." (C.) *The Complete MacTutor—The Macintosh Programming Journal*, Vol. 2, 1987.

Matthews, James. "Menus in Windows." (Pascal.) *The Definitive MacTutor—The Macintosh Programming Journal*, Vol. 4, 1989.

Sheets, Steven. "Hierarchical Menus." (Pascal.) *The Essential MacTutor—The Macintosh Programming Journal*, Vol. 3, 1988.

5 ▶ Cursors

▶ Overview of Cursors

A traditional command-line computer interface relies on a blinking cursor to indicate where the next entry of text or numbers should be, and it forces you to use arrow keys to change the entry point. The Macintosh interface allows you to point to a new insertion point or graphics object and choose it with the click of a mouse.

Most applications use some or all of the five standard cursors: arrow, I-beam, crosshairs, plus sign, and wristwatch. The routine and example in this chapter show you how to create those and other cursors, and how to switch from one type to another in the same application.

Now that color monitors are commonplace, color cursors can play a big part in the design elements of a screen. When a large screen is in use, a colorful cursor can be easy to find on a cluttered screen.

▶ Using Black-and-White and Color Cursors

FetchCursor.c compensates for some minor inconsistencies in the Toolbox managers. Say you want a window to come up automatically in color. You create the window resource. When the Window Manager goes out to open the window, it looks to see whether a 'wctb', or Window Color Table resource, exists. If one does, the manager automatically opens that resource in color, assuming that it is a color resource. The same goes for dialogs and menus.

Unfortunately, cursors and icons don't get this favorable treatment. If you have created your own color cursor and put it into your resource file, the Resource Manager will overlook your color cursor because it is looking for a black-and-white cursor. That's why you'll find FetchCursor.c useful if you want to use color cursors in your application. This routine provides a simple way to pass in the ID of a color cursor and have the cursor opened. Some cursors in the Macintosh are stored in the System file: the I-beam (resource ID = 1), the cross-hairs (resource ID = 2), the plus sign (resource ID = 3), and the wrist-watch (resource ID = 4). The arrow cursor (resource ID = 0) resides in ROM.

▶ FetchCursor.c

If you have a routine in which you want to switch from an arrow cursor to a wrist watch cursor—while the program executes something computationally intensive—then switch back to the arrow again, FetchCursor.c takes care of the switching for you. It also provides color equivalents of the five standard cursors, including a rainbow arrow. You pass into the routine the ID of the cursor you want. The cursor automatically comes up in color if you're running the application on a color machine; otherwise it comes up in black-and-white.

Listing 5-1. Getting a cursor

```
PROCEDURE FetchCursor(theID: INTEGER);

 1:  /***************************************************/
 2:  void FetchCursor(short theID)
 3:  /***************************************************/
 4:  {
 5:     #define    SysEnvironsTrap 0xA090      /* Toolbox traps */
 6:     #define    UnknownTrap    0xA89F
 7:     #define    Arrow         0
 8:     SysEnvRec   sysEnv;
 9:     char        hasColor;
10:     CCrsrHandle hCCur;
11:     CursHandle  hCur;
12:     hasColor = false;                      /* Test for color */
13:     if ((long)NGetTrapAddress(SysEnvironsTrap, OSTrap) !=
14:         (long)NGetTrapAddress(UnknownTrap, ToolTrap))
15:     {
16:         SysEnvirons(1, &sysEnv);
17:         hasColor = sysEnv.hasColorQD;
18:     }
```

```
19:     switch (theID)
20:     {
21:       case (Arrow):
22:         hCCur = nil;
23:         if (hasColor)
24:         {
25:            hCCur = GetCCursor(Arrow);
26:         }
27:         if (hCCur)
28:         {
29:            SetCCursor(hCCur);
30:            DisposCCursor(hCCur);
31:         }
32:         else
33:         {
34:            InitCursor();
35:         }
36:       default:
37:         hCCur = nil;
38:         if (hasColor)
39:         {
40:            hCCur = GetCCursor(theID);
41:         }
42:         if (hCCur)
43:         {
44:            SetCCursor(hCCur);
45:            DisposCCursor(hCCur);
46:         }
47:         else
48:            {
49:            hCur = GetCursor(theID);
50:            if (hCur)
51:            {
52:               SetCursor(*hCur);
53:            }
54:         }
55:     }
56:   }
```

To use this routine, call it and pass it the ID of the resource containing the cursor you want drawn. For example, you might have both a black-and-white and a color version of your cursor in the resource. You give each the same ID number, say 128, but the black-and-white, or monochrome, version is identified as CURS 128 and the color version as crsr 128.

Note first the two declarations on lines 5 and 6, and then skip down to the first real code on line 12, in which *hasColor* is a local variable that assumes you're using a monochrome machine.

Next you need to find out whether your program is running on a color machine, so you call the Toolbox SysEnvirons routine. Early Macintoshes with the original operating system did not come with SysEnvirons. It's a routine Apple added later, and all but the non-upgraded Macintosh 512s have it. Just to be on the safe side, however, this routine includes an if-test on lines 13–14 to determine whether SysEnvirons is present.

Here's where the two declarations on lines 5 and 6 come into play. They define the number of the System environs trap and the number of a nonexistent trap, called UnknownTrap. The if-test asks, "Does a valid trap exist?" If it does, its address, 0xA090, is returned, signifying that you do, indeed, have SysEnvirons. If it doesn't, the number 0xA89F is returned. Apple not only has assigned 0xA89F to UnknownTrap, but also guarantees that the number will continue to be reserved for that purpose. The if-test compares the two numbers. If they are equal, SysEnvirons is absent. You can then be pretty sure that the Macintosh is not a color machine. If they are not equal, SysEnvirons is present. That doesn't necessarily mean the Macintosh has color. You still have to call SysEnvirons (line 16), passing in the number 1, which returns a record containing a lot of information about the machine. The number 1 is used because Apple may some day decide to add a record saying that the machine has, for instance, a CD-ROM. At that time, it may be necessary to pass in a different number, such as 2.

One of the items in the SysEnvirons record is an indication that the machine has color QuickDraw. If the statement on line 17 is equal to 1, the machine has color; if equal to 0, the machine is black-and-white.

At this point you fall out of the if-test and go to a switch-statement on line 19 and a case-statement on line 21. The case-statement is a test on the ID. If the ID = 0, you've got the arrow cursor. You handle this cursor a little differently from the other cursors because the arrow is set much more often. You set a handle to color cursor equals 0 on line 22. Then, if you want the color arrow, notably the one in rainbow colors, lines 23–26 tell you whether you have color. If you do, a value is returned and sets a handle to the color arrow.

Now comes another if-test on lines 27–31. The if-test says, "If the handle to the color cursor does not equal 0—meaning, in negative logic, there is a valid color cursor—set the color cursor equal to the color cursor handle, hCCur." If you do not have color, then you need a black-and-white cursor. The quickest way to bring up the black-and-white cursor is to call (on line 34) the InitCursor routine from the Toolbox. You also call the routine DisposCCursor. This routine is necessary because of a quirk in Apple's approach to purging. If the earlier call to get the color cursor finds a color cursor, it puts that cursor in memory but doesn't flush it out. On the other hand, if you call for the black-and-white cursor, the call not only gets you the familiar arrow but also flushes it.

The next part of the else-statement (lines 36–46) says, "If I have color, I do what I did just before; that is, I get the handle to the color cursor. Then I run a test. If the cursor is not equal to 0, I set the color cursor and dispose of it."

Now, on lines 47–53, comes a difference in the procedure. Earlier you initialized the cursor with InitCursor; here you get a handle to the black-and-white cursor by calling GetCursor and passing it the ID. You say, "If the handle to this black-and-white cursor is not equal to 0, call SetCursor to a pointer, as opposed to a handle." The star in front of the handle (line 52) changes it to a pointer. You don't have to dispose of the black-and-white resource you read in because that is done automatically with SetCursor.

▶ A Simple Cursor Example

This section contains a pair of source code listings that demonstrate the cursor. The pair consists of one file with the extension .c and another file, containing the resources, with the extension .R. The two types of files always go together to make up an application.

▶ CursorExample.c

CursorExample.c is an example of an arrow cursor inside a dialog box. The box also contains radio buttons with indicators for five common types of cursors, any of which you can select with the arrow cursor. The routine will change the cursor to the type indicated by the selected radio button. Figure 5-1 shows the result of the code.

Listing 5-2. Example of a cursor

```
1:  /***************************************************************/
2:  void    main()                      /* Routine to test cursors */
3:  /***************************************************************/
4:  {
5:      DialogPtr   theDialog;
6:      short       itemHit;
7:      InitToolBox();
```

```
 8:    OpenResources("\pCursorExample.rsrc");  /* For development */
 9:    CenterDialog(300);
10:    OpenDialog(theDialog, 300);
11:    FrmDefItem(theDialog);
12:    PushRadioButton(theDialog, 2, 2, 6)
13:    for(;;)
14:    {
15:      MyModalDialog(&itemHit)
16:      switch (itemHit)
17:      {
18:        case (1):                          /* Quit button */
19:          break;
20:        case (2):                   /* Arrow radio button */
21:          PushRadioButton(theDialog, 2, 2, 6);
22:          FetchCursor(arrow);
23:          continue;
24:        case (3):                  /* I-beam radio button */
25:          PushRadioButton(theDialog, 3, 2, 6);
26:          FetchCursor(iBeamCursor);
27:          continue;
28:        case (4):                   /* Cross radio button */
29:          PushRadioButton(theDialog, 4, 2, 6);
30:          FetchCursor(crossCursor);
31:          continue;
32:        case (5):                    /* Plus radio button */
33:          PushRadioButton(theDialog, 5, 2, 6);
34:          FetchCursor(plusCursor);
35:          continue;
36:        case (6):                   /* Watch radio button */
37:          PushRadioButton(theDialog, 6, 2, 6);
38:          FetchCursor(watchCursor);
39:          continue;
40:        case (-updateEvt):
41:          BeginUpdate(theDialog);
42:            UpDialog(theDialog);
43:            FrmDefItem(theDialog);
44:          EndUpdate(theDialog);
45:      }
46:      break;
47:    }
48:    DisposeDialog(theDialog);
49:  }
```

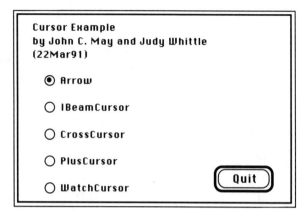

Figure 5-1. Dialog box created with CursorExample.c.

▶ CursorExample.R

This resource file brings up the CursorExample.

Listing 5-3. Resource file for example of a cursor

```
CursorExample.rsrc
rsrcRSED

Type DLOG
,300
Cursor Test                         ;; Message (Title)
50 50 278 344                       ;; Rect (T,L,B,R)
Visible NoGoAway                    ;; Flags
1                                   ;; Proc ID
1                                   ;; Refcon
300                                 ;; Resource ID of DITL list

Type DITL
,300
7

* 1
Button    Enabled
183 219 203 279                     ;; Rect (T,L,B,R)
Quit                                ;; Message

* 2
RadioButton Enabled
74 20 94 150                        ;; Rect (T,L,B,R)
Arrow                               ;; Message

* 3
RadioButton Enabled
103 20 124 150                      ;; Rect (T,L,B,R)
IBeamCursor                         ;; Message
```

```
* 4
RadioButton Enabled
133 20 153 150                          ;; Rect (T,L,B,R)
CrossCursor                             ;; Message

* 5
RadioButton Enabled
163 20 182 150                          ;; Rect (T,L,B,R)
PlusCursor                              ;; Message

* 6
RadioButton Enabled
192 20 212 150                          ;; Rect (T,L,B,R)
WatchCursor                             ;; Message

* 7
StaticText Disabled
10 10 60 280                            ;; Rect (T,L,B,R)
Cursor Example\0Dby John C. May and Judy Whittle\0D(22Mar91)         ;; Message

Type crsr=GNRL
Rainbow Arrow,0
.H
8001                                    ;; crsrType
00000060                                ;; srsrMap
00000092                                ;; crsrData
00000000                                ;; crsrXData
0000                                    ;; crsrXValid
00000000                                ;; crsrXHandle
00004000 60007000 78007C00 7E007F00 7F807C00 6C004600 06000300 01000000;; crsr1Data
C000E000 F000F800 FC00FE00 FF00FF80 FFC0FFE0 FE00EF00 CF008780 07800380;; crsrMask
.I
1 1                                     ;; crsrHotSpot
.H
00000000                                ;; crsrXTable
.L
0                                       ;; crsrID
.H
00000000                                ;; BaseAddr
8008                                    ;; rowBytes
.I
0 0 16 16                               ;; Bounds
0                                       ;; pmVersion
0                                       ;; packType
.H
00000000                                ;; packSize
00480000                                ;; hRes
00480000                                ;; vRes
.I
0                                       ;; pixelType
4                                       ;; pixelSize
1                                       ;; cmpCount
4                                       ;; cmpSize
.H
00000000                                ;; planeBytes
00000112                                ;; pmTable
.L
0                                       ;; pmReserved
.H
00000000 00000000 01000000 00000000 01100000 00000000 01210000 00000000;; PixelData
02222000 00000000 02333200 00000000 03333330 00000000 03444445 00000000
04444445 50000000 04445500 00000000 05506600 00000000 05000660 00000000
00000660 00000000 00000066 00000000 00000066 00000000 00000000 00000000
```

A Simple Cursor Example

```
00000000 00000006 0000FFFF FFFFFFFF 00010000 DB000000 0002FFFF DB000000;; CLUT
0003FFFF 4F000000 0004DB00 00000000 00059200 0000B000 00060001 0005FFFF

Rainbow IBeam,1
.H
8001                              ;; crsrType
00000060                          ;; srsrMap
00000092                          ;; crsrData
00000000                          ;; crsrXData
0000                              ;; crsrXValid
00000000                          ;; crsrXHandle
0C600280 01000100 01000100 01000100 01000100 01000100 01000100 02800C60;; crsr1Data
00000000 00000000 00000000 00000000 00000000 00000000 00000000 00000000;; crsrMask
.I
4 7                               ;; crsrHotSpot
.H
00000000                          ;; crsrXTable
.L
0                                 ;; crsrID
.H
00000000                          ;; BaseAddr
8008                              ;; rowBytes
.I
0 0 16 16                         ;; Bounds
0                                 ;; pmVersion
0                                 ;; packType
.H
00000000                          ;; packSize
00480000                          ;; hRes
00480000                          ;; vRes
.I
0                                 ;; pixelType
4                                 ;; pixelSize
1                                 ;; cmpCount
4                                 ;; cmpSize
.H
00000000                          ;; planeBytes
00000112                          ;; pmTable
.L
0                                 ;; pmReserved
.H
00001100 01100000 00000010 10000000 00000001 00000000 00000002 00000000;; PixelData
00000002 00000000 00000003 00000000 00000003 00000000 00000003 00000000
00000004 00000000 00000004 00000000 00000004 00000000 00000005 00000000
00000005 00000000 00000006 00000000 00000060 60000000 00006600 06600000
00000000 00000007 0000FFFF FFFFFFFF 00010000 DB000000 0002FFFF DB000000;; CLUT
0003FFFF 4F000000 0004DB00 00000000 00059200 0000B000 00060000 0000FFFF
00070000 00000000

Color Cross,3
.H
8001                              ;; crsrType
00000060                          ;; srsrMap
00000092                          ;; crsrData
00000000                          ;; crsrXData
0000                              ;; crsrXValid
00000000                          ;; crsrXHandle
000007C0 04600460 04607C7C 43864286 43867C7E 3C7E0460 046007E0 03E00000;; crsr1Data
0FC00FE0 0FF00FF0 FFFFFFFE FC7FFC7F FC7FFFFF 7FFF7FFF 0FF00FF0 07F003E0;; crsrMask
.I
8 8                               ;; crsrHotSpot
.H
00000000                          ;; crsrXTable
```

```
                    .L
                    0                                           ;; crsrID
                    .H
                    00000000                                    ;; BaseAddr
                    8008                                        ;; rowBytes
                    .I
                    0 0 16 16                                   ;; Bounds
                    0                                           ;; pmVersion
                    0                                           ;; packType
                    .H
                    00000000                                    ;; packSize
                    00480000                                    ;; hRes
                    00480000                                    ;; vRes
                    .I
                    0                                           ;; pixelType
                    4                                           ;; pixelSize
                    1                                           ;; cmpCount
                    4                                           ;; cmpSize
                    .H
                    00000000                                    ;; planeBytes
                    00000112                                    ;; pmTable
                    .L
                    0                                           ;; pmReserved
                    .H
                    00000000 00000000 00000222 22000000 00000200 02300000 00000200 02300000;; PixelData
                    00000200 02300000 02222200 02222200 02000011 10000230 02000010 10000230
                    02000011 10000230 02222230 00333200 02333330 00000200 02300000
                    00000200 02300000 00000222 22300000 00000033 33300000 00000000 00000000
                    00000000 00000003 0000FFFF FFFFFFFF 0001DB00 00000000 00020000 0000FFFF;; CLUT
                    00030000 00000000

                    Rainbow Plus,2
                    .H
                    8001                                        ;; crsrType
                    00000060                                    ;; srsrMap
                    00000092                                    ;; crsrData
                    00000000                                    ;; crsrXData
                    0000                                        ;; crsrXValid
                    00000000                                    ;; crsrXHandle
                    04000400 04000400 0400FFE0 04000400 04000400 04000400 00000000 00000000;; crsr1Data
                    00000000 00000000 00000000 00000000 00000000 00000000 00000000 00000000;; crsrMask
                    .I
                    5 5                                         ;; crsrHotSpot
                    .H
                    00000000                                    ;; crsrXTable
                    .L
                    0                                           ;; crsrID
                    .H
                    00000000                                    ;; BaseAddr
                    8008                                        ;; rowBytes
                    .I
                    0 0 16 16                                   ;; Bounds
                    0                                           ;; pmVersion
                    0                                           ;; packType
                    .H
                    00000000                                    ;; packSize
                    00480000                                    ;; hRes
                    00480000                                    ;; vRes
                    .I
                    0                                           ;; pixelType
                    4                                           ;; pixelSize
                    1                                           ;; cmpCount
                    4                                           ;; cmpSize
```

```
                .H
                00000000                        ;; planeBytes
                00000112                        ;; pmTable
                .L
                0                               ;; pmReserved
                .H
                00000600 00000000 00000600 00000000 00000600 00000000 00000400 00000000;; PixelData
                00000400 00000000 66644444 66600000 00000400 00000000 00000400 00000000
                00000600 00000000 00000600 00000000 00000600 00000000 00000600 00000000
                00000000 00000000 00000000 00000000 00000000 00000000 00000000 00000000
                00000000 00000007 0000FFFF FFFFFFFF 00010000 DB000000 0002FFFF DB000000;; CLUT
                0003FFFF 4F000000 0004DB00 00000000 00059200 0000B000 00060000 0000FFFF
                00070000 00000000

                Color Watch,4
                .H
                8001                            ;; crsrType
                00000060                        ;; srsrMap
                00000092                        ;; crsrData
                00000000                        ;; crsrXData
                0000                            ;; crsrXValid
                00000000                        ;; crsrXHandle
                3F003F00 3F003F00 40808440 84408460 9C608040 80404080 3F003F00 3F003F00;; crsr1Data
                3F003F00 3F003F00 7F80FFC0 FFC0FFC0 FFC0FFC0 FFC07F80 3F003F00 3F003F00;; crsrMask
                .I
                8 8                             ;; crsrHotSpot
                .H
                00000000                        ;; crsrXTable
                .L
                0                               ;; crsrID
                .H
                00000000                        ;; BaseAddr
                8008                            ;; rowBytes
                .I
                0 0 16 16                       ;; Bounds
                0                               ;; pmVersion
                0                               ;; packType
                .H
                00000000                        ;; packSize
                00480000                        ;; hRes
                00480000                        ;; vRes
                .I
                0                               ;; pixelType
                4                               ;; pixelSize
                1                               ;; cmpCount
                4                               ;; cmpSize
                .H
                00000000                        ;; planeBytes
                00000112                        ;; pmTable
                .L
                0                               ;; pmReserved
                .H
                00222222 00000000 00222222 00000000 00222222 00000000 00222222 00000000;; PixelData
                02000000 20000000 20000100 02000000 20000100 02000000 20000100 02100000
                20011100 02100000 20000000 02000000 20000000 02000000 02000000 20000000
                00222222 00000000 00222222 00000000 00222222 00000000 00222222 00000000
                00000000 00000003 0000FFFF FFFFFFFF 0001D100 3D004600 00021A36 134AC800;; CLUT
                00030000 00000000
```

▶ Summary

This chapter presented a routine that allows you to create and use cursors on a monochrome or color routine. The routine demonstrated the fastest way to bring up a black-and-white arrow cursor from a resource file. The routine also showed how you can switch cursors from one type to another and back again within an application.

▶ Recommended Reading

Gibson, Robert S. T. "Cursor Control." (C.) *MacTutor—The Macintosh Programming Journal*, Vol. 6, No. 9, September 1990.

Gordon, Bob. "Cursor Control." (C.) *MacTutor—The Macintosh Programming Journal*, Vol. 6, No. 4, June 1990.

Lesh, Richard. "Animated Color Cursors." (C.) *MacTutor—The Macintosh Programming Journal*, Vol. 7, No. 3, March 1991.

6 ▶ Windows and Dialogs

▶ Overview of Windows and Dialogs

A Macintosh window is simply a frame for viewing something. Usually a document window contains text or graphics, depending on the application. A dialog box, on the other hand, is a window through which you and the Macintosh talk to each other. The dialog prompts you to supply information that the Macintosh needs before it can do your bidding. It gets you to make decisions and to tell it exactly what you want it to do.

Document windows are highly standardized to give you a sense of familiarity and control from application to application. They are also visually responsive to give you the feeling of the "real world"; that is, you "see" the window opening and closing and can watch the position of the window change "over" the document when scrolling up or down through the document using the vertical scroll bar. The window routines in this chapter follow the conventions for standard windows. Dialogs come in two types: modal and modeless. You can use the routines here interchangeably for both types, except for the routine MyModalDialog.c.

The essential difference between modal and modeless dialogs is that a modal dialog does not have a go-away box. It sits there until you acknowledge it by selecting an OK button or a Cancel button, for instance. And it won't let you do anything else in the meantime. Suppose you need to print a file on your ImageWriter. You do the keyboard shortcut Command-P or you select Print... from the File menu. Up pops a modal dialog box that offers you a number of options. You are required to specify one of three print qualities. You are required to say whether you want to print all pages in your file or just selected pages or sections. There's no way of evading the Macintosh's insistence on answering those questions, except to say, "Aw, forget it," by clicking on the Cancel button.

Another example of a modal dialog is what appears when you close a file. The dialog asks, "Save changes before closing?" and insists that you click on a Yes, No, or Cancel button. One more example is the Delete... item in the File menu. When you select a file to delete, a modal dialog asks, "Delete file '(filename)'?" and obliges you to answer by clicking on the Yes, No, or Cancel button. This type of modal dialog is called an alert; alerts are described in Chapter 7.

A modeless dialog box is one that you can dismiss through its go-away box. You may be able to perform other operations without first answering its questions. Along the menu bar of a typical application are the names of operations such as Print Preview, Page Setup, Find, and Change whose selection will result in typical modeless dialog boxes. You can choose options in or request information from these dialogs, or you can select Cancel and return to your application window. Modeless dialogs do not demand a response from you.

▶ Dialog Records

The dialog record contains a number of entries over and above what is found in the window record. Included in the additional entries is a handle to a list of all the items in the dialog, such as buttons, static text, and edit text fields, as well as a handle to TERecord, the text edit record. This record comprises the information your application needs about all text in the dialog box, both static and edit. When you click in an edit text field, making it active, the Dialog Manager changes the pointer in the TERecord. Static text is handled pretty much the same way. Whenever an update event occurs, the Dialog Manager goes to every static text field in turn and sets the TERecord to that text. It doesn't, however, draw a rectangle around static text.

The TERecord also contains the font information used in the dialog box. On monochrome machines the same font is used throughout the dialog box; that is, you can't have different fonts for edit text and static text. You can on color machines. Apple has provided an 'ictb' resource, (Items Color Table resource). If you have an 'ictb' resource associated with a particular 'DITL' resource, you can change the font of an individual static or edit text field. The Dialog Manager changes the font in the chosen field, draws the field, then changes the font back to what it was. There is still, however, only one TERecord for an entire dialog box.

In the dialog record table is a handle to the edit text record. Immediately after that handle in the table is a variable, defined as an integer that contains the item number of the active edit text field. Interestingly, Apple stores that integer as the item number -1. So, if you have item number 10, it is stored as 9.

The next field in this dialog record is *EditOpen*. Apple uses it for its own purposes. Last of all is a field that tells which button is the default.

▶ Creating Dialogs

Creating a dialog box is simple, compared to creating many other routines. The following routine shows you how to create a new dialog box, allocate space for it in the resource file, draw it to your specifications, and then bring it to the front of the screen.

▶ OpenDialog.c

This routine opens up a dialog box on the screen. You could use three Toolbox calls to do the same thing, but if you're writing a program that requires several dialog boxes, you'll find this a real time-saver.

Listing 6-1. Opening a dialog box

```
PROCEDURE OpenDialog(UAR theDialog: DialogPtr, theID: INTEGER);
  1:  /***********************************************************/
  2:  void OpenDialog(DialogPtr *theDialog, short theID)
  3:  /***********************************************************/
  4:  {
  5:     *theDialog = GetNewDialog(theID, 0, -1);
  6:     SetPort(*theDialog);
  7:     ShowWindow(*theDialog);
  8:  }
```

On line 2 you pass in to the resource file the ID number of the dialog box that you want to open up, and it returns a pointer.

Line 5 is a call to the Toolbox routine GetNewDialog. You pass in the resource ID and also a 0 designating a variable called *dStorage*, which specifies that you want to allocate storage on the heap. If you wanted to specify storage that you had created, you would pass in a pointer. To allocate storage on the heap, you pass in a 0. The next parameter, the constant -1, specifies that you want the routine to open up your dialog box as the frontmost window.

Next, on line 6, you set the QuickDraw port to your new dialog box by calling the Toolbox routine SetPort and passing it the variable *theDialog*.

Line 7 makes the new window visible through the Toolbox routine ShowWindow. If your window is invisible, the routine makes it visible. If your window is already visible, it doesn't do anything more to it.

▶ Dialog Positioning

Sometimes a user gets frustrated trying to figure out where on the screen a dialog box will open. We've all worked with applications where one dialog box opens up in the lower right-hand corner, another in the upper left-hand corner, and another in the top center. If you have a large-screen Macintosh, this can get annoying, especially when you're trying to locate where on the screen you left your cursor.

The routine CenterDialog.c shows you how to position your dialog boxes so that they will always open in the center of the screen. If you choose to have your dialogs open in another position, you can modify the coordinates to accomplish your ends.

▶ CenterDialog.c

This routine places your dialog window in the center of the screen, horizontally, and slightly above center, vertically.

Listing 6-2. Centering a dialog box

```
PROCEDURE CenterDialog(theID: INTEGER);

1:  /****************************************************************/
2:  void CenterDialog(short theID)   /* Set dialog window to center
                  screen */
3:  /****************************************************************/
4:  {
5:      Rect         screenRect;                /* Screen rect */
6:      Rect         theRect;                   /* Dialog rect */
7:      long         menuHeight;          /* Height of menu bar */
8:      Handle       theHandle;           /* Hdl to DLOG template */
9:      DialogTPtr   thePointer;          /* Ptr to DLOG template */
10:     short        h, v;                      /* H and V offsets */
11:     screenRect = screenBits.bounds;         /* Get screen rect */
12:     menuHeight = MBarHeight;            /* Get menu bar height */
13:     theHandle = GetResource('DLOG', theID); /*Get hndl to DLOG */
```

```
14:     if (theHandle != 0)                    /* Valid handle? */
15:     {
16:        thePointer = *(DialogTHndl)theHandle; /* Get ptr to DLOG */
17:        theRect = thePointer->boundsRect;    /* Get dialog rect */
18:        h =
19:           -theRect.left +
20:           ((screenRect.right - screenRect.left) -/*Comp.offsets */
21:           (theRect.right - theRect.left)) / 2;
22:        v =
23:           -theRect.top +
24:           (((screenRect.bottom - screenRect.top -
25:           menuHeight) -
26:           (theRect.bottom - theRect.top)) / 3) +
27:           menuHeight;
28:        OffsetRect(&theRect, h, v);          /* Set new location */
29:        thePointer->boundsRect = theRect;
30:     }
31:  }
```

Note that the syntax follows certain conventions of C programming. For instance, the first character of a variable name begins with a lowercase letter, and each additional word begins with an uppercase letter; hence, *screenRect*. In contrast, each word in a function name begins with an uppercase letter, as in GetResource. Acronyms such as ID are in all capital letters.

In line 2 of the declaration, *void* states that there is no value to return, and short *theID* means that the value to be passed in (the ID number of the dialog) is 2 bytes in length.

On lines 5–10 are several declarations of variables. They are explained in the comments.

Program execution statements follow the standard Pascal calling sequence as applied to the Toolbox. They begin with line 11, which passes in the rectangle represented by the variable (&*screenRect*). Being a variable, *screenRect* is preceded by the ampersand character (&). Line 12 returns the default height of the menu bar.

In line 13, GetResource is a Toolbox routine. If no resource of type 'DLOG' with this ID exists, the GetResource routine returns a 0. The next line states that if *theHandle* is not equal to 0, execute all the indented lines.

Line 16 turns the handle into a pointer and gets the information to which the handle points. This statement shows how strict C is in regard to type casting. For that matter, so is Pascal. You've already declared the pointer as a DialogTPointer (line 9) and the handle as simply a handle. When you call GetResource, it returns just an ordinary handle. It is necessary to convert this first to a dialog template handle, then to a dialog template pointer. Because C is so strict, it forces us to declare that this handle is a dialog template handle. If you don't, C will say your statement is invalid.

Line 17 gets the rectangle from the dialog template. The pointer is pointing to a structure that contains a lot of information. The statement here instructs the pointer to pull out the dimensions of the dialog box and put them into a local variable for later computation.

Next come two lengthy statements, beginning with lines 18 and 22, that determine where the dialog box appears on the screen. They compute how far up or down and right or left you have to move the dialog box to have it centered. Getting the horizontal offset is rather complicated. You take the left-hand coordinate of the dialog box and add it to the right-hand coordinate of the whole screen minus the left-hand coordinate of the whole screen, then subtract from that value the right-hand coordinate of the dialog box minus the left-hand coordinate of the dialog box. Finally you divide the result by 2 and invert the signs.

You convert vertical offset in a similar manner, except that you have to figure in the height of the menu bar. Also, you divide by 3 in the interest of esthetics: A rectangle appearing above center is more pleasing to the eye than one centered.

Line 28 calls the Toolbox routine OffsetRect and passes in the horizontal and vertical coordinates. The ampersand is placed before *theRect* to denote that the rectangle is bigger than 4 bytes and is being changed by OffsetRect; *h* and *v* do not have an ampersand in front because they are only 2 bytes long and are not being changed.

Now that the rectangle has been computed, you need to put it back into the structure. That's what line 29 does.

▶ Window Positioning

Window positioning is accomplished in much the same way as dialog positioning. Unlike dialogs, which you may want to offset for emphasis, you probably will always want your windows to come up centered so that you can take full advantage of the screen.

▶ CenterWindow.c

CenterWindow.c allows you to position your window so that it will always open in the center of the screen. If you want to open your window in some other position, you can modify the horizontal and vertical coordinates in this routine.

Listing 6-3. Centering a window

```
PROCEDURE CenterWindow (theID: INTEGER);

 1:  /***************************************************************/
 2:  void CenterWindow(short theID)   /* Set window center screen */
 3:  /***************************************************************/
 4:  {
 5:     Rect         screenRect;                  /* Screen rect    */
 6:     Rect         theRect;                     /* Dialog rect    */
 7:     long         menuHeight;          /* Height of menu bar     */
 8:     Handle       theHandle;           /* Hdl to DLOG template   */
 9:     DialogTPtr   thePointer;          /* Ptr to DLOG template   */
10:     short        h, v;                /* H and V offsets        */
11:     short        titleBarHeight;      /* Height of title bar    */
12:     screenRect = screenBits.bounds;           /* Get screen rect */
13:     menuHeight = MBarHeight;                  /* Get menu bar height */
14:     titleBarHeight = 20;
15:     theHandle = GetResource('WIND', theID); /*Get hndl to WIND */
16:     if (theHandle != 0)                       /* Valid handle? */
17:     {
18:        thePointer = *(DialogTHndl)theHandle; /* Get ptr to WIND */
19:        theRect = thePointer->boundsRect;     /* Get window rect */
20:        h =
21:          -theRect.left +
22:          ((screenRect.right - screenRect.left) -/*Comp offsets */
23:          (theRect.right - theRect.left)) / 2;
24:        v =
25:          -theRect.top +
26:          (((screenRect.bottom - screenRect.top -
27:          menuHeight) -
28:          (theRect.bottom - (theRect.top - titleBarHeight)))
29:          / 3) + menuHeight;
30:        OffsetRect(&theRect, h, v);           /* Set new location */
31:        thePointer->boundsRect = theRect;
32:     }
33:  }
```

The CenterWindow.c routine is almost a replica of the CenterDialog.c routine. You will see the differences in CenterWindow in the form of extra lines of code (lines 11 and 14) dealing with title bar height. Since modal dialogs do not have title bars, CenterDialog.c does not reference them.

▶ Window Stacking

In most cases, when you open more than one window on the screen, you find that the window in front obscures the windows in back. Often, you have to close the front window to see what lies behind. However, you can control the position and appearance of those windows by stacking them, assuring that the title bars of the windows behind are in clear view.

▶ StackWindow.c

This routine stacks windows that are already open so that each successive window is to the right of and just below the title bar of the window behind.

Listing 6-4. Stacking windows

PROCEDURE StackWindows(theWindowList: WindowList);

```
 1:  /******************************************************/
 2:  void StackWindows(WindowLst theWindowList)
 3:  /******************************************************/
 4:  {
 5:     GrafPtr         savePort;              /* Old grafPort */
 6:     short           numWindows;            /* Number of windows */
 7:     Rect            screenRect;            /* Screen rect */
 8:     WindowPtr       tempW;
 9:     Rect            newRect;
10:     short           vStaggerFactor;
11:     short           hStaggerFactor;
12:     short           n;
13:     short           h, v;
14:     short           nh, nv;
15:     short           windowTitleHeight;
16:     short           hSlop, vSlop;
17:     vSlop = 10;
18:     hSlop = 10;
19:     GetPort(&savePort);
20:     numWindows = sizeof(WindowList) / 4; /* Get number of ptrs */
21:     if (numWindows > 1)                  /* More than one? */
22:     {
23:        screenRect = screenBits.bounds;
24:        windowTitleHeight = 20;
25:        screenRect.top = screenRect.top + MBarHeight +
                windowTitleHeight + vSlop;
26:        screenRect.left = screenRect.left + hSlop;
```

```
27:        vStaggerFactor = vSlop + windowTitleHeight;
28:        hStaggerFactor = hSlop;
29:        v = 0;
30:        h = 0;
31:        for (n = 1; n <= numWindows, n++)      /* Cycle through */
32:        {
33:          newRect.top = screenRect.top;
34:          newRect.left = screenRect.left;
35:          newRect.bottom = newRect.top + 1;
36:          newRect.right = newRect.left + 1;
37:          OffsetRect(&newRect, h, v);
38:          tempW = theWindowList[n];
39:          SetPort(tempW);
40:          HideWindow(tempW);
41:          nh = newRect.left;
42:          nv = newRect.top;
43:          MoveWindow(tempW, nh, nv, true);
44:          ShowWindow(tempW);
45:          v = v + vStaggerFactor;
46:          h = h + hStaggerFactor;
47:        }
48:     }
49:     SetPort(savePort);
50:  }
```

This routine requires that you set up a special structure called a WindowList. This is an array of window pointers that need to be stacked. You pass in the WindowList on line 2.

The first real code starts on lines 17 and 18, where you set the vertical and horizontal *slop*. The slop refers to the indentation and lowering, or overlap factor, of the windows. In this case, you set those factors to 10 pixels for *v* and 10 pixels for *h*.

You get and save the port on line 19. On line 20 you get the number of windows that will be stacked through WindowList, which tells the size of the list in bytes. Each window on the list is a window pointer, which is 4 bytes long. You divide the number of pointers by 4 to get the number of windows.

Line 21 states that if the number of windows is greater than 1, the if-test will continue. However, if the number of windows is less than 1, the routine will end automatically with this line of code.

Line 23 sends a call to the Toolbox, which returns the size of the screen in global coordinates.

Line 24 sets the window title height to 20 pixels.

Line 25 allows for menu bar height and window title height. You reduce the screen height by lowering the menu bar height. You compensate for the menu bar and title bar and then go down about 10 more pixels for the stagger slop. When you draw the window, you want the title bar to be about 10 pixels below the menu bar. This is where the stacking starts.

On line 26 you start drawing 10 pixels over from the left-hand side of the screen. Then you compute the vertical and horizontal stagger factors on lines 27 and 28.

On lines 29 and 30 you set the constants for vertical and horizontal to 0.

Line 31 starts a for-loop. You loop through all the windows, starting with number 1 and incrementing by 1, until you reach the last window.

Lines 33–36 represent the top left position for the new rectangle, which is equal to the screen rectangle top and screen rectangle left. The bottom of the rectangle is equal to the screen rectangle top plus 1 pixel and the screen rectangle left plus 1 pixel.

Line 37 offsets that rectangle by nothing the first time through the loop because *h* and *v* are set to 0. In each successive loop, *h* and *v* are incremented by the stagger factor.

On line 38 you get a variable called *tempW*. That's the pointer to the first window in the window list. On line 39 you set the port to that first window, and you hide that window on line 40.

Then, on lines 41 and 42, you compute two variables called *nh* and *nv*, which are equal to the new rectangle left and the new rectangle top.

The Toolbox routine MoveWindow on line 43 moves the window to the front and makes it active if the window is TRUE, that is, if it is the last window on the list. The factors *nh* and *nv* are offsets. On line 44, you make the window visible again.

You compute a new vertical and horizontal on lines 45 and 46 by adding the stagger factors: 10 pixels down and 10 pixels over. You then loop through again until you reach the last window.

On line 49 you set the port back to what it was when you started and fall out of the routine.

▶ Writing Your Own Modal Dialog Routine

The Apple Dialog Manager has a routine in the Toolbox called ModalDialog that returns the number of the item (such as Fast Save, Make Backup, Save, Cancel, and so on, in a Save As...dialog box) when you press a button. The same routine also handles EditText. It does not, however, handle updates or maintain the cursor in EditText or in any Apple modal dialogs. To do this, you have to write your own modal dialog routine.

▶ MyModalDialog.c

The MyModalDialog.c routine shows you how to customize your dialog box. With this routine you can update, or redraw, your dialog box and maintain the cursor so that it changes to the appropriate type as it passes over static and active *EditText* fields.

MyModalDialog returns the item number of an item requiring a response. If the item number is negative, it is returned as an event. Because the event number is always a negative number, it will not be confused with the item number, which has to be a positive number.

Listing 6-5. Customizing a dialog box

```
PROCEDURE MyModalDialog(VAR itemHit: INTEGER);

 1:   /*************************************************/
 2:   void MyModalDialog(short *itemHit)
 3:   /*************************************************/
 4:   {
 5:     short         itemType, tempItem;      /* type of item */
 6:     Rect          itemRect;                /* size of user item */
 7:     Handle        item;                             /* not used */
 8:     EventRecord   event;                          /* Event Stuff */
 9:     short         eventMask;
10:     char          eventFlag;
11:     DialogPtr     theDialog;               /* The dialog handle */
12:     WindowPtr     theWindow;
13:     char          click;
14:     char          dialogEvent;
15:     short         mouseLoc;
16:     eventMask = everyEvent;
17:     *itemHit = 0;
18:     theDialog = FrontWindow();
19:     for (;;)
20:     {
21:       if (wEvent)
22:       {
23:         eventFlag = WaitNextEvent(eventMask, &event, 9, 0);
24:       }
25:       else
26:       {
27:         SystemTask();
28:         eventFlag = GetNextEvent(eventMask, &event);
29:       }
30:         /* Insert cursor maintenance routine here - see Vol 2 */
31:       if (eventFlag)
```

```
32:     {
33:        dialogEvent = IsDialogEvent(event);
34:        switch (event.what)
35:        {
36:          case (nullEvent):
37:            break;
38:          case (mouseDown):
39:            mouseLoc = FindWindow(event.where, &theWindow);
40:            if ((dialogEvent) && (theWindow == theDialog) &&
                    (mouseLoc == inContent))
41:            {
42:              click = DialogSelect(&event, theDialog,
                    *itemHit);
43:              if (click)
44:              {
45:                GetDItem(theDialog, *itemHit, &itemType, &item,
                      &itemRect);
46:                if ((itemType == 5) || (itemType == 6))
47:                {
48:                  SetCtlValue(item, 1 - GetCtlValue(item));
49:                }
50:                break;
51:              }
52:            }
53:            else
54:            {
55:              SysBeep(16);
56:            }
57:            break;
58:          case (mouseUp):
59:            if (dialogEvent)
60:            {
61:              *itemHit = -mouseUp;
62:              break;
63:            }
64:          case (keyDown):
65:            if (dialogEvent)
66:            {
67:              *itemHit = -KeyDown;
68:              if (CommandIsDown())
69:              {
70:                if (theDialog->editField != 65535)
71:                {
72:                  switch (event.message && charCodeMask)
73:                  {
74:                    case (0x5A):          /* Undo - Command Z */
75:                    case (0x7A):
```

```
76:                    break;
77:                case (0x58):         /* Cut - Command X */
78:                case (0x78):
79:                    TECut(((DialogPeek)theDialog)->textH);
80:                    break;
81:                case (0x43):         /* Copy - Command C */
82:                case (0x63):
83:                    TECopy(((DialogPeek)theDialog)->textH);
84:                    break;
85:                case (0x56):         /* Paste - Command V */
86:                case (0x76):
87:                    TEPaste(((DialogPeek)theDialog)->textH);
88:                    break;
89:                case (0x55):         /* Upper - Command U */
90:                case (0x75):
91:                    TEUpper(((DialogPeek)theDialog)->textH);
92:                    break;
93:                case (0x4C):         /* Lower - Command L */
94:                case (0x6C):
95:                    TELower(((DialogPeek)theDialog)->textH);
96:                    break;
97:                case (0x52):      /* Chg Case - Command R */
98:                case (0x72):
99:                    TEChgCase(((DialogPeek)theDialog)
100:                            - >textH);
100:                    break;
101:                case (0x3B):         /* Caps - Command K */
102:                case (0x6B):
103:                    TECapitalize(((DialogPeek)theDialog)
                                ->textH);
104:                    break;
105:                case (0x41):       /* Sel All - Command A */
106:                case (0x61):
107:                    TESelectAll(((DialogPeek)theDialog)
                                ->textH);
108:                    break;
109:                default:
110:                    break;
111:            }
112:            continue;
113:        }
114:    }
115:    else
116:    {
117:        click = DialogSelect(&event, theDialog,
                    tempItem);
118:        if (click)
```

```
119:            {
120:              *itemHit = tempItem;
121:            }
122:            if (event.message && charCodeMask == 0x0D)
123:            {
124:              *itemHit = ((DialogPeek)theDialog)->aDefItem;
125:            }
126:          break;
127:        }
128:      }
129:    case (keyUp):
130:      if (dialogEvent)
131:      {
132:        *itemHit = -keyUp;
133:        break;
134:      }
135:    case (autoKey):
136:      if (dialogEvent)
137:      {
138:        *itemHit = -autoKey;
139:        break;
140:      }
141:    case (updateEvt):
142:      if (dialogEvent)
143:      {
144:        *itemHit = -updateEvt;
145:        break;
146:      }
147:    case (diskEvt):
148:      if (dialogEvent)
149:      {
150:        *itemHit = -diskEvt;
151:        break;
152:      }
153:    case (activateEvt):
154:      if (dialogEvent)
155:      {
156:        *itemHit = -activateEvt;
157:        break;
158:      }
159:    case (abort):
160:      if (dialogEvent)
161:      {
162:        *itemHit = -abort;
163:        break;
164:      }
165:    case (networkEvt):
```

```
166:        if (dialogEvent)
167:        {
168:           *itemHit = -networkEvt;
169:           break;
170:        }
171:     case (driverEvt):
172:        if (dialogEvent)
173:        {
174:           *itemHit = -driverEvt;
175:           break;
176:        }
177:     case (app1Evt):
178:        if (dialogEvent)
179:        {
180:           *itemHit = -app1Evt;
181:           break;
182:        }
183:     case (app2Evt):
184:        if (dialogEvent)
185:        {
186:           *itemHit = -app2Evt;
187:           break;
188:        }
189:     case (app3Evt):
190:        if (dialogEvent)
191:        {
192:           *itemHit = -app3Evt;
193:           break;
194:        }
195:     case (app4Evt):
196:        if (dialogEvent)
197:        {
198:           *itemHit = -app4Evt;
199:           break;
200:        }
201:      }
202:    }
203:   }
204: }
```

The large event loop is central to this routine because you are looking for any event: mouse-down, update, copy, cut, paste, and so on. The Macintosh Toolbox's version of ModalDialog actually calls a couple of other routines, IsDialogEvent and DialogSelect, to do the work inside of ModalDialog. The MyModalDialog routine calls on IsDialogEvent (line 33) and DialogSelect (line 42) as well, but it handles more events than Apple's ModalDialog.

After many lines of declarations, the for-loop begins on line 19. The two semicolons in parentheses indicate that this is an infinite for-loop, and it will branch out only when you hit a break statement at the right time.

On lines 21–29, you try to see if there is an event by calling either WaitNextEvent (line 23) or GetNextEvent (line 28). So, starting with if (wEvent), you can use WaitNextEvent by setting the flag to 1 or GetNextEvent by setting the flag to 0. Both routines return information from the event record when an event occurs.

If you send for the disk that contains the routines in this book, you will receive an additional routine, MaintainCursor.c which could be inserted on line 30. MaintainCursor searches for the cursor. If it finds the cursor over an active edit text field, for example, it will change the cursor to an I-beam. If it finds the cursor over a static field, it will change the cursor to an arrow. This all happens while you are still searching for events. If an event has happened, an event flag will be set on line 31.

Then, on line 33, you call the Toolbox routine IsDialogEvent to tell you if the event has anything to do with your dialog box. You set a flag called *dialogEvent* and pass it the event record.

Now you need to find out what kind of event occurred. Line 34 starts a switch-statement to check on what the event is. If the event is a null event, as on line 36, you do nothing. If it's a mouse-down event (line 38), you first need to call the Toolbox routine FindWindow (line 39) to get the location of the mouse in the window. Then you set up an if-test (lines 40–52) that states, "If the window that was returned on line 39 is equal to my dialog window, and if it's a dialog event, and if the mouse location is within the content region of the screen, I'm going to continue. If, however, one of those parameters is not true, I'm going to beep (lines 53–57)."

Now go back to line 42 where you see DialogSelect. This routine handles mouse-down events like inserting and deleting text in an edit text field and many other chores. Here, DialogSelect returns click, which says, "If the event is a mouse-down event and if everything on line 40 is TRUE, then DialogSelect returns click as TRUE. If anything on line 40 is not TRUE, then click returns as FALSE."

If click returns as TRUE, the code on lines 43–52 performs a toggling routine to insert or take out click marks in radio buttons and check boxes. The routine calls GetDItem, passes it the item, and tests on the item type. If the item type is a 5 (radio button) or a 6 (check box), it will toggle the value by calling SetCtlValue on line 48, passing it the item handle, and subtracting the old value (either a 1 or a 0) from 1.

If it's a **mouse-up** event (line 58) and a dialog event, you set *itemHit* equal to a negative mouse-up and break out (lines 59–63).

A key-down event on line 64 works much the same as a mouse-down event. If you have a key-down event and a dialog event, you first set the item type to negative key-down. Then you find out if the Command key is down (line 68). If it is, the user may be trying to do a copy, cut, or paste, which is possible in MyModalDialog. So, on line 70, you have to begin an if-test that says, "Since all these things that I'm going to be doing deal with edit text field, if an edit text field does not appear in the dialog box, forget the whole thing!" If the dialog edit text field is equal to 65535, there can be no edit text field. If the edit text field is equal to a number smaller than 65535, an edit text field exists. Suppose, for now, that it does exist. The switch-statement on line 72 gets an event message, which is a 16-bit message. You then mask out the upper 8 bits of the event message with a *charCodeMask*. From this point, you test to see if the Command key event is any of the following:

- Undo, lines 74–76
- Cut, lines 77–80
- Copy, lines 81–84
- Paste, lines 85–88
- Upper Case, lines 89–92
- Lower Case, lines 93–96
- Change Case, lines 97–100
- All Caps, lines 101–104
- Select All, lines 105–108

For any Command key event listed above except Undo, you pass in the text edit record. For any other key-down event, you let DialogSelect handle the event (lines 111–127). Within this DialogSelect routine is a code statement that handles a carriage return (line 122). This allows you to set the *itemHit* back to the default item (line 124). Pressing the Return or Enter key is the same as clicking on the OK button.

Skip now to line 129 for a key-up case-statement. Here again, if it's a key-up event and a dialog event, you set the *itemHit* to a negative key-up (lines 130–134). You continue case-statements for a series of events, as follows:

- Auto-key event, lines 135–140
- Update event, lines 141–146
- Disk-inserted event, lines 147–152
- Activate event, lines 153–158
- Abort, lines 159–164
- Network event, lines 165–170
- Device driver event, lines 171–176
- Four user-definable events, lines 177–200

After looping through to the last possible item, the code branches out of the routine (lines 201–204).

▶ Changing the Default Dialog Font

Usually the font for static and active text fields in a dialog box is Chicago 12-point. There may be times when you want to have another font in one of those fields for emphasis. Or perhaps you don't like the Chicago font and you want to change it for purely esthetic reasons.

▶ SetDFont.c

This routine shows you how to change a dialog font from the system font to another font of your choice.

Listing 6-6. Changing the font in a dialog box

```
PROCEDURE SetDFont(theDialog: DialogPtr, fontName: Str255,
  fontSize: INTEGER, fontStyle: INTEGER, copyMode: INTEGER);

 1:  /***************************************************************/
 2:  void SetDFont(DialogPtr theDialog, Str255 fontName,
 3:     short fontSize, short fontStyle, short copyMode)
 4:  /***************************************************************/
 5:  {
 6:     GrafPtr    savePort;                      /* Old grafPort */
 7:     short      fontNumber;
 8:     GetPort(&savePort);
 9:     SetPort(theDialog);
10:     GetFNum(fontName, &fontNumber);
11:     (*((DialogPeek)theDialog)->textH)->txFont = fontNumber;
12:     (*((DialogPeek)theDialog)->textH)->txSize = fontSize;
13:     (*((DialogPeek)theDialog)->textH)->txFace = fontStyle;
14:     (*((DialogPeek)theDialog)->textH)->txMode = copyMode;
15:     TextFont(fontNumber);
16:     TextFace(fontStyle);
17:     TextMode(copyMode);
18:     TextSize(fontSize);
19:     SetPort(savePort);
20:  }
```

On lines 2 and 3 SetDFont requires you to pass in the dialog box pointer; the font name (a Pascal string that might be, for example, Monaco); the font size (which might be 9-point); the font style (plain, italic, boldface, and so forth); and copy mode. Copy mode has to do with how the text you draw interacts with the text and graphics already drawn on the screen. You can overlay existing text, invert it, blend with it, or paint over it. Suppose half of your dialog box is on a white background and the other half is on a black background. You may want the words on the white background to be black and the words on the black background to be white, or "reversed out."

After two lines of declarations, you begin the real code on lines 8 and 9, where you save and set the port. Line 10 is a Toolbox routine that returns a font number when you pass it a font name.

Now you must change the font information both in the TextEditRecord and in the GrafPort. Each has its own font. If you don't save the new font information in the GrafPort and you call the QuickDraw routine DrawString, QuickDraw will draw it in the Chicago font. Lines 11–14, which exemplify the terseness of C, cast the pointer as a pointer to a true dialog record and not just as a pointer to a window. That way you can get the information in a dialog window that a regular window does not have.

On line 11, for example, the statement DialogPeek in front of *theDialog* casts *theDialog* into a true dialog record. The rest of the line gets out the text font with a pointer. (The handle is now a pointer because you put an asterisk (*) at the beginning of the line.) In short, all that messiness on line 11 allows you to set the text font. Line 12 sets the size; line 13 the style; and line 14 the copy mode.

Lines 15–18 are Toolbox routines that affect the GrafPort font, style, copy mode, and size, respectively.

Line 19 sets and saves the port back to what it was.

▶ Creating a General-Purpose About Dialog Routine

An About dialog box displays information about an application and may be viewed by selecting the About item from the Apple menu. The routine AboutDialog.c, brings up a dialog box with, typically, the name of the application, its version number, and the name and logo of the software developer. Although some developers bring up a copyright notice in the About box, we prefer to keep such a notice separate for the convenience of the user. Our copyright dialog routine, described in the next section, dismisses itself after a few seconds or the moment you click anywhere on the screen. The About dialog stays up until you dismiss it.

► AboutDialog.c

This routine gives you the tools to create your own About dialog box.

Listing 6-7. Creating a general-purpose About dialog box

PROCEDURE AboutDialog(theID: INTEGER);

```
 1:  /***************************************************/
 2:  void    AboutDialog(short theID)
 3:  /***************************************************/
 4:  {
 5:     EventRecord    event;                       /* Event Stuff */
 6:     short          eventMask;
 7:     char           eventFlag;
 8:     DialogPtr      theDialog;                   /* The dialog handle */
 9:     short          itemHit;                             /* Item info */
10:     short          itemType;
11:     Rect           itemRect;
12:     Handle         itemHandle;
13:     char           wEvent = true;               /* Event type flag */
14:     eventMask = everyEvent;
15:     CenterDialog(theID);                        /* Open dialog */
16:     OpenStandardDialog(&theDialog, theID);
17:     GetDefItem(theDialog, itemHit);    /* if def item a button */
18:     GetDItem(theDialog, itemHit, &itemType, &itemHandle,
                  &itemRect);
19:     switch (itemType)
20:     {
21:       case (4):
22:       case (132):
23:          FrameDefItem(theDialog);              /* Frame it */
24:          break;
25:       default:
26:          break;
27:     }
28:     for (;;)
29:     {
30:       if (wEvent)
31:       {
32:          eventFlag = WaitNextEvent(eventMask, &event, 9, 0);
33:       }
34:       else
35:       {
36:          SystemTask();
```

```
37:          eventFlag = GetNextEvent(eventMask, &event);
38:        }
39:        if (eventFlag)
40:        {
41:          switch (event.what)
42:          {
43:            case (mouseDown):
44:              break;
45:            case (keyDown):
46:              break;
47:            case (updateEvt):
48:              BeginUpdate(theDialog);
49:                UpDialog(theDialog);
50:              EndUpdate(theDialog);
51:              continue;
52:            default:
53:              continue;
54:          }
55:          break;
56:        }
57:     }
58:     DisposeDialog(theDialog);
59:  }
```

Line 2 passes in the ID 300. Let's skip over the declarations and go to lines 14 and 15 where the two statements say you want the dialog box to be centered. Line 16 opens the dialog, drawing it on the screen. You need to know what the default item is, so you use the call GetDefItem on line 17. You pass into this routine your pointer to the dialog box, and back comes the answer 1. This is always the number of the default item, unless you have set it specifically.

Now that you have the default item, you need certain information about it. Line 18 calls GetDItem and passes in the dialog pointer and the itemHit, which happens to be the default item. We use the term *itemHit* because we return something called Item later in this program, and we want to distinguish it from the item handle. What you get back are the item type, the item handle, and the item rectangle. For this routine, you need only the item type.

Lines 19–22 test to see whether item type 4 or item type 132 is present in the About box. Type 4 is a button, and type 132 is an enabled button. If either type is there, you give it the distinctive double frame of the default item on lines 23–27, thus making sure that an OK button in the About box does indeed look the way a default button should. Any other type of item, such as a picture, is rightfully ignored.

Line 28 begins an endless for-loop waiting for an event to happen. Many events—mouse-down, mouse-up, key-down, key-up, as well as application-specific and network events—can occur in the Macintosh. When an event happens, the Event Manager returns some information about the event. A variable, *event*, is passed into either line 32 or line 37, depending on a flag, wEvent. The event record has several different parts, including What, which asks, "What kind of event?" and others that cover the gamut of when, why, and how.

In this loop, you're interested only in mouse-down (line 43), key-down (line 45), and update events (line 47). When you get either a mouse-down or a key-down, you dispose of the dialog. That implements a useful feature: Click anywhere on the screen or press any key, and the dialog box disappears. When an update event occurs, a call to the Toolbox begins the update process. For example, the user might click on an inactive window to make it active. That requires the portions of the now-active window that were hidden to be redrawn.

Line 58 disposes the dialog box and ends the routine.

▶ The About Example

This section contains a pair of source code listings that demonstrate the About item in the Apple menu. The pair consists of one file with the extension .c and another file, containing the resources, with the extension .R. The two types of files always go together to make up an application.

▶ AboutExample.c

AboutExample.c brings up the About dialog box and tests the AboutDialog.c routine.

Listing 6-8. Example of an About dialog box

```
1:  /*************************************************************/
2:  void  main()                    /* Routine to test about boxes */
3:  /*************************************************************/
4:  {
5:     InitToolBox();
6:     OpenResources("\pAbout.rsrc");          /* For development */
7:     AboutDialog(300);
8:  }
```

This main program demonstrates the Toolbox routine InitToolBox mentioned in Chapter 2. Being a main, it starts executing with the declaration on line 2 and has only three statements within the pair of braces. The first statement on line 5 calls the routine to initialize the Toolbox, initializing its various managers, clearing up the event queue, and so on.

Next comes a routine on line 6 that opens the file About.rsrc and gets all the resources contained in that file so they are accessible while this application is open. When developing an application, it's a good practice to keep the source code in one file and the executable object code, also called the code resources, in another file. When at last you merge everything into one application, you delete the OpenResources line from the code and recompile the file.

The last statement, on line 7, calls the About dialog box and brings it up on the screen. That's all there is to a routine so important that it deserves a place in every program.

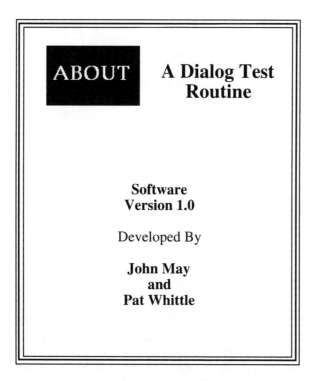

Figure 6-1. About dialog box created with AboutDialog.c routine

▶ AboutExample.R

This routine brings up the About box.

Listing 6-9. Resource file for example of an About dialog box

```
About.rsrc
rsrcRSED

Type DLOG
***About Dialog
About Dialog,300
About Dialog
21 185 317 421
Visible NoGoAway
1
300
300

Type DITL
*** About Dialog
About Dialog,300
1

* 1
PictItem Enabled
0 0 296 236
300

Type PICT=GNRL
,300
.H
4534            ;; Picture Length
.I
45 475 341 711    ;; Bounding Rectangle
.H
```

In this routine you create a resource, About.rsrc, that contains a dialog box with the ID 300. This box contains only one item, type 'DITL', item 1, which is enabled. It has the rectangular coordinates 0 0 296 236. The figure 300 is the ID in the 'PICT' resources. It identifies the picture you're going to put into the About box. 'GNRL' is a PICT resource containing the length of the picture in bytes: 4534. The size of the picture is expressed as its bounding rectangle.

Every 8 bits represent a color on the screen. This routine refers to a screen in which a pixel can have any of 256 colors. Color IDs range from 00 (black) to FF (white), both of which are reserved by the system. Numbers in between represent the palette of colors.

If you wanted the arrow cursor to have rainbow colors, you would add the following line.

```
Type crsr=GNRL Rainbow Arrow
```

▶ Creating a General-Purpose Copyright Routine

The Code of Federal Regulations offers a choice of ways for a software developer to let users know that the program is copyrighted. The copyright notice should appear in such manner and location as to give reasonable notice of the claim of copyright. One popular way is to make the notice come up on the user's terminal at sign-on.

Bringing up a copyright notice at the start of your application sounds easy. It usually isn't, but the CopyrightDialog.c routine makes it simple.

▶ CopyrightDialog.c

This routine brings up your copyright notice as a prelude to opening your application.

Call the CopyrightDialog.c routine, and pass it the ID of the dialog box you've set up in the resource file. After installing this routine, your copyright box will come up as soon as your application starts. The box stays up for the length of time you specify in the constant for delay time, then dismisses itself. Five to ten seconds should be more than enough. This feature contrasts with one well-known resource editor whose copyright graphic never times out. A little jack-in-the-box sticks his head in and out of the box until the MTBF of the machine expires or you click the mouse, whichever comes sooner.

To avoid irritating users, the CopyrightDialog.c routine not only dismisses the copyright notice after a few seconds, but also allows the user to click the mouse or tap any key to send it away.

The CopyrightDialog.c routine has a lot in common with the routine AboutDialog.c discussed earlier in this chapter. To cut down on repetition, we talk here about differences between the two. The main difference is that the CopyrightDialog.c routine automatically brings up the copyright dialog as soon as an application is opened. The AboutDialog.c routine lies dormant until the user needs information about the application and selects the About item in the Apple pull-down menu.

A fringe benefit of the CopyrightDialog.c routine is that it can warn the programmer of problems with program development. You may find that, if something is wrong with the program you're writing, the error will manifest itself when you call the copyright dialog. One example is an absent resource file.

Listing 6-10. Bringing up a copyright dialog at the beginning of an application

```
PROCEDURE CopyrightDialog(theID: INTEGER);

 1:  /****************************************************************/
 2:  void    CopyrightDialog(short theID)
 3:  /****************************************************************/
 4:  {
 5:    EventRecord   event;                          /* Event Stuff */
 6:    short         eventMask;
 7:    char          eventFlag;
 8:    DialogPtr     theDialog;                      /* The dialog handle */
 9:    long          oldTick;                        /* Ticks */
10:    long          newTick;
11:    short         itemHit;                        /* Item info */
12:    short         itemType;
13:    Rect          itemRect;
14:    Handle        itemHandle;
15:    char          wEvent = true;                  /* Event type flag */
16:    long          delayTime = 7 * 60;             /* In 1/60 of second */
17:    eventMask = everyEvent;
18:    CenterDialog(theID);                          /* Open dialog */
19:    OpenStandardDialog(&theDialog, theID);
20:    GetDefItem(theDialog, itemHit);    /* if def item a button */
21:    GetDItem(theDialog, itemHit, &itemType, &itemHandle,
                &itemRect);
22:    switch (itemType)
23:    {
24:      case (4):
25:      case (132):
26:        FrameDefItem(theDialog);                  /* Frame it */
27:        break;
28:      default:
29:        break;
30:    }
31:    oldTick = TickCount();                        /* Wait for response */
32:    for (;;)
33:    {
34:      newTick = TickCount();
```

```
35:        if (newTick - oldTick > delayTime) break;
36:        if (wEvent)
37:        {
38:          eventFlag = WaitNextEvent(eventMask, &event, 9, 0);
39:        }
40:        else
41:        {
42:          SystemTask();
43:          eventFlag = GetNextEvent(eventMask, &event);
44:        }
45:        if (eventFlag)
46:        {
47:          switch (event.what)
48:          {
49:            case (mouseDown):
50:              break;
51:            case (keyDown):
52:              break;
53:            case (updateEvt):
54:              BeginUpdate(theDialog);
55:                UpDialog(theDialog);
56:              EndUpdate(theDialog);
57:              continue;
58:            default:
59:              continue;
60:          }
61:          break;
62:        }
63:      }
64:      DisposeDialog(theDialog);
65:      FlushEvents(everyEvent, 0);
66:    }
```

Line 2 passes in the ID of this dialog. Skip the declarations and go down to the for-loop on line 32, which starts with a call to a Toolbox routine called TickCount. This returns the number of ticks that have occurred since the system started up. Each tick is 1/60 second, so five seconds would equal 300 ticks and 100 seconds would equal 6000 ticks. The tick count is likely to be a large number, depending on the time elapsed since start-up.

Line 34 returns the tick count at the very moment the request is made. Then you say what amounts to, "If the new tick count minus the old tick count equals the number I have set as my delay time, wipe the copyright notice off the screen." In this example, you defined the delay on line 16 as 7 * 60 ticks, or seven seconds. To set a different delay time, change the first figure in this constant to the desired number of seconds.

During the delay period, you want the user to have the option of clicking on the screen to get rid of the copyright notice before it times out. The remainder of the for-loop, which is identical to that in the AboutDialog.c routine, allows for that. When you get either a mouse-down or a key-down event, you dispose of the dialog. Therefore, you can click anywhere on the screen or press any key, and the dialog box disappears. Lines 53–59 take care of an update event by redrawing a now-active window.

▶ Summary

This chapter presented routines for

- Creating, opening, positioning, and changing the font in dialog boxes and windows
- Customizing a modal dialog
- Developing a copyright dialog

You also saw an example of an About box to test the AboutDialog.c routine and the resource file for that example.

▶ Recommended Reading

Apple Technical Note No. 203 "Don't Abuse the Managers"

Chor, Jack Edward. "The About Box." (Pascal.) *MacTutor—The Macintosh Programming Journal*, Vol. 7, No. 1, January 1991.

Denny, Bob. "Mac's Window Technology." (C.) *The Best of MacTutor—The Macintosh Programming Journal*, Vol. 1, 1986.

———. "Window Dynamics." (C.) *The Best of MacTutor—The Macintosh Programming Journal*, Vol. 1, 1986.

Gordon, Bob. "Beginning Windows." (C.) *The Complete MacTutor—The Macintosh Programming Journal*, Vol. 2, 1987.

———. "Menus and Windows in LightSpeed." (C.) *The Complete MacTutor—The Macintosh Programming Journal*, Vol. 2, 1987.

———. "Window Structures." (C.) *The Best of MacTutor—The Macintosh Programming Journal*, Vol. 5, 1990.

Potts, Paul. "Extending Modal Dialogs." (C.) *MacTutor—The Macintosh Programming Journal*, Vol. 6, No. 4, April 1990.

Rausch, William. "Breaking the Four Window Barrier." (C.) *The Definitive MacTutor—The Macintosh Programming Journal*, Vol. 4, 1989.

Wootton, Alan. "Custom Dialog Box for Input." (Pascal.) *The Best of MacTutor—The Macintosh Programming Journal*, Vol. 1, 1986.

7 ▶ Alerts

▶ Overview of Alerts

Alerts, which are a type of modal dialog box, come in three types—Note, Caution, and Stop—in increasing order of seriousness. Each escalation is called a stage.

Deciding when to put an alert into a program and what type of alert to use is the prerogative of the programmer. Our preference is to use a Note alert when we want to impart what we consider useful information. If the user ignores the alert, no harm is done. Say, for example, you're writing a routine to initialize a disk. The note might say, in effect, "Dear user, forgive us for pointing out the obvious, but you're initializing an 800K disk." The user probably knows that, but you include this gentle reminder.

A Caution alert says, "Watch it! What you've done isn't drastic yet, but think of the consequences before you go on." An example would be to mark a place in the program where the user wishes to initialize a disk, but to warn that doing so will wipe out all the data on that disk. The acknowledgment would be to press either the OK button or the Cancel button.

A Stop alert tells the user, "No! No! Catastrophe looms. Cease and desist at once!" Imagine a point in the program where the user is initializing a disk and something nightmarish happens. Instead of a floppy disk, the hard disk is getting initialized and its data are being eaten alive. That's when a Stop alert could save what's left.

▶ A General-Purpose Alert Routine

In this section you'll find general routines for each of the alerts mentioned in the overview. NoteAlert.c, CautionAlert.c, and StopAlert.c have only minor differences, which we describe after each routine.

▶ NoteAlert.c

NoteAlert.c opens a Note alert box on the screen. The note offers users interesting information. Unlike the consequences foretold in a Caution alert or a Stop alert, no harm befalls the user who disregards your Note alert.

Listing 7-1. Bringing up a Note alert

```
PROCEDURE Note(theID: INTEGER, theString: Str 255);

 1:  /**************************************************************/
 2:  void    Note(short theID, Str255 theString)
 3:  /**************************************************************/
 4:  {
 5:     short                   itemHit;
 6:     AlertTHndl              hALRT;
 7:     AlertTPtr               pALRT;
 8:     Ptr                     thePointer;
 9:     Rect                    screenRect;
10:     short                   MenuHeight;
11:     short                   h, v;
12:     ErrorSound(0);
13:     ParamText(theString, 0, 0, 0);
14:     screenRect = screenBits.bounds;
15:     MenuHeight = MBarHeight;
16:     hALRT = (AlertTHndl)GetResource('ALRT', theID);
17:     pALRT = *hALRT;
18:     h = -pALRT->boundsRect.left +
19:         ((screenRect.right - screenRect.left) -
20:         (pALRT->boundsRect.right -
21:         pALRT->boundsRect.left)) / 2;
22:     v = -pALRT->boundsRect.top +
23:         (((screenRect.bottom - screenRect.top -
24:         MenuHeight) -
25:         (pALRT->boundsRect.bottom -
26:         pALRT->boundsRect.top)) / 3) + MenuHeight;
27:     OffsetRect(&pALRT->boundsRect, h, v);
28:     itemHit = NoteAlert(300, 0);
29:     ParamText(0, 0, 0, 0);
30:  }
```

To begin the routine, you pass in the resource ID for the Note alert on line 2. This resource ID (300) is the same for any generic alert.

Line 12 reflects our preference for not allowing the Macintosh to beep at you when an alert comes up. Beeping can be an annoyance, so it's best to reserve the sound for other purposes, especially to warn of something absolutely horrible. Remember the old fable of the boy and the wolf? Anyway, this call turns off the beep.

Your next call is to a Toolbox routine on line 13. This indicates that you're selecting only one of four possible text strings to get printed out from the resource file. The three zeros say, "Forget the other three text strings."

Lines 14-27 have the effect of centering the alert box. Our routine to esthetically center the dialog is inapplicable here because you want to dead-center the alert.

Line 28 tells the program to wait for someone to click the OK button.

Line 29 sets all four items of text to 0, meaning there's no parameter text. This avoids the possibility that text from this routine might appear later in an alert box of some other program you've written.

▶ CautionAlert.c

CautionAlert.c opens a Caution alert box on the screen.

Listing 7-2. Bringing up a Caution alert

```
PROCEDURE Caution(theID: INTEGER, theString: Str255);

 1:  /*************************************************************/
 2:  void    Caution(short theID, Str255 theString)
 3:  /*************************************************************/
 4:  {
 5:      short               itemHit;
 6:      AlertTHndl          hALRT;
 7:      AlertTPtr           pALRT;
 8:      Ptr                 thePointer;
 9:      Rect                screenRect;
10:      short               MenuHeight;
11:      short               h,v;
12:      ErrorSound(0);
13:      ParamText(theString, 0, 0, 0);
14:      screenRect = screenBits.bounds;
15:      MenuHeight = MBarHeight;
16:      hALRT = (AlertTHndl)GetResource('ALRT', theID);
17:      pALRT = *hALRT;
18:      h = -pALRT->boundsRect.left +
19:          ((screenRect.right - screenRect.left) -
```

```
20:            (pALRT->boundsRect.right -
21:            pALRT->boundsRect.left)) / 2;
22:     v = -pALRT->boundsRect.top +
23:            (((screenRect.bottom - screenRect.top -
24:            MenuHeight) -
25:            (pALRT->boundsRect.bottom -
26:            pALRT->boundsRect.top)) / 3) + MenuHeight;
27:     OffsetRect(&pALRT->boundsRect, h, v);
28:     itemHit = CautionAlert(300, 0);
29:     ParamText(0, 0, 0, 0);
30: }
```

CautionAlert.c is the same as NoteAlert.c with one exception, which you'll find on line 28 of the listing. This instruction brings up the Caution alert icon instead of the Note alert icon. See the "NoteAlert.c" section for more details.

▶ StopAlert.c

StopAlert.c opens a Stop alert box on the screen. It lets the Macintosh tell you that, for instance, you're running out of memory or facing some catastrophe, so you'd better take heed and act without delay.

Listing 7-3. Bringing up a Stop alert

```
PROCEDURE Stop(theID: INTEGER, theString: Str255);

 1: /***************************************************************/
 2: void    Stop(short theID, Str255 theString)
 3: /***************************************************************/
 4: {
 5:     short              itemHit;
 6:     AlertTHndl         hALRT;
 7:     AlertTPtr          pALRT;
 8:     Ptr                thePointer;
 9:     Rect               screenRect;
10:     short              MenuHeight;
11:     short              h, v;
12:     ErrorSound(0);
13:     ParamText(theString, 0, 0, 0);
14:     screenRect = screenBits.bounds;
15:     MenuHeight = MBarHeight;
16:     hALRT = (AlertTHndl)GetResource("ALRT", theID);
17:     pALRT = *hALRT;
18:     h = -pALRT->boundsRect.left +
```

```
19:         ((screenRect.right - screenRect.left) -
20:         (pALRT->boundsRect.right -
21:         pALRT->boundsRect.left)) / 2;
22:   v = -pALRT->boundsRect.top +
23:         (((screenRect.bottom - screenRect.top -
24:         MenuHeight) -
25:         (pALRT->boundsRect.bottom -
26:         pALRT->boundsRect.top)) / 3) + MenuHeight;
27:   OffsetRect(&pALRT->boundsRect, h, v);
28:   itemHit = StopAlert(300, 0);
29:   ParamText(0, 0, 0, 0);
30: }
```

StopAlert.c is identical to NoteAlert.c except that the instruction on line 28 brings up the Stop alert icon instead of the Note alert icon. See the "NoteAlert.c" section for further explanation of the code.

▶ A Standard Confirmation Alert Routine

You can require the user's confirmation of an action in a large variety of situations. The Save As command is typical. If you request the File Manager to save a file, and a file of the same name already exists, a confirmation alert will ask, "Replace existing (file name)?" You then have the opportunity to select the Yes or the No button. If you select No, you can cancel out of the Save As command.

The following routine shows you how to build an alert box to call whenever you want to ask the user a yes-or-no question.

▶ Confirmation.c

Confirmation.c presents an alert dialog box that requires the user to confirm a command.

Listing 7-4. Bringing up a standard confirmation alert

```
FUNCTION Confirmation(theID: INTEGER, theString: Str255): BOOLEAN;
1:  /*************************************************************/
2:  char    Confirmation(short theID, Str255 theString)
3:  /*************************************************************/
4:  {
5:    Handle      theDialog;
6:    short       itemHit;
7:    GrafPtr     savePort;              /* Old grafPort          */
```

```
 8:      GetPort(&savePort);
 9:      CenterDialog(theID);
10:      OpenStandardDialog(&theDialog, theID);
11:      FrmDefItem(theDialog);
12:      ParamText(theString, 0, 0, 0);
13:      for(;;)
14:      {
15:        MyModalDialog(&itemHit);
16:        switch (itemHit)
17:        {
18:          case (1):
19:             return(true);
20:             break;
21:          case (2):
22:             return(false);
23:             break;
24:          case (-updateEvt):              /* Update events      */
25:             BeginUpdate(theDialog);
26:                UpDialog(theDialog);
27:                FrmDefItem(theDialog);
28:             EndUpdate(theDialog);
29:             continue;
30:          default:                        /* All other events   */
31:             continue;
32:        }
33:        break;
34:      }
35:      DisposeDialog(theDialog);
36:      SetPort(savePort);
37:   }
```

This routine uses almost the same calls as the alert routines described earlier in this chapter.

Line 2 declares a function in C that will return a short value. The ID is the number of the confirmation alert box you want to bring up, and *theString* asks the question, "Are you sure you want to do this?" The only contents of the resource are the string, a Yes button, a No button, and the dialog box outline. This modal dialog insists that the user answers yes or no; otherwise, it just sits there and stares defiantly.

On lines 9–12, you make three calls to the Toolbox that center the dialog box, open it, and frame the default button.

Next comes a for-loop on lines 13–31 in which you call MyModalDialog (line15) and wait for a button to be pressed. You set the confirmation to TRUE if the Yes button is pressed, and to FALSE if the No button is pressed. Calls to begin and end the update redraw previously hidden regions of the screen as necessary (lines 25–28).

▶ The Alert Example

This section describes a pair of source code listings that demonstrate the three basic types of alert boxes: Note, Caution, and Stop. The pair consists of one file with the extension .c and another file, containing the resources, with the extension .R. The two types of files always go together to make up an application.

▶ AlertExample.c

AlertExample.c is a demonstration application that brings up the three basic types of alert boxes, one after another, in which they say what they are (Figure 7-1).

Listing 7-5. Example of three basic types of alerts

```
 1: /**************************************************************/
 2: void    main()                       /* Routine to test alerts */
 3: /**************************************************************/
 4: {
 5:    InitToolBox();
 6:    OpenResources("\pAlert.rsrc");    /* For devel. purposes */
 7:    Note ("\pThis is a Note alert.");
 8:    Caution ("\pThis is a Caution alert.");
 9:    Stop ("\pThis is a Stop alert.");
10: }
```

This routine begins by initializing the Toolbox and opening the resource file Alert.rsrc. It uses the routines presented earlier to call the three basic types of alert and passes into each the text shown in quotation marks.

84 ▶ Chapter 7 Alerts

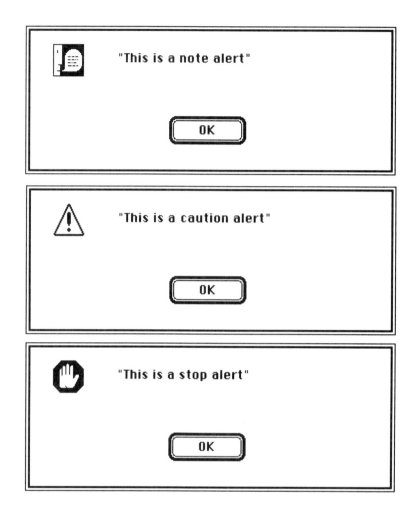

Figure 7-1. Alert boxes created with AlertExample.c and AlertExample.R

▶ AlertExample.R

AlertExample.R is the resource file that goes with AlertExample.c to make a demonstration program of the Note, Caution, and Stop alert boxes.

Listing 7-6. Resource file for AlertExample.c

```
 1:  Alert.rsrc
 2:  rsrcRSED
 3:
 4:  Type ALRT
 5:  ***Generic Alert
 6:       ,300                    ;;Resource ID
 7:  50   40   181   401          ;;Top left bottom right
 8:  399                          ;;ID of item list
 9:  7777                         ;;Stages word
10:
11:  Type DITL
12:  ***Alert Dialog
13:       ,399                    ;;Resource ID
14:  2                            ;;Number of controls in list
15:
16:  * 1   OKay
17:  BtnItem Enabled              ;;Push button
18:  85   143   105   213         ;;Top left bottom right
19:  OK                           ;;Message
20:
21:  * 2   Text
22:  StaticText Enabled           ;;Static text
23:  16   85   76   333           ;;Top left bottom right
24:  "^0"                         ;;Message
```

Line 1 contains the name of a file that you want to create as an output, a directive to the compiler saying you want the output of the compiled resource in the file Alert.rsrc. The resource compiler you run this through is RMaker, and Alert.rsrc is the correct format for the name of an RMaker file.

Line 2 names the file type and file creator. Every Macintosh file has a file type and a file creator—for instance, Microsoft Word files have 'wordMSWD'—whose purpose is to start up the application program automatically when the user double-clicks on the program icon or the file name in a menu list. The output of this file is something you might look at in ResEdit. The ResEdit program edits resources; RMaker creates resources from a resource file. After you've used RMaker to create a program, you can use ResEdit to tweak it. Here you use the default file for ResEdit. When you double-click on the file you've created by compiling this source code, it automatically runs ResEdit.

Line 4 refers to a generic alert box to which we have given the resource ID of 300. It resembles the dialog box. After giving the coordinates of the rectangle, you give the 'DITL' the ID of 399 (line 8).

The number 7777 says you don't wish to include stages in your alert. Stages are a means of escalating the cautions if the user goes on making the same mistake. For example, the machine might first beep to say "Ahem, you can't do that." The next time the mistake is made, it beeps again, meaning, "Watch it!" Finally it brings up the alert box, with or without another beep. Such multistage alerts are uncommon, and this routine doesn't include them.

Lines 11 and 12 refer to a standard dialog in the 'DITL' resource. Number 399 in the alert resource calls up this 'DITL'.

The digit 2 (line 14) says you have two items in the 'DITL'. Line 16 denotes the first item, an enabled button containing the text "OK." It is the default item. Line 21 lists the second item, enabled static text. Line 24 means you're going to be passing in a phrase (identified by the number 0) that gets printed out from a call to a Toolbox routine called ParamText. The numbers 0 through 4 represent four different pieces of static text, of which you use only 0.

▶ Summary

This chapter provided you with an overview of alerts and showed you how to create three generic alert boxes as well as an alert that requires confirmation. It also gave you the source code and resource file to generate an example of three alert boxes.

▶ Recommended Reading

Wootton, Alan. "Custom Dialog Box for Input." (Pascal.) *The Best of MacTutor—The Macintosh Programming Journal*, Vol. 1, 1986.

8 ▶ Resources

▶ Overview of Resources

Resources are little packages of information stored in the file that contains your application. When used, they tell your program how to do certain things such as draw windows or menus. If you look into a typical file on any IBM PC-compatible computer (which, for convenience' sake we'll refer to as a PC), you'll find nothing but bytes. It may be an ASCII file, or it may be an executable file containing the bytes to be executed and the corresponding instructions. The file may have a header that tells you the size of the file or some attributes, but the rest of the information is just what you'd get on the screen when you edit the program.

Look in a Macintosh file and you'll find something different. The first few bytes also are a header that gives the operating system some information about the file. Next is a fork consisting of two offsets. The first, an offset to the data fork of the program, points to the location in memory where the data of interest begins. For instance, when Microsoft Word opens a file, it has to go to the place in memory where the data fork is contained, at the beginning of the file. That place tells Word where to look in the data file so that it can find and retrieve the data. Although this procedure may seem cumbersome, the Macintosh handles it well and transparently.

The second kind of offset points to the beginning of the resource map, where it finds another offset that points to the various types of resources in the map. Having found the right location in the map, the Toolbox then encounters yet another offset that directs it to the sought-after resource.

If, for example, it is instructed to find a resource called 'DLOG', the Toolbox uses the three offsets to reach that resource. Then it has to go to the place in memory where 'DLOG' is stored. Because these steps to a resource take a little longer than is needed to retrieve data, you wouldn't dream of storing data in a resource. If you don't want to access a resource, the resource fork may be zeroed out.

Every resource is identified by a resource type, such as 'DLOG', and an ID number, such as 300. You can have several 'DLOG' resources, but each will have its unique ID, so the Toolbox won't get them mixed up. Even if you goof and try to give two 'DLOG's the same ID, ResEdit won't let you. Another type of resource, such as 'ICON', can have the ID of 300, but there won't be any problem, because "ICON 300" and "'DLOG' 300" are uniquely different.

Resources are nothing more than streams of data bytes stored in memory. Interestingly, the data fork in the Macintosh is less sophisticated than the resource fork, but it still does a good job with the Toolbox File Manager and the support of certain compilers. You may prefer the resource fork because it is better for storing window information and so forth and is easier to use because it has a more convenient interface from the Toolbox point of view. It has its own Toolbox manager, the Resource Manager, which has all the tools you need to manipulate the resource fork. For example, if you want to get the handle to a particular resource, such as 'DLOG' = 300, you call the GetResource routine. The Toolbox returns the handle, whereupon you pass in the type 'DLOG' and the ID of 300.

Now let's compare programming on a Macintosh and programming in a DOS or OS/2 environment so as to highlight the Macintosh's advantages of having a resource fork and a data fork. Suppose you've written and compiled code for a word processing program. On the PC, the executable code would reside in one file. You might have some preferences you've created for the program, such as defaults for the word processing. They might go in another file. Perhaps you got fancy and put windows and menus into your program. They would go into a third file. In contrast to the three files on the PC, the Macintosh combines them all into one file. The code goes into a code resource. The data for the preferences could be stored in the data fork. Information on the windows and menus would go into a resource fork.

If you want to make a change in your PC program—increase the size of a window, maybe—you have to go in and change the program, then do a recompile. This procedure is fraught with danger. You might mess up the program and have it abort at run time. Your program might be so big that when you try to rebuild it you forget and leave out parts. You might link the wrong routines back in again. Wouldn't it be wonderful if you had a tool that would let you change just the resource instead of disturbing the code portion of the program and having to recompile? Well, the Macintosh provides that tool. With the resources separate from the program code, you are able to use ResEdit to alter the size of a window, move an OK button, revise some static text, add a couple of check boxes, or whatever. You don't have to touch the program code.

Resources are arranged in a hierarchy. It works like this. Suppose you open the dialog box with the ID of 5000. The Macintosh takes a series of steps until it finds the dialog. It looks first in the resources your program contains, then in the files the program has opened. Next it looks through all the resources the operating system has opened in the Finder and the System file. In the Macintosh II or later models, the search continues into the ROM resources.

Another capability of the resource approach comes into play if you want to customize a font for use in a particular word processing program. An example would be adding a special character to the 12-point Courier font for use in Word but not in Word Perfect when you have both programs on the machine. You create this special font and put it into the resources of the Word program. Because of the hierarchy, the Resource Manager would search in the Word program, find the font there, and look no further. Suppose, instead, you want to use the special font in just one document. You create the font and put it into the resource map of the Word file you're going to edit. The Resource Manager would peek into the Word program. The font would not be there, so the manager would turn its attention to the file you had opened. Voilà!

Source code is a set of ASCII characters. You present that set to a compiler, which produces machine code. The machine code knows nothing about routines the source code may have called. The compiler plucks out of their individual files all the routines you have created. Next it compiles them into separate object files and links them together, creating an executable file. One convention in the world of computers is to give an executable file the file name extender .EXE and an object file the extender .OBJ.

From this point on in the programming process, the Macintosh stands apart from most other computers because of its revolutionary feature, resources. With non-Macintosh machines you can go ahead and execute your executable file, and that's all there is to it. With the Macintosh one more step is necessary. Since your executable file is a code resource, you have to include the resources you've created by means of ResEdit, RMaker, Rez, or a similar resource editor or compiler. You end up with your application ready to run.

Figure 8-1 gives you a map of programming steps for creating an application for the Macintosh.

90 ▶ Chapter 8   Resources

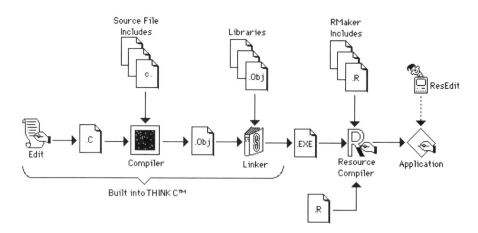

Figure 8-1. Programming steps for creating an application for the Macintosh

A map at the beginning of your resource file contains offsets to various resources contained in that file. One of the places to which the offsets point holds dialogs, which contain all the information on your dialog boxes; another has your executable source code; yet another has menus. Each of these is a resource. Just about everything but the kitchen sink is called a resource on the Macintosh. This feature offers a number of advantages. One is that whenever you want to make modifications—for example, suppose you've misspelled a word—you don't have to go back to the source code, modify it, recompile, relink, and produce an executable file. You simply access the resource editor and make the change there. There's no need to recompile.

The resource feature benefits not only the programmer but also the power user, who can customize a program. One example is to modify a font such as Helvetica by putting a slash through the digit 0 so that it looks different from the letter O. Without the modification (∅), 0 and O almost look the same. Most confusing! Until the world of typography agrees to make every zero have a slash, you have to do it yourself.

| By the Way ▶ | Resources are the reason viruses work so well on the Macintosh. They disguise themselves as resources. The 'WDEF' virus is just one. It takes a pretty sophisticated program to ferret out these pestilential infections. |

Resource names always have four characters. If you see three, the space counts as the fourth. Every resource should have an ID number. Apple reserves all IDs up to 127 for its own purposes, so be sure to start your numbering with 128 or above.

How can you keep track of what resources the IDs signify? The ID number appears in the Get Information dialog box or the New Dialog dialog box in ResEdit. Also, you can put your comments in the box to associate a name with the ID number. When you open the 'DLOG' resource in ResEdit, you get a scrolling list of each 'DLOG' ID number and its size. You can enter a name for each ID.

Suppose you lose track and try to give the same ID to a different dialog. No problem: Up comes an alert. You don't even have to think of an ID, because ResEdit will give it a number for you, and it has thousands to choose from.

Use ResEdit to look at what the dialog ('DLOG' resource) contains. You can select a code presentation or a graphic, just the way it would come up when your application is running.

The first piece of information is the boundary rectangle, which is the size of the window. The Macintosh always deals with sizes by describing the position of the box in terms of its position on the screen with respect to two corners: upper left and lower right. It assumes that if you go to the top left, just under the menu bar, the coordinates are 0,0. Position is reckoned in pixels across and down. Both the Macintosh Plus and the Macintosh SE computers have nine-inch-diagonal screens, 512 pixels by 342 pixels, bitmapped.

There are two ways to describe a location on the screen. One way is to specify a pixel point by two numbers. The first number indicates the number of pixels horizontally from the left; the other number indicates the number of pixels vertically from the top. Extreme top left is 0,0. Extreme bottom right is 512,342 on the standard nine-inch screen and is indicated by much larger numbers on a bigger screen.

The other way to describe a location is by the four coordinates of a rectangle. Oddly enough, the convention for this is the reverse of the point method. In rectangle 50,60, 238,364, the numbers signify that its top left is 50 pixels down and 60 across, while its bottom right is 238 pixels down and 364 across.

Every dialog box has a global location and a size. Global location is where the box is going to open on the desktop. Next, in specifying a window is a ProcID, short for procedure ID. Each type of window has its distinctive ID, a simple number, so you don't have to go into a lot of detail, such as spelling out that you want a title bar with the name of the dialog and so on.

If you want the dialog box to be visible when it first comes up, enable the True radio button. You may, however, prefer to keep the dialog box invisible. This preference can be useful if the window has a lot of information. Things will go more quickly if everything is drawn to the screen before the dialog box appears so that users will not have to drum their fingers with impatience.

The next flag is goAwayFlag. It puts a go-away box into the title bar. If your dialog doesn't have a title bar, a go-away flag has no effect.

Also in the 'DLOG' resource is a refCon. Apple includes refCon for possible use by a programmer.

Every dialog box has items. ItemsID, which describes the resource ID of the items, is always stored under 'DITL'.

▶ Resource Compilers

Once you know what resources you want to use, you can create them through a resource compiler that takes a text description of your resources and compiles them into resource files. RMaker and Rez are the two resource compilers that are most common.

Going back a few years, resources on the Macintosh came into being on its forerunner, the Lisa computer. The Lisa came with a set of program development tools that included RMaker. This tool was adapted and tweaked to run on the Macintosh. The examples in this book use RMaker to compile resource files.

Rez was created by Apple Computer for their Macintosh Programmer's Workshop (MPW) development program. Rez is C-oriented and resembles UNIX, so a programmer used to UNIX might feel more comfortable with MPW. Rez is a more recent resource maker than RMaker and uses a different syntax. Because Rez runs under MPW, you'll need MPW if you want to use Rez.

Several graphical tools are available under the MPW umbrella. Commando is one. It gives you menus from which it generates the necessary commands. Apple's C Compiler is another MPW tool. In addition, several proprietary compilers and other tools run under MPW. THINK C, the popular integrated development environment, runs under Finder, not MPW.

▶ Resource Editors

Much more interactive than a resource compiler, a resource editor works on a file containing the resources, changing them graphically. It both edits and creates resources.

▶ Special-Purpose Editors and Builders

Many special-purpose resource editors and builders exist in the public domain; Apple provides others. This kind of tool creates or edits one type of resource only. Examples are Icon Builder and ICON Designer, which offer the ability to design icons. Menu Builder does the same for menus, and Dialog Creator does the same for dialogs. Special-purpose editors and builders tend to be more powerful and versatile than ResEdit for such specialized tasks.

▶ Resource Decompiler

This type of tool undoes the work of a resource compiler. It produces a text description from a compiled resource file. DeRez is the most popular resource decompiler. It decompiles a resource into a Rez format. REdit is a public domain decompiler that decompiles a resource into an RMaker format.

▶ RMaker Program Syntax

An RMaker file can have comments similar to those in other source code files such as those created with compilers for Pascal, FORTRAN, and C. Comments are remarks that make code more understandable. Not being instructions, they are ignored by the program. Think of them as you would notes handwritten in the margin of a book.

One kind of comment is a single-line comment; the other is a four-line, or end-of-line, comment. A one-line comment begins with an asterisk, or star (*); two semicolons (;;) denote an end-of-line comment. In the RadioButton.R example, whose listing appears later in this chapter, the "* 1" on line 14 is a one-line comment. RMaker ignores some spaces, such as the space after the star. You can put them in or leave them out according to what you think looks better. Some spaces, however, are essential. One instance is the space in a declaration like Type 'DLOG'.

RMaker files also can include compiler directives. (These use the forward slash [/]. The backward slash [\] serves a different purpose—for example, with a hexidecimal number to indicate a carriage return. The two types of slash are not interchangeable.) One compiler directive is a /Quit. This tells RMaker to quit as soon as it has finished building the new resource file. Otherwise, you would need to go to the File menu and select Quit or Open. Another compiler directive is /Noscroll. This directive speeds up the compiling process. It does so by turning off a window that scrolls through your code, line by line, as the compiler reads your code, interprets it, and compiles the resource. Although the scrolling offers the benefit of letting you see where you are in the compilation, the trade-off is a dramatic slowing of the compiler because writing each line to the screen takes a long time.

The general format of the resources consists of a type definition. The RadioButton.R example is type 'DLOG'. This is one of only twelve resource types that RMaker supports. Each is a four-character symbol. The symbols and what they stand for are listed in Table 8-1.

Table 8-1. The Twelve RMaker Resource Types

Four-character symbol	Resource type	Notes
ALRT	Alert	
BNDL	Bundle	
CNTL	Control	
DITL	Dialog item list	
DLOG	Dialog	Used for a description of the dialog box
FREF	File reference	
GNRL	General	
MENU	Menu	
PROC	Procedure	
STR	String	The space after STR is mandatory
STR#	String number	
WIND	Window	

Apple has more than one hundred predefined resources, compared with a piffling twelve supported by RMaker. In reality, RMaker is more versatile than it seems. The twelve resources are by far the most popular, and the 'GNRL' type of resource gives the opportunity to describe more than the twelve listed.

▶ RadioButton.R

Listing 8-1. RMaker file for a radio button resource

```
 1:   RadioButton.rsrc
 2:   rsrcRSED
 3:
 4:   Type DLOG
 5:   ,300
 6:   Pop-up Test
 7:   50 50 236 372
 8:   Visible NoGoAway
 9:   1
10:   300
11:   300
12:
13:   Type DITL
14:   ,300
15:   7
16:
17:   * 1
18:   Button
19:   150 252 170 312
20:   Quit
21:
22:   * 2
23:   RadioButton
24:   87 14 107 74
25:   80m
26:
27:   * 3
28:   RadioButton
29:   87 75 107 135
30:   40m
31:
32:   * 4
33:   RadioButton
34:   87 136 107 196
35:   20m
36:
37:   * 5
38:   RadioButton
39:   87 197 106 257
40:   15m
41:
```

```
42:   * 6
43:   RadioButton
44:   87 258 107 318
45:   10m
46:
47:   * 7
48:   StaticText Disabled
49:   10 9 60 279
50:   Radio Button Example\0Dby John May and Judy Whittle\0D
         Mar91)
51:
52:   Type crsr=GNRL
53:   Rainbow Arrow,0
54:   .H
55:   8001                                              ;; crsrType
56:   00000060                                          ;; srsrMap
57:   00000092                                          ;; crsrData
58:   00000000                                          ;; crsrXData
59:   0000                                              ;; crsrXValid
60:   00000000                                          ;; crsrXHandle
61:   00004000 60007000 78007C00 7E007F00
      7F807C00 6C004600 06000300 01000000               ;; crsr1Data
62:   C000E000 F000F800 FC00FE00 FF00FF80
      FFC0FFE0 FE00EF00 CF008780 07800380               ;; crsrMask
63:   .I
64:   1 1                                               ;; crsrHotSpot
65:   .H
66:   00000000                                          ;; crsrXTable
67:   .L
68:   0                                                 ;; crsrID
69:   .H
70:   00000000                                          ;; BaseAddr
71:   8008                                              ;; rowBytes
72:   .I
73:   0 0 16 16                                         ;; Bounds
74:   0                                                 ;; pmVersion
75:   0                                                 ;; packType
76:   .H
77:   00000000                                          ;; packSize
78:   00480000                                          ;; hRes
79:   00480000                                          ;; vRes
80:   .I
81:   0                                                 ;; pixelType
82:   4                                                 ;; pixelSize
83:   1                                                 ;; cmpCount
84:   4                                                 ;; cmpSize
85:   .H
```

```
 86:   00000000                              ;; planeBytes
 87:   00000112                              ;; pmTable
 88:   .L
 89:   0                                     ;; pmReserved
 90:   .H
 91:   00000000 00000000 01000000 00000000   ;; PixData
 92:   01100000 00000000 01210000 00000000
 93:   02222000 00000000 02333200 00000000
 94:   03333330 00000000 03444445 00000000
 95:   04444445 50000000 04445500 00000000
 96:   05506600 00000000 05000660 00000000
 97:   00000660 00000000 00000066 00000000
 98:   00000066 00000000 00000000 00000000
 99:   00000000 00000006 0000FFFF FFFFFFFF   ;; CLUT
100:   00010000 DB000000 0002FFFF DB000000
101:   0003FFFF 4F000000 0004DB00 00000000
102:   00059200 0000B000 00060001 0005FFFF
```

The first two lines of the listing constitute the header. Line 1 is the name of the compiler output file. Line 2 says the file type is a resource file and the creator is ResEdit, for which the symbol is 'RSED'. Uppercase and lowercase are significant. The creator tells the Macintosh what program to open when you select a file. Actually, the creator in routine RadioButton.R is RMaker, not ResEdit, but showing 'RSED' as the creator enables you to double-click on the resource file and bring up ResEdit automatically.

The comma on line 4 means "null name," signifying that you don't want to give the dialog a name and ID at this point. If you do, and the name is, let's say, "Mimosa" with an ID of 567, the line should read as follows.

```
4: Mimosa, 567
```

You could follow this with attributes signifying, for instance, that the dialog is purgeable. In the absence of specified attributes, the routine uses default attributes stated on lines 7–10.

The groups of code from line 11 to line 41 constitute what are called the type-specific data.

Now, on line 41, the \0D is the hexadecimal equivalent of a carriage return. Thus, this piece of static text appears in three lines as the title of the radio button dialog box.

On lines 42 and 43, the expression 'GNRL' allows you to create your own type of resource. Rainbow Arrow is the name of this resource, and

0 is its ID. One of the Apple resources is the familiar cursor arrow, and it has the same ID, 0. You want to jazz up this dowdy black arrow by endowing it with the colors of the rainbow. Here's where the Macintosh's lookup hierarchy makes it easy. As you read in the "Overview" section of this chapter, the first place the Macintosh looks for the resource is in the program. That's where the ID = 0 resides, so up comes the cursor in rainbow hues. You'll find the rainbow cursor specified for many of the routines in this book.

Going to line 44, .H signifies that the data following it is going to be hexadecimal, which is expressed in 16-bit integers. Icons are described as 128 bytes; 32 bits by 32 bits equals 1024 bits, divided by 8 equals 128 bytes. Double semicolons (;;) mark the end of a line of code and precede a comment. The program ignores comments, so you're free to enter any remarks that will make your code listing more understandable.

When you get to the .I on line 55, the code switches from hexadecimal notation to decimal integers. It reverts to hex at the next .H, on line 57. Then .L on line 59 switches from the 16 bits of a hex integer to the 32 bits of a long integer. Other valid types of statements you can use are .P for a Pascal string, .S for a regular string, and .R for a file name. A Pascal string starts with the number of characters in the string, whereas a regular string contains just the characters. The .R says you want to open and read data from another file. This statement can be useful if you want to include a picture consisting of many pixels.

Be sure to enter a blank line at the very end of your program. Remember, a statement of resource type requires a blank line above and below it.

▶ Resource File Merging and Overwriting

If you put a bang, or exclamation point (!), in front of the first line of Listing 8-1 so that it reads !RadioButton.rsrc, RMaker would look for an existing resource file with that name. If it found one, RMaker would merge the resources created here into that file, overwriting if necessary. Say, for example, you already had a 'DLOG' resource with the ID 300 in the file; RMaker would replace it with the new 'DLOG' 300.

Putting an exclamation point in front of the file type and creator has another effect. The exclamation point makes it unnecessary to specify the resource type and ID unless you are changing it. For example, you could leave out lines 3 and 4 and the machine would know you wanted 'DLOG' 300. If you entered "Type DLOG" and ",301" instead, the machine would replace the resource 'DLOG' 300 with 'DLOG' 301 in your 'RSED' resource file.

Another way to merge resources is to use an include statement. Say your resource is 'DLOG' 566. You enter "Include DLOG" on one line and ",566" on the next, and RMaker adds 'DLOG' 566 to the resource file.

▶ Summary

This chapter provided an overview of resources—one of the most important aspects of programming the Macintosh. This chapter also gave you a survey of resource compilers and editors, special-purpose editors and builders, and resource decompilers; a detailed review of RMaker program syntax; and a discussion of file merging and overwriting.

▶ Recommended Reading

Alley, Peter and Carolyn Strange. *ResEdit Complete.* Reading, MA: Addison-Wesley, 1991.

Andrews, Mark. *Programmer's Guide to MPW, Volume 1: Exploring the Macintosh Programmer's Workshop.* Reading, MA: Addison-Wesley, 1990.

Apple Computer. *ResEdit Reference*, for ResEdit 2.0b2. Cupertino, CA and Reading, MA: Apple Computer and Addison-Wesley, 1990. APDA No. MM0015LL/C.

Symantec Corporation. *The THINKC User's Manual*, Version 4.0. Cupertino, CA: Symantec Corporation, 1989.

West, Joel. "All About Resource Editors." *The Complete MacTutor—The Macintosh Programming Journal*, Vol. 2, 1987.

———. "No Rez-ervations Needed!" *The Essential MacTutor—The Macintosh Programming Journal*, Vol. 3, 1988.

———. *Programming with Macintosh Programming Workshop.* New York: Bantam Books, 1988.

9 ▶ Buttons

▶ Overview of Buttons

In the Apple Desktop Interface, buttons are simple little rectangles with rounded corners and a word or two (a label) inside. They are called buttons because they resemble the buttons you press on your stereo set, television, or telephone. The default button is distinguished by its double-line border. That means you can either click on the button or press Return or Enter to get the desired action.

Much fancier versions of buttons, such as those in the NeXT computer's interface, are quite realistic. They not only look more like the real thing, but they also can be made to respond visually to a mouse click the way a real button does, appearing to sink down when pressed and pop back up when let go.

▶ Routine to Draw the Outline of a Default Button

The Macintosh Toolbox contains a routine for drawing standard buttons, as specified in the Human Interface Guidelines. Surprisingly, though, the Toolbox doesn't contain a routine for creating a default button. You're left to figure out how to frame the default item by drawing the required bold frame outside the skinny one. The routine in this section, FrmDefItem.c, supplies the missing instructions. Once you keyboard the code or install it from disk, you only need call the routine by name to have the default button outline appear.

Chapter 9 Buttons

For readers who are not experienced programmers, we use this routine as a tutorial. The review of the source code goes into greater detail here than in other parts of the book, and the programming principles apply to all the routines.

▶ FrmDefItem.c

This routine puts a double frame around a default button, signaling the user that pressing the Enter or Return key will have the same effect as clicking on the double-framed button.

Listing 9-1. Putting a double frame around the default item in a dialog box

```
PROCEDURE FrmDefItem(theDialog: DialogPtr);

 1:  /****************************************************************/
 2:  void FrmDefItem(DialogPtr theDialog)
 3:  /****************************************************************/
 4:  {
 5:     short        theItemID;              /* Dialog item   */
 6:     short        itemType;               /*   Not used    */
 7:     Rect         itemRect;               /* Rectangle item */
 8:     Handle       itemHandle;             /*   Not used    */
 9:     PenState     penStuff;
10:     short        curveFactor;
11:     GrafPtr      savePort;               /* Old grafPort  */
12:     short        hasColor = 0;
13:     AuxCtlHndl   auxCtlHndl = NIL;
14:     RGBColor     newRGB;
15:     RGBColor     oldRGB;
16:     SysEnvRec    sysEnvRec;              /* Environment record */
17:     #define      SysEnvironsTrap 0xA090  /* Toolbox traps */
18:     #define      UnknownTrap     0xA89F
19:     if ((long)NGetTrapA#ddress(SysEnvironsTrap, OSTrap) !=
20:        (long)NGetTrapAddress(UnknownTrap, ToolTrap))
21:     {
22:        SysEnvirons(1, &sysEnvRec);
23:        hasColor = sysEnvRec.hasColorQD;
24:     }
25:     theItemID = ((DialogPeek)theDialog->aDefItem;/* Get def item */
26:     GetPort(&SavePort);
27:     SetPort(theDialog);
28:     GetPenState(&penStuff);
29:     GetDItem(theDialog, theItemID, &itemType, &itemHandle,
                    &itemRect);
```

Routine to Draw the Outline of a Default Button

```
30:    if (hasColor)                              /* Get frame color */
31:    {
32:      if (!GetAuxCtl(itemHandle, &auxCtlHndl))
33:      {
34:        if (GetAuxCtl(0, &auxCtlHndl))
35:        {
36:        }
37:      }
38:      newRGB = (*(*auxCtlHndl)->acCTable)-
               >ctTable[cFrameColor].rgb;
39:      GetForeColor(&oldRGB);
40:      RGBForeColor(&newRGB);
41:    }
42:    PenNormal();                               /* Draw Frame */
43:    PenSize(3, 3);
44:    InsetRect(&itemRect, -4, -4);
45:    curveFactor = (itemRect.bottom + 8 - itemRect.top) / 2;
46:    FrameRoundRect(&itemRect, curveFactor, curveFactor);
47:    SetPenState(&penStuff);
48:    if (hasColor)
49:    {
50:      RGBForeColor(&oldRGB);
51:    }
52:    SetPort(savePort);
53:  }
```

Call the routine on line 2 and pass it the dialog box that contains the default item. Every item in the box has a distinct number. The OK button usually has the number 1, but there can be exceptions. One example is a confirmation dialog box where you ask the user a question like, "Do you want to delete this file?" and offer Yes, No, or Cancel as the response buttons. You might want the No button as the default response.

In the dialog box's record is a constant that tells this program and the Dialog Manager which item is the default. You could write three routines, one each for the Yes, No, and Cancel responses. That would do it; but why give yourself extra work? Better to write just one routine that brings up all three buttons and allows you to change the default item. You need to pass in only the item number of the button you want outlined.

Lines 5–18 are declarations that have a global effect on the routine. For example, they set the values associated with constants, state which data types are used in the routine, and disclose other fixed information that remains in effect for the entire routine.

Starting the code listing at line 19, the routine leads off with an if-statement (lines 19–24) to determine whether SysEnvirons is present. The system environment record is a collection of essential information about the machine. Is it a Macintosh II, an SE, or a Plus? What's the version number of the System? What processor? Does it have a floating-point unit? What type of keyboard? Does it have color?

On line 25 you can pass in the item ID and the statement returns the dialog and the default item.

The statements on lines 26 and 27 refer to the grafPort. Every window in the Macintosh is known as a grafPort. You can think of a grafPort as a way to define a graphical environment in which QuickDraw will operate. You tell the machine which grafPort you are going to be in. Say you want to draw a line in a window. If you don't call SetPort, the Macintosh will assume you are using the coordinate system of the last window in which it called SetPort. That window might be down near the bottom right of the screen, yet the Macintosh will call it 0,0. Any other set of coordinates you draw will be referenced to the same 0,0. If you want to draw your new window up near the top of the screen, that also will be 0,0. With the GetPort call, you tell the Macintosh you are using another grafPort and its coordinates are 0,0 but you want it drawn higher on the screen.

Getting grafPorts confused is one aspect of the Macintosh that spells trouble for some programmers. If something strange is going on, the probability is high that the grafPort isn't set up right. It's painfully easy to forget to set it.

| Important ▶ | • Always make sure you set the grafPort to what you want.
• Always make sure you set it back when you're through.
• Call the routine GetPort to get the old port. Then do the graphics you want. Next use SetPort to set things back to what they were. |

Line 28 gets the present state of the pen and stores it away for recall. The pen can be used several ways in grafPorts. It can be 1, 2, 3, or more pixels wide. It can draw lines that are solid or patterned. If used to draw over another graphic, it can erase or not erase. Later, on line 47, you'll want to set the pen back to what it was. You don't want the pen to be drawing a line 2 pixels wide, then suddenly switch to 4 pixels wide.

The call on line 29 returns the item and its ID, type, and rectangle.

The if–statement from line 30 to line 41 sets the default color of the frame. If the user is running the program on a color machine, the routine will use the same color to frame the button as to draw the button. Frame color is the same as foreground color. Lines 32–34 return information on the color table for the control. Lines 38–40 pull out the red, green, and blue for the frame. Line 39 saves the current foreground color, and line 40 returns the new foreground color. By saving the old foreground color, you avoid having the wrong color appear when you resume work on your previous program.

The statement on line 42 sets the pen back to its initial defaults of size, mode, and pattern. The pen size reverts to 1 pixel vertical, 1 pixel horizontal. The pen pattern reverts to black, which gives a solid line. Then line 43 sets the pen size to 3 pixels wide for drawing the vertical sides of the frame and also to 3 pixels for the top and bottom of the frame. That width happens to be standard for a default button frame.

The statement on line 44 outsets the rectangle 4 pixels on all sides. Insetting the rectangle by a negative amount to make it bigger sounds like a joke, but that is the convention. A negative inset is called an outset. If you substitute positive 4 for negative 4 on line 44, you shrink the rectangle 4 pixels, getting a 4-pixel inset.

The code on line 45 is necessary because the corners of a button are rounded. The Macintosh computes the curve automatically for its standard button resource. Such a curve radius simply would not do for the default frame, which has to fit outside the regular button. This statement gives the Macintosh the curve factor needed for its computation.

Line 46 calls the FrameRoundRect routine, passes it the rectangle item you had outset, and passes it the curve factor. You get a frame 3 pixels wide around the button rectangle. Frame color has been set to the color of the button, so the two colors are matched.

Having completed its task of double framing the default button, the program restores your original settings for the pen, the foreground color (if color is available), and the grafPort. Just to do something as simple as framing a rectangle, the program has made sixteen different Toolbox calls and one of our own.

▶ A Simple Button Example

This section contains a pair of source code listings that demonstrate the Macintosh default button. The pair consists of one file with the extension .c and another file, containing the resources, with the extension .R. The two types of files always go together to make up an application.

ButtonExample.c

The button example tests the routine FrmDefItem.c and produces a Quit button in a dialog box (see Figure 9-1).

Listing 9-2. Example of a default button

```
/********************************************************************/
void    main()                          /* Routine to test button frame */
/********************************************************************/
{
  DialogPtr             theDialog;
  short                 itemHit;
  InitToolBox();
  OpenResources("\pButtonExample.rsrc"); /*For development purposes */
  CenterDialog(300);
  OpenDialog(&theDialog,300);
  FrmDefItem(theDialog);
  for(;;)
  {
    MyModalDialog(&itemHit);
    switch (itemHit)
    {
      case (1):
        break;
      case (-updateEvt):
        BeginUpdate(theDialog);
          UpDialog(theDialog);
          FrmDefItem(theDialog);
        EndUpdate(theDialog);
        continue;
      default:                                    /* All other events */
        continue;
    }
    break;
  }
  DisposeDialog(theDialog);
}
```

▶ A Simple Button Example   107

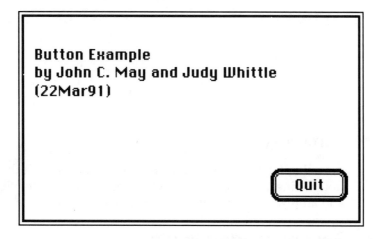

Figure 9-1. Dialog box with example of a default button

▶ ButtonExample.R

This section contains the resource file for ButtonExample.

Listing 9-3. Resource file for example of a default button

```
ButtonExample.rsrc
rsrcRSED

Type DLOG
,300
Cursor Test                   ;; Message (Title)
50 50 278 344                 ;; Rect (T,L,B,R)
Visible NoGoAway              ;; Flags
1                             ;; Proc ID
1                             ;; RefCon
300                           ;; Resource ID of DITL list

Type DITL
,300
2
```

```
183 219 203 279              ;; Rect (T,L,B,R)
Quit                         ;; Message

* 2
StaticText Disabled
10 10 60 280                 ;; Rect (T,L,B,R)
Button Example\0Dby John C. May and Judy Whittle\0D(22Mar91);; Message
```

▶ Summary

This chapter provided a routine for framing a default button with a double line, an example of a default button complete with source code, and an RMaker file containing the resources used.

▶ Recommended Reading

Apple Computer. *Inside Macintosh,* Vol. 1. Reading, MA: Addison-Wesley, 1985.

10 ▶ Check Boxes

▶ Overview of Check Boxes

A Macintosh check box is a little square outline sitting in a dialog window. It can be likened to a latching toggle switch on your stereo set. The toggle switch gives you two choices: When it sticks out, its function is off; when it is pressed in, its function is on, and it stays pushed in until pushed again. When a Macintosh check box is not selected, it is empty. When you select it by clicking on it, an "X" appears in the box. Unlike radio buttons, which are mutually exclusive within a functional group (that is, only one can be selected at one time), check boxes are functionally independent in that you can have one or more in a group selected at the same time. A good example is the Preferences item in Microsoft Word's Edit menu, whose dialog offers a number of check boxes that give you the option to show hidden text, use picture placeholders, show table gridlines, and so forth.

▶ Getting and Setting the Check Box State

The value 1 or 0 in the check box represents either of two states, selected (1) or not selected (0). The two routines in this section perform the function of getting the value in the check box or setting the value in the check box.

You can write your program so that, for instance, clicking in a check box sets the value 1 denoting "on" and puts an X in the box. PutCheckBox.c turns the check boxes on or off to reflect the user's decisions. However, nothing else happens unless you click on the OK button. As soon as the user selects OK, the GetCheckBox.c routine gets that value so that your program can take the desired action.

▶ PutCheckBox.c

This routine puts a value in a check box, making it on or off. Using a voice-mail program for an example, you might have a check box with which the user can reply to the question, "Do you want the system to answer the phone?" The default reply would be yes, turning the box on.

The routine requires you to pass in the item number of the check box and the value to which you want it set: 0 for off, 1 for on.

Listing 10-1. Setting the value in a check box

```
PROCEDURE PutCheckBox(theDialog: DialogPtr,itemHit: INTEGER,
        value: INTEGER);

 1: /***************************************************************/
 2: void PutCheckBox(DialogPtr theDialog, short itemHit, short
     value)
 3: /***************************************************************/
 4: {
 5:   short           itemType;                        /* Not used */
 6:   Rect            itemRect;                        /* Not used */
 7:   Handle          itemHandle;            /* Handle to edit text */
 8:   GrafPtr         savePort;                    /* Old grafPort */
 9:   GetPort(&savePort);                          /* Save old port */
10:   SetPort(theDialog);
11:   GetDItem(theDialog, itemHit, &itemType,
12:           &itemHandle, &itemRect);    /* Get edit text handle */
13:   if (value)
14:   {
15:     SetCtlValue(itemHandle, 1);
16:   }
17:   else
18:   {
19:     SetCtlValue(itemHandle, 0);
20:   }
21:   HiliteControl(itemHandle, 0);
22:   SetPort(savePort);                          /* Restore old port */
23: }
```

Just as in the corresponding get routine, GetCheckBox.c, described next, this put routine leads off with getting and setting ports on lines 9 and 10. Lines 11 and 12 get the dialog items, ignoring all but the item handle.

Lines 13-20 do an if-test on the value by calling the SetCtlValue Toolbox routine, saying, "If the value is true, set the control value equal to 1; if the value is not greater than 0, set the control value to 0."

The routine uses the call on line 21 to highlight the check box. Highlighting, or making a control active, is the opposite of giving it the dim, grayed-out look of an inactive control. To make a control active, you pass it the value 0, making the reasonable assumption that a programmer setting a value for a control wants to make it active. If for some reason you wanted to make it inactive, you could pass it the number 255 instead of 0 on line 21. The number 255 is equivalent to all ones, hex FF. Line 21 would then make the check box inactive.

The last statement, on line 22, sets the port back to its default.

▶ GetCheckBox.c

GetCheckBox.c has much in common with GetEditShort.c (reviewed in Chapter 15), which gets a value out of an edit text field. GetCheckBox.c does the same for a check box.

Listing 10-2. Getting the value from a check box

```
FUNCTION GetCheckBox(theDialog: DialogPtr,itemHit: INTEGER): INTEGER;
 1:  /*****************************************************************/
 2:  short    GetCheckBox(DialogPtr theDialog, short itemHit)
 3:  /*****************************************************************/
 4:  {
 5:      short         itemType;                    /* Not used */
 6:      Rect          itemRect;                    /* Not used */
 7:      Handle        itemHandle;         /* Handle to edit text */
 8:      GrafPtr       savePort;                 /* Old grafPort */
 9:      short         value;                 /* Check box value */
10:      GetPort(&savePort);                    /* Save old port */
11:      SetPort(theDialog);
12:      value = 0;
13:      GetDItem(theDialog, itemHit,&itemType,
14:              &itemHandle, &itemRect);    /* Get edit text handle */
15:      if (GetCtlValue(itemHandle))
16:      {
17:         value = 1;
18:      }
```

112 ▶ Chapter 10 Check Boxes

```
19:    return(value);                      /* Return short value */
20:    SetPort(savePort);                  /* Restore old port */
21: }
```

After the usual preamble of getting and saving the old grafPort, then setting the dialog box needed for your program on lines 10 and 11, the statement on line 12 sets the check box value to 0. Next, lines 13 and 14 get you the item handle you need.

The if-statement on lines 15–18 say, "If the value is not a 0, then make it a 1." This thinking goes along with the basic idea that the check box is merely an off or on toggle requiring a value of 0 for off and 1 for on. GetCtlValue is a Toolbox routine.

What GetCheck-Box.c does is to save a couple of calls to the Toolbox. Without it, you'd have to call the GetDItem routine to get the handle, then call to get the value, then figure out whether the value was 0 or 1.

▶ Toggling the Check Box State

The first two check box routines in this chapter either get a value from a check box or put a value into a check box. The following routine handles the most frequent check box event, toggling, which is a switching back and forth between off and on. When you point into an empty check box and click the mouse, you expect an X to appear in the box to indicate that the function it represents is selected. Conversely, when you click in a box that has the X, you expect the X to disappear. One of the surprises of the Macintosh Toolbox is that although it automatically draws the check box on the screen, it does not automatically draw the X when you click in it. It will draw the X only if you supply a value of 1.

▶ ToggleCheckBox.c

ToggleCheckBox.c provides the necessary code to toggle the check box.

Listing 10-3. Toggling the value in a check box

```
PROCEDURE ToggleCheckBox(theDialog: DialogPtr,itemHit: INTEGER);

1:  /*************************************************************/
2:  void    ToggleCheckBox(DialogPtr theDialog, short itemHit)
3:  /*************************************************************/
4:  {
```

```
 5:        short           itemType;                        /* Not used */
 6:        Rect            itemRect;                        /* Not used */
 7:        Handle          itemHandle;         /* Handle to edit text */
 8:        GrafPtr         savePort;                  /* Old grafPort */
 9:        short           value;
10:        GetPort(&savePort);                       /* Save old port */
11:        SetPort(theDialog);
12:        GetDItem(theDialog, itemHit, &itemType,
13:              &itemHandle, &itemRect);     /* Get edit text handle */
14:        value = 1 - GetCtlValue(itemHandle)             /* Toggle */
15:        SetCtlValue(itemHandle, value);
16:        SetPort(savePort);                    /* Restore old port */
17:     }
```

This simple routine is similar to the various get and put routines in this book. After the usual grafPort calls, the routine gets the handle to the check box on lines 12 and 13. Line 14 says that *value*, which is a temporary variable, is equal to 1 minus the control value. You pass it the handle to the item. Suppose the control value is 0, then 1 minus 0 equals 1; if the control value is 1, then 1 minus 1 equals 0. What that boils down to is that the value is going to be either to 0 or 1. That's the essence of toggling.

Line 15 sets the control value to 0 or 1, as the case may be.

Ending the routine is the customary instruction to set the grafPort back to its default state.

▶ A Simple Check Box Example

This section contains a pair of source code listings that demonstrate the GetCheckBox, PutCheckBox, and ToggleCheckBox routines. The pair consists of one file with the extension .c and another file, containing the resources, with the extension .R. The two types of files always go together to make up an application.

▶ CheckBoxExample.c

CheckBoxExample.c produces a dialog box containing two check boxes, an icon representing a speaker, an icon representing a telephone, static text, and an OK button (see Figure 10-1).

Chapter 10 Check Boxes

Listing 10-4. Example of a check box

```
/*****************************************************************/
void     main()                        /* Routine to test check boxes */
/*****************************************************************/
{
  DialogPtr         theDialog;
  short             itemHit;
  InitToolBox();
  OpenResources("\pCheckboxExample.rsrc");     /*For devel purposes */
  CenterDialog(300);
  OpenDialog(&theDialog,300);
  FrmDefItem(theDialog);
  for(;;)
  {
    MyModalDialog(&itemHit)
    switch (itemHit)
    {
      case (1):
        break;
      case (2):                                   /* Speaker icon */
        TogCheckBox(theDialog, 4);
        continue;
      case (3):                                   /* Telephone icon */
        TogCheckBox(theDialog, 5);
        continue;
      case (-updateEvt):
        BeginUpdate(theDialog);
          UpDialog(theDialog);
          FrmDefItem(theDialog);
        EndUpdate(theDialog);
        continue;
      default:                                    /* All other events */
        continue;
    }
    break;
  }
  DisposeDialog(theDialog);
}
```

▶ A Simple Check Box Example   115

Figure 10-1. Dialog box with example of check boxes

▶ CheckBoxExample.R

This section contains the resource file for CheckBoxExample.c.

Listing 10-5. Resource file for a check box example

```
CheckBoxExample.rsrc
rsrcRSED

Type ICON=GNRL
,311
.H
00000000 00000000 00000000 00000000 00000000 00000000 00000000 00000000
   ;; Icon
00000000 003FFE00 01FFFFC0 03FC1FE0 07EFFBF0 07EFFBF0 07DE3DF0 003BEE00
00363600 0073E700 00FC1F80 00FFFF80 00FFFF80 00FFFF80 00FFFF80 00E00380
00000000 00000000 00000000 00000000 00000000 00000000 00000000 00000000

,310
.H
00000000 00000000 00000000 00000000 00000000 00000000 00000000 00000000
   ;; Icon
00000000 00008000 0000C000 0088E000 0110F000 0220FE00 0220FE00 0220FE00
0220FE00 0220FE00 0220FE00 0110F000 0088E000 0000C000 00008000 00000000
00000000 00000000 00000000 00000000 00000000 00000000 00000000 00000000
```

Chapter 10 Check Boxes

```
Type DLOG
,300
Playback Setup                  ;; Message (Title)
34 32 200 248                   ;; Rect (T,L,B,R)
Visible NoGoAway                ;; Flags
1                               ;; Proc ID
300                             ;; RefCon
300                             ;; Resource ID of DITL list


Type DITL
,300
6

* 1
Button     Enabled
129 147 149 202                 ;; Rect (T,L,B,R)
OK                              ;; Message

* 2
IconItem   Enabled
46 54 78 86                     ;; Rect (T,L,B,R)
310                             ;; ID

* 3
IconItem   Enabled
85 54 117 86                    ;; Rect (T,L,B,R)
311                             ;; ID

* 4
CheckBox   Enabled
56 90 69 178                    ;; Rect (T,L,B,R)
Speaker                         ;; Message

* 5
CheckBox   Enabled
96 90 108 186                   ;; Rect (T,L,B,R)
Telephone                       ;; Message

* 6
StaticText Enabled
21 16 42 170                    ;; Rect (T,L,B,R)
Playback Through ...            ;; Message
```

▶ Summary

This chapter provided three routines that help you manipulate the value in a check box.

- Getting a value from a check box
- Putting a value in a check box
- Toggling the value in a check box

It also gave an example of a check box created with a combination of the three routines, plus the source code and the resource file for the example.

11 ▶ Radio Buttons

▶ Overview of Radio Buttons

Radio buttons—the little open or bull's-eye circles in a dialog window—got their name because they act like the station selection buttons on a car radio. They are designed so that only one button in the group can be active at one time. After all, who would want two or more stations playing through the same speakers at the same time, even if it were possible? Until recently, car radio buttons were electromechanical contraptions, and all buttons in the group were interlocked by a mechanism. Now the interlock is done with flip-flops and transistor latches, but the effect is the same.

A radio button in the standard Macintosh graphical interface is a plain circle that you click on to select. The chosen one shows a solid dot in the middle, like a small bull's-eye. Microsoft Word's Page Setup item in the File menu on the Macintosh Plus is a good example. Its dialog has a group of five radio buttons that allow you to select only one paper format at a time, such as US Letter or US Legal.

▶ Setting the Radio Button State

The routines in this section work a lot like the get and put routines for check boxes, described in Chapter 10. In fact, a radio button and a check box are indistinguishable to the Macintosh Toolbox and in the control definitions written by Apple. Functionality distinguishes one type of control from the other: Whereas you can have several in a group of check boxes on at a time, only one radio button in a functional group can be on at once.

Our radio button routines make several assumptions—that the radio buttons are grouped, that they are numbered contiguously, and that the selection of one radio button deselects the others. Contiguous numbering is not essential, but it's strongly recommended. If, for instance, you numbered four radio buttons 5, 6, 8, and 9 and later gave a different type of item the number 7, your program would mess up.

All three routines use the familiar calls to save the old port while you bring up a different one, then restore the old port to its original setting.

▶ GetRadioButton.c

This routine gets the value from a radio button, returning the ID of the radio button that is pressed. First you need to pass in the ID of the first and last radio buttons in a group. All the ID numbers must be contiguous for this routine to work right.

Listing 11-1. Getting the value from a radio button

```
FUNCTION GetRadioButton(theDialog: DialogPtr, firstItem: INTEGER,
        lastItem: INTEGER): INTEGER;

 1: /*************************************************************/
 2: short   GetRadioButton
 3:         (DialogPtr theDialog, short firstItem, short lastItem)
 4: /*************************************************************/
 5: {
 6:    short        itemType;                      /* Not used */
 7:    Rect         itemRect;                      /* Not used */
 8:    Handle       itemHandle;         /* Handle to edit text */
 9:    short        value;              /* Which radio is down */
10:    GrafPtr      savePort;                   /* Old grafPort */
11:
12:    GetPort(&savePort);                       /* Save old port */
13:    SetPort(theDialog);
14:    for (value = firstItem;value <= lastItem; value++)
15:    {
16:      GetDItem(theDialog, itemNo, &itemType,
17:           &itemHandle, &itemRect);      /* Get edit text handle */
18:      if (GetCtlValue(itemHandle))
19:      {
```

```
20:         return(value);
21:         break;
22:      }
23:   }
24:   SetPort(savePort);                    /* Restore old port */
25: }
```

After several lines of declarations and getting and setting the port, line 14 says that this function returns a value denoting that a radio button is pressed or not pressed.

Like the other routines in the get and put category, this routine requires the pointer to the dialog. Unlike the others, is that it also requires the IDs of the first and last items. With, for example, three radio buttons numbered 5, 6, and 7, radio button number 5 would be the first and number 7 the last. So, line 14 says, "For a value equal to the first item, loop as long as the value is equal to or less than the last item, and increment this item with each loop." In our example, the looping continues until the value reaches 8.

Lines 16 and 17 get the handle to the dialog item number, which in our example is 5.

Lines 18–22 amount to: "If the control value returns any number but 0, the value will be returned, and the break-statement will branch you out of the for-loop." In the example of radio buttons numbered 5 through 7, you'll branch out of the loop after one cycle if radio button number 5 is pressed and after three cycles if number 7 is pressed. If no button is pressed, the value 8 will be returned after four cycles, whereupon you branch out of the loop.

The routine assumes that only one radio button is pressed. Don't worry about what will happen if two or more are pressed. PushRadioButton.c in this chapter takes care of that eventuality.

▶ PutRadioButton.c

This routine is the put counterpart of GetRadioButton.c just described. It puts a value in a radio button, making it on or off. The routine requires you to pass in the item number of the radio button and the value to which you want it set: 0 for off, 1 for on.

Listing 11-2. Setting the value in a radio button

```
PROCEDURE PutRadioButton(theDialog: DialogPtr,itemHit: INTEGER,
         value: INTEGER);
```

```
 1:  /***************************************************************/
 2:  void PutRadioButton(DialogPtr theDialog, short itemHit, short
 3:          value)
 4:  /***************************************************************/
 5:  {
 6:    short           itemType;                     /* Not used */
 7:    Rect            itemRect;                     /* Not used */
 8:    Handle          itemHandle;          /* Handle to edit text */
 9:    GrafPtr         savePort;                  /* Old grafPort */
10:    GetPort(&savePort);                       /* Save old port */
11:    SetPort(theDialog);
12:    GetDItem(theDialog, itemHit, &itemType,
13:             &itemHandle, &itemRect);    /* Get edit text handle */
14:    if (value)
15:    {
16:      SetCtlValue(itemHandle, 1);
17:    }
18:    else
19:    {
20:      SetCtlValue(itemHandle, 0);
21:    }
22:    HiliteControl(itemHandle, 0);
23:    SetPort(savePort);                      /* Restore old port */
24:  }
```

Just as in the corresponding get routine, GetRadioButton.c, this put routine leads off with getting and setting ports on lines 10 and 11. Lines 12 and 13 get the dialog items, ignoring all but the item handle.

Lines 14–21 do an if-test on the value by calling the SetCtlValue Toolbox routine, saying, "If the value is true, set the control value equal to 1; if the value is not greater than 0, set the control value to 0."

The routine uses the call on line 22 to highlight the radio button. Highlighting an active control is the opposite of giving it the dim, grayed-out look of an inactive control. To make a control active, you pass it the value 0, making the reasonable assumption that a programmer setting a value for a control wants to make the it active. If for some reason you wanted to make it inactive, you could pass it the number 255 instead of 0 on line 22. The number 255 is equivalent to all ones, hex FF. Line 22 would then make the radio button inactive.

The last statement, on line 23, sets the port back to its default.

▶ Grouping Radio Buttons

Radio buttons must, to comply with the Human Interface Guidelines, be mutually exclusive within a group. Click on one to select it, and all the others are deselected.

▶ PushRadioButton.c

This routine, PushRadioButton.c, gives the radio buttons in a group the necessary attribute of exclusivity.

Listing 11-3. Making radio buttons within a group mutually exclusive

```
PROCEDURE PushRadioButton(theDialog: DialogPtr,itemHit: INTEGER,
         firstItem: INTEGER, lastItem: INTEGER);

 1:  /**************************************************************/
 2:  void    PushRadioButton
 3:          (DialogPtr theDialog, short itemHit, short firstItem,
 4:              short lastItem)
 5:  /**************************************************************/
 6:  {
 7:    short         itemType;                    /* Not used */
 8:    Rect          itemRect;                    /* Not used */
 9:    Handle        itemHandle;          /* Handle to edit text */
10:    short         value;               /* Which radio is down */
11:    GrafPtr       savePort;                 /* Old grafPtr */
12:    GetPort(&savePort);                     /* Save old port */
13:    SetPort(theDialog);
14:    for (value = firstItem;
15:        value <= lastItem; value++)      /* Reset all buttons */
16:    {
17:      GetDItem(theDialog, value, &itemType, &itemHandle,
           &itemRect);
18:      SetCtlValue(itemHandle,0);
19:    }
20:    if ((itemHit < firstItem) ||
21:        (itemHit > lastItem))           /* Is button valid? */
22:    {
23:      for (value = firstItem;
24:         value <= lastItem; value++)    /* Set buttons inactive */
25:      {
26:        GetDItem(theDialog, value, &itemType, &itemHandle,
             &itemRect);
```

```
27:         HiliteControl(itemHandle, 255);
28:      {
29:      }
30:      else
31:      {
32:        for (value = firstItem;
33:             value <= lastItem; value++)    /* Set buttons active */
34:        {
35:          GetDItem(theDialog, value, &itemType, &itemHandle,
                &itemRect);
36:          HiliteControl(itemHandle,0);
37:        }
38:        GetDItem(theDialog, itemHit, &itemType,
39:              &itemHandle, &itemRect);      /* Set the button */
40:        SetCtlValue(itemHandle, 1);
41:      }
42:      SetPort(savePort);                    /* Restore old port */
43: }
```

PushRadioButton.c is a subroutine as opposed to a function. As shown on lines 3 and 4, it requires the dialog pointer, the item representing the pushed button, and the first and last items in the list of buttons. Assumptions are that all the items are contiguously numbered radio buttons and that the button to be pressed is in that group.

After several lines of declarations and getting and saving the port, line 14 starts a for-loop that bumps up the value of the radio button with each loop. Within the for-loop, lines 17 and 18 reset all the radio buttons to off, meaning that none is in the pressed condition.

Line 20 starts an if-test that says, "If the item you're going to press is less than the first item or greater than the last item—in other words, if the item isn't within the range of contiguous allocated numbers—then go through the for-loop on lines 23–28, which makes every radio button inactive."

If, however, the item you press is within the valid range, the routine does another for-loop on lines 30–37 that is identical to the previous for-loop, except that this one makes all the valid buttons active.

On line 38 you call the Toolbox routine GetDItem and pass it the item number of the button you want to press.

Line 40 calls the Toolbox routine SetCtlValue. You pass it the handle of the desired button and pass it the number 1, which says, "Press that button."

After restoring the port to the old settings on line 42, you finish the routine. Your radio button group has become mutually exclusive.

▶ A Simple Radio Button Example

This section contains a pair of source code listings that demonstrate the routine PushRadioButton.c, as seen in Figure 11-1. The pair consists of one file with the extension .c and another file, containing the resources, with the extension .R. The two types of files always go together to make up an application.

▶ RadioButtonExample.c

This example tests the routine PushRadioButton.c.

Listing 11-4. Example of radio buttons

```
/*********************************************************************/
void    main()                         /* Routine to test radio button */
/*********************************************************************/
{
  DialogPtr     theDialog;
  short         itemHit;
  InitToolBox();
  OpenResources("\pRadioButtonExample.rsrc"); /*For dev purpose */
  CenterDialog(300);
  OpenDialog(&theDialog,300);
  FrmDefItem(theDialog);
  PushRadioButton(theDialog, 2, 2, 6);
  for(;;)
  {
    MyModalDialog(itemHit);
    switch (itemHit)
    {
      case (1):
        break;
      case (2):
      case (3):
      case (4):
      case (5):
      case (6):
        PushRadioButton(theDialog, itemHit, 2, 6);
        continue;
      case (-updateEvt):
        BeginUpdate(theDialog);
          UpDialog(theDialog);
          FrmDefItem(theDialog);
        EndUpdate(theDialog);
        continue;
```

```
        default:                              /* All other events */
            continue;
      }
      break;
   }
   DisposeDialog(theDialog);
}
```

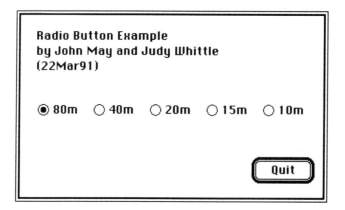

Figure 11-1. Dialog box with example of radio buttons

▶ RadioButtonExample.R

This section contains the resource file for RadioButtonExample.c.

Listing 11-5. Resource file for example of radio buttons

```
RadioButtonExample.rsrc
rsrcRSED

Type DLOG
,300
Radio Button Test
50 50 236 372
Visible NoGoAway
1
300
300
```

```
Type DITL
,300
7

* 1
Button
150 252 170 312
Quit

* 2
RadioButton
87 14 107 74
80m

* 3
RadioButton
87 75 107 135
40m

* 4
RadioButton
87 136 107 196
20m

* 5
RadioButton
87 197 106 257
15m

* 6
RadioButton
87 258 107 318
10m

* 7
StaticText Disabled
10 9 60 279
Radio Button Example\0Dby John May and Judy Whittle\0D(22Mar91)
```

▶ Summary

This chapter presented three routines for handling radio buttons.

- Getting the value of a radio button
- Setting the value of a radio button
- Making a group of radio buttons mutually exclusive

The chapter also included an example that tests the routine PushRadioButton.c as well as the source code and resource file for the example.

12 ▶ Icons

▶ Overview of Icons

Icons, in the Apple Desktop Interface, typically represent familiar objects such as disks, folders, applications, documents, and so on. Often these icons are static, so that when you click on them, they do nothing or, in the case of an application or document, they open up. However, icons can be used in dialog boxes as control buttons that, when pressed, perform some function.

The routines in this chapter deal with two classes of icons: button and toggle. Real-world buttons can be of the "button" or "toggle" type. When you push a doorbell button, it goes down; when you release, it pops back. When you press a latching toggle switch on your stereo set, it stays pressed until you push it again.

For each button or toggle icon, you actually need two icons. You need to show a button that is pushed and a button that is not pushed or a toggle switch that is up or down, or on or off. In this way you can give your application a little animation, at least two frames of it. Animated icons can be nice to look at, but they can be overused. You might use an icon for a Find function, but you would not use one for an Okay function: What could you illustrate with an icon for an okay? The example in this chapter uses a toggle icon to represent the on and off positions of a switch in a dialog box.

▶ Using Icons as Control Buttons

The routines in this section provide three capabilities for icon buttons. The first routine draws the icon, the second handles a mouse-down event inside the icon, and the third disposes of the icon.

Included as a prologue are some declarations (Listing 12-1) that need to go into your application globally so that all the routines have access to them. In C, you put global declarations outside of the curly braces. If you put them inside the curly braces, they become local declarations for that routine only.

Listing 12-1. Global code defining the structure for three button icon routines

```
 1:  typedef struct
 2:  {
 3:    DialogPtr oDialog;
 4:    short oItem;
 5:    Handle switchA;
 6:    Handle switchB;
 7:    char inColor;
 8:    short valueA;
 9:    short valueB;
10:  } iconBut, *pIconBut,  **hIconBut;
```

This type definition structure creates a variable called an iconBut. The structure has five items in it: the pointer to the dialog box that contains the button icon; the item in the dialog box that, when hit, represents the button icon; two icons—one icon to be drawn when the button is on and one icon to be drawn when it is off; and information on whether the icon is in color.

▶ GetButtonIcon.c

GetButtonIcon.c draws the button icon on the screen. In order to use button icons, you have to create in the dialog box an item that is the exact size of the icon that will be drawn on the screen. The item can be either a user item or an icon item. Normally, icon items inside a dialog box don't do anything. For example, the icons on alerts are static; you can click on them, but nothing happens. The icons in these routines perform a function.

Listing 12-2. Drawing a button icon

```
FUNCTION GetButtonIcon (theDialog: DialogPtr, itemHit: INTEGER, icon1:
INTEGER, icon2: INTEGER): hIconBut;

 1:   /***************************************************************/
 2:   hIconBut   GetButtonIcon (DialogPtr theDialog,
 3:                             short itemHit,short icon1,short icon2)
 4:   /***************************************************************/
 5:   {
 6:     GrafPtr           savePort;                  /* Old grafPort */
 7:     SysEnvRec         sysEnvRec;                 /* Environment */
 8:     short             itemType;
 9:     Rect              itemRect;
10:     Handle            itemHandle;
11:     hButtonIcon       hButIcon;
12:     pButtonIcon       pButIcon;
13:     #define           SysEnvironsTrap 0xA090     /* Toolbox traps */
14:     #define           UnknownTrap 0xA89F
15:
16:     GetPort(&savePort);
17:     SetPort(theDialog);
18:     if ((long)NGetTrapAddress(SysEnvironsTrap, OSTrap) !=
19:         (long)NGetTrapAddress(UnknownTrap, ToolTrap))
20:     {
21:        SysEnvirons(1, &sysEnvRec);
22:     }
23:     hButIcon = (hButtonIcon)NewHandle (sizeof(iconBut));
24:     HLock(hButIcon);
25:     pButIcon = *hButIcon;
26:     pButIcon->oDialog = theDialog;
27:     pButIcon->oItem = itemHit;
28:     pButIcon->switchA = nil;
29:     pButIcon->switchB = nil;
30:     if (sysEnvRec.hasColorQD)
31:     {
32:       pButIcon->switchA =  (Handle)GetCIcon(icon1);
33:       pButIcon->switchB = (Handle)GetCIcon(icon2);
34:       pButIcon->inColor = true;
35:     }
36:     else
37:     {
38:       pButIcon->switchA = (Handle)GetIcon(icon1);
39:       pButIcon->switchB = (Handle)GetIcon(icon2);
40:       pButIcon->inColor = false;
41:     }
42:     GetDItem(theDialog, itemHit, &itemType, &itemHandle,
             &itemRect);
```

```
43:     pButIcon->valueA = true;
44:     pButIcon->valueB = false;
45:     if (pButIcon->inColor)
46:     {
47:       PlotCIcon(&itemRect, pButIcon->switchA);
48:     }
49:     else
50:     {
51:       PlotIcon(&itemRect, pButIcon->switchA);
52:     }
53:     SetDItem(theDialog, itemHit, itemType, pButIcon->switchA,
54:         &itemRect);
55:     HUnlock(hButIcon);
56:     SetPort(savePort);
57:     return(hButIcon);
58: }
```

To begin, line 2 returns a handle to all the items in the type definition. When you call the routine, it requires that you pass in a pointer to the dialog box that contains the icon, the item number for the icon, and the ID of two icon resources: 'cicn' for a color icon or 'ICON' for a black-and-white icon.

After ten lines of declarations, the first active code on lines 16 and 17 gets, saves, and sets the port.

Lines 18–22 determine if a SysEnvirons record is present and if the machine has color. (The review of FrmDefItem.c in Chapter 9 includes a discussion of SysEnvirons.)

Line 23 gets the memory for the items that are stored in the type definition structure by calling the Toolbox Memory Manager routine NewHandle, which returns a handle to a specified number of bytes of memory on the heap. If your type definition requires 10 bytes of memory, that is what the Memory Manager allocates. Also, because the call to NewHandle returns a generic handle, the statement (hButtonIcon) before NewHandle casts it as a handle to the button icon.

Since the heap moves things around in memory, and the routine does not want this allocation of memory moved, it locks the handle to the button icon with the statement on line 24.

Line 25 dereferences the handle and gets a pointer to it. Lines 26–29 store the pointers to the dialog box and the item in the allocated spot in memory and set the values of the switches to nil.

The if-statement on lines 30–35 says, "If I have color available, then I want the handles to icons 1 and 2 to be in color." The Toolbox routine GetCIcon does this. However, if color is not available, the else-statement on lines 36–41 gets handles to black-and-white icons through the Toolbox routine GetIcon.

At this point, the routine has set up the icons, but they have not yet been drawn on the screen. Line 42 calls the Toolbox routine GetDItem and passes it the dialog and the item hit. It returns, among other things, the item rectangle, which is passed into the Toolbox routines PlotCIcon and PlotIcon when the icon is drawn (lines 47–51).

The assumption on lines 43 and 44 is that the first icon to be drawn will be the off-position icon, which is icon A. Line 43 sets the A value to true, and line 44 sets the B (on-position icon) value to false.

The if-statement on lines 45–52 plots the icon on the screen. The statement says, "If I have color, then draw icon A in color; if I don't have color, draw icon A in black-and-white."

The call on line 53 returns the handle to the icon.

To finish the routine, line 55 unlocks the handle to the icon, line 56 sets the port back to the original position, and line 57 returns the handle to the structure where all the values were placed.

▶ DoButtonIcon.c

Whenever the mouse button is pressed inside of the icon, DoButtonIcon.c performs the required function. If the icon is a push button, which it is in this particular case, then DoButtonIcon.c changes the button to the on position. When the mouse button is released, the routine changes the button back to the off position.

Listing 12-3. Acting on a mouse-down event inside a button icon

PROCEDURE DoButtonIcon(hButIcon: hIconBut);

```
 1:    /****************************************************************/
 2:    void DoButtonIcon(hButtonIcon hButIcon)
 3:    /****************************************************************/
 4:    {
 5:        GrafPtr         savePort;                   /* Old grafPort */
 6:        DialogPtr       theDialog;
 7:        short           itemType;
 8:        Rect            itemRect;
 9:        Handle          itemHandle;
10:        pButtonIcon     pButIcon;
11:        short           itemHit;
12:        HLock(hButIcon);
13:        pButIcon = *hButIcon;
14:        theDialog = pButIcon->oDialog;
15:        itemHit = pButIcon->oItem;
16:        GetPort(&savePort);
```

```
17:     SetPort(theDialog);
18:     GetDItem(theDialog, itemHit, &itemType,
19:             &itemHandle, &itemRect);
20:     if (pButIcon->valueA)
21:     {
22:       pButIcon->valueA = false;
23:       pButIcon->valueB = true;
24:       if (pButIcon->inColor)
25:       {
26:         PlotCIcon(&itemRect, pButIcon->switchB);
27:       }
28:       else
29:       {
30:         PlotIcon(&itemRect, pButIcon->switchB);
31:       }
32:       SetDItem(theDialog, itemHit, itemType,
33:               pButIcon->switchB, &itemRect);
34:       while (Button())
35:       {
36:       }
37:       pButIcon->valueA = true;
38:       pButIcon->valueB = false;
39:       if (pButIcon->inColor)
40:       {
41:         PlotCIcon(&itemRect, pButIcon->switchA);
42:       }
43:       else
44:       {
45:         PlotIcon(&itemRect, pButIcon->switchA);
46:       }
47:       SetDItem(theDialog, itemHit, itemType,
48:               pButIcon->switchA, &itemRect);
49:     }
50:     else
51:     {
52:       pButIcon->valueA = true;
53:       pButIcon->valueB = false;
54:       if (pButIcon->inColor)
55:       {
56:         PlotCIcon(&itemRect, pButIcon->switchA);
57:       }
58:       else
59:       {
60:         PlotIcon(&itemRect, pButIcon->switchA);
61:       }
62:       SetDItem(theDialog, itemHit, itemType,
63:               pButIcon->switchA, &itemRect);
64:       while (Button())
```

```
65:        {
66:        }
67:        pButIcon->valueA = false;
68:        pButIcon->valueB = true;
69:        if (pButIcon->inColor)
70:        {
71:           PlotCIcon(&itemRect, pButIcon->switchB);
72:        }
73:        else
74:        {
75:           PlotIcon(&itemRect, pButIcon->switchB);
76:        }
77:        SetDItem(theDialog, itemHit, itemType,
78:               pButIcon->switchB, &itemRect);
79:     }
80:     HUnlock(hButIcon);
81:     SetPort(savePort);
82: }
```

After several lines of local declarations, the first active code on line 12 locks the handle to the type definition stored in the allocated memory. Line 13 dereferences it and gets a pointer.

The statements on lines 14 and 15 pull the dialog and the item out of memory.

Lines 16 and 17 play the get port, save port, and set port game, but, in this case, the port is set to the dialog.

The call on lines 18 and 19 returns the rectangle, as well as other items that are not used here.

The if-statement on lines 20–49 simply says, "If icon A is now drawn on the screen, then draw icon B, wait for the mouse button to come back up, and redraw icon A."

In the meantime, the while-statement on lines 34–36 (and again on lines 64–66) comprises a do-nothing loop; that is, while the mouse button is down, nothing should change. As soon as the mouse button is released, the routine falls out of that loop.

Lines 37 and 38 set the value of A (off position) to true and value B (on position) to false. Line 39–49 then plot icon A in either color or black-and-white.

The else-statement on lines 50–79 says that if the reverse is true—that is, if icon B instead of icon A is drawn on the screen—then draw icon A, wait for the mouse button to come back up, then redraw icon B.

Line 80 unlocks the handle to the button icon, line 81 resets the port, and the routine is finished.

▶ DispButtonIcon.c

DispButtonIcon.c disposes the button icon after the mouse button has been released.

Listing 12-4. Disposing the button icon

```
PROCEDURE DispButtonIcon(hButIcon: hIconBut);

1:  /***************************************************************/
2:  void DispButtonIcon(hButIcon)
3:  /***************************************************************/
4:  {
5:    DisposHandle(hButIcon);
6:  }
```

We include this routine to be consistent with the Get–Do–Dispose sequence, since it is necessary to dispose the button icon. Line 5 calls the Toolbox routine DisposHandle, and it disposes the handle to the button icon.

▶ Using Icons as Toggle Switches

Instead of using icons as buttons that you press and release with the mouse, the routines in this section use icons as toggles. You do not release a toggle icon; once you click the mouse on it, it stays that way until you click on it again. As with the button icon routines, we've included some global declarations for your toggle icon routines.

Listing 12-5. Global code defining the structure for five toggle icon routines

```
typedef struct
{
  DialogPtr oDialog
  short oIitem;
  Handle switchA;
  Handle switchB;
  char inColor;
    short valueA;
  short valueB;
} iconTog, *pIconTog, **hIconTog;
```

This type definition structure creates a variable called *IconTog*. Like the structure for the button icon routines, this has five items in it: the pointer to the dialog box that contains the toggle icon; the item in the dialog box that, when hit, represents the toggle icon; two icons—one icon to be drawn when the toggle is on and one icon to be drawn when it is off—and information on whether the icon is in color.

▶ GetToggleIcon.c

GetToggleIcon.c draws the toggle icon on the screen.

Listing 12-6. Drawing a toggle icon

```
FUNCTION GetToggleIcon (theDialog: DialogPtr, itemHit: INTEGER, icon1:
        INTEGER, icon2: INTEGER): hIconTog;
```

```
 1:  /****************************************************************/
 2:  hToggleIcon GetToggleIcon (DialogPtr theDialog,
 3:                   short itemHit,short icon1,short icon2)
 4:  /****************************************************************/
 5:  {
 6:    GrafPtr      savePort;                  /* Old grafPort */
 7:    SysEnvRec    sysEnvRec;                 /* Environment */
 8:    short        itemType;
 9:    Rect         itemRect;
10:    Handle       itemHandle;
11:    hIconTog hTogIcon;
12:    pIconTog pTogIcon;
13:    #define      SysEnvironsTrap 0xA090     /* Toolbox traps */
14:    #define      UnknownTrap     0xA89F
15:    #define      sizeTogIconRecord  28      /* Size of record */
16:    GetPort(&savePort);
17:    SetPort(theDialog);
18:    if ((long)NGetTrapAddress(SysEnvironsTrap, OSTrap) !=
19:    (long)NGetTrapAddress(UnknownTrap, ToolTrap))
20:    {
21:      SysEnvirons(1, &sysEnvRec);
22:    }
23:    hTogIcon = (hToggleIcon)NewHandle(sizeof(iconTag));
24:    HLock(hTogIcon);
25:    pTogIcon = *hTogIcon;
26:    pTogIcon->oDialog = theDialog;
27:    pTogIcon->oItem = itemHit;
28:    pTogIcon->switchA = nil;
29:    pTogIcon->switchB = nil;
```

```
30:     if (sysEnvRec.hasColorQD)
31:     {
32:       pTogIcon->switchA = (Handle)GetCIcon(icon1);
33:       pTogIcon->switchB = (Handle)GetCIcon(icon2);
34:       pTogIcon->inColor = true;
35:     }
36:     else
37:     {
38:       pTogIcon->switchA = (Handle)GetIcon(icon1);
39:       pTogIcon->switchB = (Handle)GetIcon(icon2);
40:       pTogIcon->inColor = false;
41:     }
42:     GetDItem(theDialog, itemHit, &itemType, &itemHandle,
                 &itemRect);
43:     pTogIcon->valueA = true;
44:     pTogIcon->valueB = false;
45:     if (pTogIcon->inColor)
46:     {
47:       PlotCIcon(&itemRect, pTogIcon->switchA);
48:     }
49:     else
50:     {
51:       PlotIcon(&itemRect, pTogIcon->switchA);
52:     }
53:     SetDItem(theDialog, itemHit, itemType, pTogIcon->switchA,
54:              &itemRect);
55:     HUnlock(hTogIcon);
56:     SetPort(savePort);
57:     return(hTogIcon);
58: }
```

The code for GetToggleIcon.c is exactly the same, line for line, as the code for GetButtonIcon.c. The only difference is in the name of the item: Substitute "ToggleIcon" for "ButtonIcon" in this routine. See the review of GetButtonIcon.c earlier in this chapter for a detailed discussion of the source code.

▶ DoToggleIcon.c

DoToggleIcon.c is a simple version of DoButtonIcon.c. It is far easier to toggle these icons than it is to await mouse-up events and return the icons to their original state. This routine changes whatever state the icon is in; if it is in the off position, the routine turns it to on, and vice versa.

Listing 12-7. Toggling a toggle icon

```
PROCEDURE DoToggleIcon(hTogIcon: hIconTog);

 1:   /*****************************************************************/
 2:   void DoToggleIcon(hToggleIcon hTogIcon)
 3:   /*****************************************************************/
 4:   {
 5:      GrafPtr       savePort;                          /* Old grafPort */
 6:      DialogPtr     theDialog;
 7:      short         itemType;
 8:      Rect          itemRect;
 9:      Handle        itemHandle;
10:      pToggleIcon   pTogIcon;
11:      short         itemHit;
12:      HLock(hTogIcon);
13:      pTogIcon = *hTogIcon;
14:      theDialog = pTogIcon->oDialog;
15:      itemHit = pTogIcon->oItem;
16:      GetPort(&savePort);
17:      SetPort(theDialog);
18:      GetDItem(theDialog, itemHit, &itemType, &itemHandle,
                  &itemRect);
19:      if (pTogIcon->valueA)
20:      {
21:         pTogIcon->valueA = false;
22:         pTogIcon->valueB = true;
23:         if (pTogIcon->inColor)
24:         {
25:            PlotCIcon(&itemRect, pTogIcon->switchB);
26:         }
27:         else
28:         {
29:            PlotIcon(&itemRect, pTogIcon->switchB);
30:         }
31:         SetDItem(theDialog, itemHit, itemType, pTogIcon->switchB,
32:               &itemRect);
33:      }
34:      else
35:      {
36:         pTogIcon->valueA = true;
37:         pTogIcon->valueB = false;
38:         if (pTogIcon->inColor)
39:         {
40:            PlotCIcon(&itemRect, pTogIcon->switchA);
41:         }
42:         else
```

```
43:        {
44:            PlotIcon(&itemRect, pTogIcon->switchA);
45:        }
46:        SetDItem(theDialog, itemHit, itemType, pTogIcon->switchA,
47:            &itemRect);
48:    }
49:    HUnlock(hTogIcon);
50:    SetPort(savePort);
51: }
```

The first active code on line 12 locks the handle to the toggle icon, and line 13 dereferences it.

Lines 14 and 15 get the dialog and the item from the structure.

Lines 16 and 17 get and set the port and save it to the dialog box.

The call on line 18 returns the necessary rectangle.

The if-statement on lines 19–48 says: "If the value A is false (that is, if the icon is in the off position), then plot icon B, which is in the on position. Also, plot it in color if color is available; otherwise, plot it in black-and-white. On the other hand, if the value B is true (if the icon is in the on position), change B to false and A to true (the off position)."

Line 49 unlocks the handle, line 50 resets the port, and the routine is finished.

▶ DispToggleIcon.c

This routine for disposing the toggle icon is functionally the same as the one for disposing the button icon presented earlier in this chapter. It is here for the purpose of consistency.

Listing 12-8. Disposing a toggle icon

```
PROCEDURE DispToggleIcon(hTogIcon: hIconTog);

1: /****************************************************************/
2: void DispToggleIcon(hToggleIcon hTogIcon)
3: /****************************************************************/
4: {
5:    DisposHandle(hTogIcon);
6: }
```

On line 5, the Toolbox routine DisposHandle takes care of disposing of the toggle icon.

▶ IconOff.c

Although this routine and its companion IconOn.c strongly resemble the three toggle icon routines just presented, there is an important difference. The routine here does not toggle the toggle icon, but rather it assures that the toggle icon is always set to off, even if it was already in the off position. The notion comes in handy when you want to make sure that the items in a dialog box always appear in the same state when they are drawn to the screen.

Listing 12-9. Setting the toggle icon to the off position

```
PROCEDURE IconOff(hTogIcon: hIconTog);

 1:   /***************************************************************/
 2:   void IconOff(hToggleIcon hTogIcon)
 3:   /***************************************************************/
 4:   {
 5:      GrafPtr        savePort;                    /* Old grafPort */
 6:      DialogPtr      theDialog;
 7:      short          itemType;
 8:      Rect           itemRect;
 9:      Handle         itemHandle;
10:      pToggleIcon    pTogIcon;
11:      short          itemHit;
12:      HLock(hTogIcon);
13:      pTogIcon = *hTogIcon;
14:      theDialog = pTogIcon->oDialog;
15:      itemHit = pTogIcon->oItem;
16:      GetPort(&savePort);
17:      SetPort(theDialog);
18:      GetDItem(theDialog, itemHit, &itemType,
19:            &itemHandle, &itemRect);
20:      pTogIcon->valueA = true;
21:      pTogIcon->valueB = false;
22:      if (pTogIcon->inColor)
23:      {
24:         PlotCIcon(&itemRect, pTogIcon->switchA);
25:      }
26:      else
27:      {
28:         PlotIcon(&itemRect, pTogIcon->switchA);
29:      }
30:      SetDItem(theDialog, itemHit, itemType,
31:            pTogIcon->switchB, &itemRect);
32:      HUnlock(hTogIcon);
33:      SetPort(savePort);
34:   }
```

The first nineteen lines of code for this routine are functionally identical to DoToggleIcon.c. The main difference in the routines appears here on lines 20 and 21, where the value A is set to true, and the value B is set to false. Period. The only if-statements in the routine say: "If I have color available, plot the icon in color. Otherwise, plot it in black-and-white."

Line 32 unlocks the handle, line 33 resets the port, and the routine is finished.

▶ IconOn.c

This routine is the companion to IconOff.c. It sets the toggle icon to the on position, even if it was already in the on position.

Listing 12-10. Setting the toggle icon to the on position

```
PROCEDURE IconOn(hTogIcon: hIconTog);

 1:  /****************************************************************/
 2:  void IconOn(hToggleIcon hTogIcon)
 3:  /****************************************************************/
 4:  {
 5:     GrafPtr        savePort;                    /* Old grafPort */
 6:     DialogPtr      theDialog;
 7:     short          itemType;
 8:     Rect           itemRect;
 9:     Handle         itemHandle;
10:     pToggleIcon    pTogIcon;
11:     short          itemHit;
12:     HLock(hTogIcon);
13:     pTogIcon = *hTogIcon;
14:     theDialog = pTogIcon->oDialog;
15:     itemHit = pTogIcon->oItem;
16:     GetPort(&savePort);
17:     SetPort(theDialog);
18:     GetDItem(theDialog, itemHit, &itemType,
19:          &itemHandle, &itemRect);
20:     pTogIcon->valueA = false;
21:     pTogIcon->valueB = true;
22:     if (pTogIcon->inColor)
23:     {
24:        PlotCIcon(&itemRect, pTogIcon->switchB);
25:     }
26:     else
27:     {
```

```
28:        PlotIcon(&itemRect, pTogIcon->switchB);
29:     }
30:     SetDItem(theDialog, itemHit, itemType,
31:         pTogIcon->switchB, &itemRect);
32:     HUnlock(hTogIcon);
33:     SetPort(savePort);
34: }
```

This routine is the exact opposite of the IconOff.c routine just presented. Instead of setting the value A to true on line 20, it sets it to false; it also sets value B to true on line 21; and on lines 24 and 28 the switch is to B instead of A. See the review of IconOff.c for details.

▶ A Simple Icon Example

This section contains a pair of source code listings that demonstrate the routines GetToggleIcon.c, DoToggleIcon.c, and DispToggleIcon.c. The pair consists of one file with the extension .c and another file, containing the resources, with the extension .R. The two types of files always go together to make up an application.

▶ IconExample.c

This example tests the routines GetToggleIcon.c, DoToggleIcon.c, and DispToggleIcon.c.

Listing 12-11. Example of a toggle icon

```
/*******************************************************************/
void    main()                          /* Routine to test Icon Switch */
/*******************************************************************/
{
  DialogPtr     theDialog;
  short         itemHit;
  iconTog       theSwitch, **hSwitch;
  InitToolBox();
  OpenResources("\pIconSwitchExample.rsrc");   /* For devel purposes */
  CenterDialog(300);
  OpenDialog(&theDialog, 300);
  FrmDefItem(theDialog);
  hSwitch = (hIconTog)GetTogIcon(theDialog, 2, 2000, 2001);
  for(;;)
  {
```

```
      MyModalDialog(&itemHit);
      switch (itemHit)
      {
        case (1):                                         /* Quit */
          break;
        case (2):                                         /* The Switch */
          DoTogIcon(hSwitch);
          continue;
        case (-updateEvt):                                /* Update */
          BeginUpdate(theDialog);
            UpDialog(theDialog);
            FrmDefItem(theDialog);
          EndUpdate(theDialog);
          continue;
        default:                                          /* All other events */
          continue;
      }
      break;
    }
  DispTogIcon(hSwitch);
  DisposeDialog(theDialog);
}
```

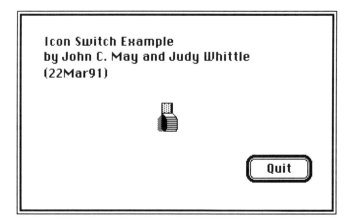

Figure 12-1. Dialog box with example of a toggle icon

▶ IconExample.R

This section contains the resource file for IconExample.c.

Listing 12-12. Resource file for example of a toggle icon

```
IconSwitchExample.rsrc
rsrcRSED

Type DLOG
,300
Icon Switch Test
50 50 238 364
Visible NoGoAway
1
300
300

Type DITL
,300
3

* 1
Button
140 233 160 293
Quit

* 2
IconItem
82 136 114 168
2000

* 3
StaticText Disabled
13 25 63 295
Icon Switch Example\0Dby John C. May and Judy Whittle\0D(22Mar91)
```

Chapter 12 Icons

```
Type ICON=GNRL
,2000
00000000 00000000 03FFC000 0244C000 0311C000 0244C000 0311C000 0244C000
0311C000 0244C000 0311C000 0244C000 03FFC000 03002000 03801000 07C00800
0BFFFC00 17E00400 2BFFFE00 17F00200 2BFFFE00 17F00200 2BFFFE00 17F00200
2BFFFE00 17F00200 2BFFFE00 17F00200 2BFFFE00 15E00400 0AFFFC00 00000000

Type ICON=GNRL
,2001
00000000 00000000 03FFC000 03002000 07801000 0BC00800 17FFFC00 2BE00400
17FFFE00 2BF00200 17FFFE00 2BF00200 17FFFE00 2BF00200 17FFFE00 2BF00200
17FFFE00 2BF00200 17FFFE00 2AE00400 057FFC00 0244C000 0311C000 0244C000
0311C000 0244C000 0311C000 03FFC000 03FFC000 00000000 00000000 00000000

Type cicn=GNRL
,2000
00000000 80100000 00000020 00200000 00000000 00000048 00000048 00000000
00040001 00040000 00000000 00000000 00000000 00000004 00000000 00200020
00000000 00040000 00000020 00200000 0000FFFF FFFFFFFF FFFFFFFF FFFFFFFF
FFFFFFFF FFFFFFFF FFFFFFFF FFFFFFFF FFFFFFFF FFFFFFFF FFFFFFFF FFFFFFFF
FFFFFFFF FFFFFFFF FFFFFFFF FFFFFFFF FFFFFFFF FFFFFFFF FFFFFFFF FFFFFFFF
FFFFFFFF FFFFFFFF FFFFFFFF FFFFFFFF FFFFFFFF FFFFFFFF FFFFFFFF FFFFFFFF
FFFFFFFF FFFFFFFF FFFFFFFF FFFFFFFF FFFF0000 00000000 000003FF C0000244
C0000311 C0000244 C0000311 C0000244 C0000311 C0000244 C0000311 C0000244
C00003FF C0000300 20000380 100007C0 08000BFF FC0017E0 04002BFF FE0017F0
02002BFF FE0017F0 02002BFF FE0017F0 02002BFF FE0017F0 02002BFF FE0017F0
02002BFF FE0015E0 04000AFF FC000000 00000000 00000000 00050000 FFFFFFFF
FFFF0001 00000000 FFFF0002 A867A7B9 FFFF0003 DCE4DBC8 DDFF0004 99FF99FF
99FF0005 00000000 00000000 00000000 00000000 00000000 00000000 00000000
00000000 00000000 00000000 00555555 55555500 00000000 00000000 00533333
33335500 00000000 00000000 00533333 33335500 00000000 00000000 00533333
33335500 00000000 00000000 00533333 33335500 00000000 00000000 00533333
33335500 00000000 00000000 00533333 33335500 00000000 00000000 00533333
33335500 00000000 00000000 00533333 33335500 00000000 00000000 00533333
33335500 00000000 00000000 00111111 11111100 00000000 00000000 00112222
22222210 00000000 00000000 00111222 22222221 00000000 00000000 04111122
22222222 10000000 00000000 44111111 11111111 11000000 00000004 44111112
22222222 21000000 00000044 44111111 11111111 11100000 00000044 44111111
22222222 22100000 00000044 44111111 11111111 11100000 00000044 44111111
22222222 22100000 00000044 44111111 11111111 11100000 00000044 44111111
22222222 22100000 00000044 44111111 11111111 11100000 00000044 44111111
22222222 22100000 00000044 44111111 11111111 11100000 00000044 44111111
22222222 22100000 00000044 44111111 11111111 11100000 00000004 44411112
22222222 21000000 00000000 44441111 11111111 11000000 00000000 00000000
00000000 00000000 0000
```

```
Type cicn=GNRL
,2001
00000000 80100000 00000020 00200000 00000000 00000048 00000048 00000000
00040001 00040000 00000000 00000000 00000000 00000004 00000000 00200020
00000000 00040000 00000020 00200000 0000FFFF FFFFFFFF FFFFFFFF FFFFFFFF
FFFFFFFF FFFFFFFF FFFFFFFF FFFFFFFF FFFFFFFF FFFFFFFF FFFFFFFF FFFFFFFF
FFFFFFFF FFFFFFFF FFFFFFFF FFFFFFFF FFFFFFFF FFFFFFFF FFFFFFFF FFFFFFFF
FFFFFFFF FFFFFFFF FFFFFFFF FFFFFFFF FFFFFFFF FFFFFFFF FFFFFFFF FFFFFFFF
FFFFFFFF FFFFFFFF FFFFFFFF FFFFFFFF FFFF0000 00000000 000003FF C0000300
20000780 10000BC0 080017FF FC002BE0 040017FF FE002BF0 020017FF FE002BF0
020017FF FE002BF0 020017FF FE002BF0 020017FF FE002BF0 020017FF FE002AE0
0400057F FC000244 C0000311 C0000244 C0000311 C0000244 C0000311 C00003FF
C00003FF C0000000 00000000 00000000 00000000 00000000 00050000 FFFFFFFF
FFFF0001 99FF99FF 99FF0002 DCE4DBC8 DDFF0003 A867A7B9 FFFF0004 00000000
FFFF0005 00000000 00000000 00000000 00000000 00000000 00000000 00000000
00000000 00000000 00000000 00444444 44444400 00000000 00000000 00443333
33333340 00000000 00000000 01444333 33333334 00000000 00000000 11444433
33333333 40000000 00000001 11444444 44444444 44000000 00000011 11444443
33333333 34000000 00000011 11444444 44444444 44400000 00000011 11444444
33333333 33400000 00000011 11444444 44444444 44400000 00000011 11444444
33333333 33400000 00000011 11444444 44444444 44400000 00000011 11444444
33333333 33400000 00000011 11444444 44444444 44400000 00000011 11444444
33333333 33400000 00000011 11444444 44444444 44400000 00000011 11444444
33333333 33400000 00000011 11544444 44444444 44400000 00000001 11524443
33333333 34000000 00000000 11522444 44444444 44000000 00000000 00522222
22225500 00000000 00000000 00522222 22225500 00000000 00000000 00522222
22225500 00000000 00000000 00522222 22225500 00000000 00000000 00522222
22225500 00000000 00000000 00522222 22225500 00000000 00000000 00555555
55555500 00000000 00000000 00555555 55555500 00000000 00000000 00000000
00000000 00000000 00000000 00000000 00000000 00000000 00000000 00000000
00000000 00000000 0000
```

▶ Summary

This chapter presented eight routines to manipulate icons of the button and toggle types.

- Three routines—to draw, execute, and dispose button icons
- Three routines—to draw, execute, and dispose toggle icons
- Two routines—to switch icons off and on

It also presented a global definition of the structure for the routines of each type as well as an icon switch example and the source code and resource files for the example.

13 ▶ Pictures

▶ Overview of Pictures

Picture scripts, commonly referred to as "Picts," come in two types: PICT files and 'PICT' resources. PICT files store their pictures in the data fork of the file. We won't cover that type in this book.

The resource 'PICT' contains three different pieces of information:

1. The size of the picture
2. The picture frame or rectangle
3. The picture itself

The picture data contain a set of QuickDraw commands that are executed each time the picture is drawn, much like record and playback on a tape recorder.

▶ Drawing a Picture

If you want to enter a picture into a dialog, you can do so through ResEdit by creating a new dialog item inside of the 'DITL' resource. You create a Picture item and assign it an ID number. When you pass in the ID number, ModalDialog draws the picture automatically in your window.

This method sounds simple enough, but there are problems involved with drawing a picture this way. First, you have to watch out for the *dialog* ID number as opposed to the *resource* ID number of the PICT.

For example, an OK button in the dialog will have 1 as the ID, and the Cancel button will almost always have 2 as the ID. If your resource ID number is larger than the dialog numbers, ModalDialog draws the PICT last because it draws from the lowest number to the highest number. And, to make matters worse, the drawing sequence in ResEdit is the opposite of what it is in ModalDialog, thereby requiring you to set up everything backwards in ResEdit.

Suppose you have a picture of a horse, and you want to be able to touch certain parts of that picture—the head, mane, forelocks, withers, and so on—with the mouse pointer, click the mouse, and have a box of information about that particular area appear on the screen. To do this, you have to create sensitive areas on the picture. Trouble is, if ModalDialog draws the picture on top of the sensitive areas, then a mouse-down event tells you that a button has been pressed, but not where on that picture the button was pressed. You need to draw your picture first, then assign the sensitive areas on top of it. You can't do this with ModalDialog, but you can with the DrawPict.c routine in this section.

In addition, ModalDialog does not handle animation. If you want to have a moving figure in a dialog or a copyright box, you can achieve that as well with the DrawPict.c routine. To provide animation, you need to create a PICT file, which needs to contain an 'INFO' resource and a 'PICT' resource. In the 'PICT' resource, the first picture has to contain the background; it defines the overall size of the picture for the total animation. Each additional frame contains the animated characters. The 'INFO' resource has to contain information like whether the picture is in black-and-white or color, its depth, its speed in frames per second—ideally, 30 frames per second—the version number of the PICT file, who created it, and the size of the largest frame in bytes.

▶ DrawPict.c

This routine uses 'PICT' resources, which have a defined format. The first 2 bytes are the link to the overall picture in bytes. The next 8 bytes are the size of the rectangle of the picture; that is, top left and bottom right. The rest of the bytes contain the data of the picture, and they may be a collection of bytes or pixels depending on whether the picture is in black-and-white or color.

You can use a variety of means to develop your picture, such as a draw or a paint program or a picture that has been scanned into a file. But it has to be in the PICT format to use it in this routine.

Listing 13-1. Drawing a picture

```
PROCEDURE DrawPict(theID: INTEGER);

1:  /*************************************************************/
2:  void DrawPict(short theID)
3:  /*************************************************************/
4:  {
5:      PicHandle hPict;
6:      hPict = (PicHandle)GetResource('PICT', theID);
7:      DrawPicture(hPict, &(*hPict)->picFrame);
8:  }
```

On line 2 you pass in the resource ID number of the picture that you want to draw.

Next, on line 6, you call the Toolbox routine GetResource. The resource type you want is 'PICT'. You pass it the ID number of the picture, and it returns the handle to the picture. You want to cast that to a PICT handle, because GetResource returned you a generic handle. You cast it with the expression (PicHandle).

On line 7 you call the QuickDraw Toolbox routine DrawPicture, pass it the handle to the picture and the picture frame, which is the rectangle of the picture, by converting the picture handle into a pointer. It then draws the picture, and you're through with the routine.

▶ A Simple Picture Example

This section contains a pair of source code listings that demonstrate the routine DrawPict.c. The pair consists of one file with the extension .c and another file, containing the resources, with the extension.R. The two types of files always go together to make up an application.

▶ PictExample.c

This sample routine tests DrawPict.c and produces a picture of a generic ten-speed bicycle with 25 call-outs in various places along the frame of the bicycle (see Figure 13-1). Each circle in the call-out is actually a radio button. When you click on one of the circles, a box containing the name of the part and a description of its function appears below the picture of the bicycle. When you click on another circle, the first description disappears, and information about the current selection then appears on the screen.

152 ▶ Chapter 13   Pictures

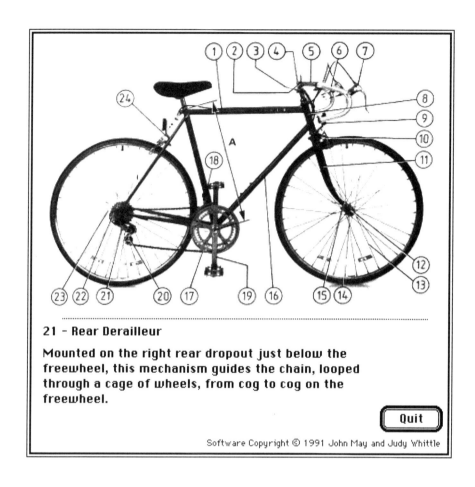

Figure 13-1. Picture created with the PictExample.c routine

Listing 13-2. Example of a picture created with the routine DrawPict.c

```
1:  /****************************************************************/
2:  void    main()                          /* Routine to test PICTS */
3:  /****************************************************************/
4:  {
5:      DialogPtr       theDialog;
6:      short           itemHit;
7:      Str255          theString;
8:      InitToolBox();
9:      OpenResources("\pPictExample.rsrc");    /* For dev. purposes */
```

```
10:     CenterDialog(300);
11:     OpenDialog(theDialog,300);
12:     FrmDefItem(theDialog);
13:     DrawDottedLine(theDialog, 28);
14:     DrawPict(300);
15:     DrawPict(301);
16:     for(;;)
17:     {
18:        MyModalDialog(&itemHit)
19:        switch (itemHit)
20:        {
21:          case (1):
22:             break;
23:          case (2):
24:          case (3):
25:          case (4):
26:          case (5):
27:          case (6):
28:          case (7):
29:          case (8):
30:          case (9):
31:          case (10):
32:          case (11):
33:          case (12):
34:          case (13):
35:          case (14):
36:          case (15):
37:          case (16):
38:          case (17):
39:          case (18):
40:          case (19):
41:          case (20):
42:          case (21):
43:          case (22):
44:          case (23):
45:          case (24):
46:          case (25):
47:          case (26):
48:             GetStrNum(300, itemHit-1, theString);
49:             PutEdString(theDialog, 29, theString);
50:             GetStrNum(301, itemHit-1, theString);
51:             PutEdString(theDialog, 31, theString);
52:          case (-updateEvt):
53:             BeginUpdate(theDialog);
54:                UpDialog(theDialog);
```

```
55:            FrmDefItem(theDialog);
56:            DrawDottedLine(theDialog, 28);
57:            DrawPict(300);
58:            DrawPict(301);
59:          EndUpdate(theDialog);
60:       }
61:       break;
62:    }
63:    DisposeDialog(theDialog);
64: }
```

After three lines of declarations (lines 5–7), you initialize the Toolbox on line 8.

Next, on line 10, you center the dialog, and line 11 opens it up. On line 12 you frame the default item, which is the Quit button in the lower right-hand corner of the picture.

You draw in the dotted line with the call on line 13, the picture of the bicycle (ID 300) on line 14, and the text in the lower right-hand corner (ID 301) on line 15.

Line 16 begins a for-loop, in which you call MyModalDialog (line 18) and wait for an item to be hit. If the item number hit is 1, that is the Quit button, and you break.

Line 19 begins a case-statement.

Lines 23–47 contain the item numbers of the names and definitions of parts of the bicycle. If any of these item numbers is hit, the routine skips to the GetStrNum call on line 48. When you pass in the ID 300 and the number of the item hit minus 1, this call gets the *name* of the item from a set of strings in the resource file. Note that you pass in the number of the item hit minus 1 because item number 1 is the Quit button and does not refer to any of the numbers of the strings in the resource file.

The statement on line 49 places that string in space 29 on the screen.

When you pass in the ID 301 and the number of the item hit minus 1 on line 50, the GetStrNum call returns the *definition* of the item that was hit.

The statement on line 51 places that definition string in space 31 on the screen.

If you have an update event on line 52, the routine updates, frames, and redraws the picture through the statements on lines 53–59.

▶ PictExample.R

PictExample.R is the resource file that forms a pair with PictExample.c to bring up the picture example on the screen.

Listing 13-3. Resource file for the picture example

```
Pict.rsrc
rsrcRSED

Type DLOG
,300
New Dialog                ;; Message (Title)
82 78 516 522             ;; Rect (T,L,B,R)
Visible NoGoAway          ;; Flags
1                         ;; Proc ID
300                       ;; Refcon
300                       ;; Resource ID of DITL list


Type DITL
,300
30                        ;; Number of items

* 1
Button      Enabled
391 378 411 438           ;; Rect (T,L,B,R)
Quit                      ;; Message

* 2
UserItem    Enabled
5 183 25 203              ;; Rect (T,L,B,R)

* 3
UserItem    Enabled
5 205 25 225              ;; Rect (T,L,B,R)

* 4
UserItem    Enabled
5 228 25 248              ;; Rect (T,L,B,R)

* 5
UserItem    Enabled
5 251 25 271              ;; Rect (T,L,B,R)

* 6
UserItem    Enabled
5 287 25 307              ;; Rect (T,L,B,R)
```

```
* 7
UserItem    Enabled
4 318 24 338                    ;; Rect (T,L,B,R)

* 8
UserItem    Enabled
4 345 24 365                    ;; Rect (T,L,B,R)

* 9
UserItem    Enabled
54 410 74 430                   ;; Rect (T,L,B,R)

* 10
UserItem    Enabled
76 411 96 431                   ;; Rect (T,L,B,R)

* 11
UserItem    Enabled
97 411 117 431                  ;; Rect (T,L,B,R)

* 12
UserItem    Enabled
119 410 139 430                 ;; Rect (T,L,B,R)

* 13
UserItem    Enabled
230 408 250 428                 ;; Rect (T,L,B,R)

* 14
UserItem    Enabled
251 407 271 427                 ;; Rect (T,L,B,R)

* 15
UserItem    Enabled
262 323 282 343                 ;; Rect (T,L,B,R)

* 16
UserItem    Enabled
262 300 282 320                 ;; Rect (T,L,B,R)

* 17
UserItem    Enabled
262 249 282 269                 ;; Rect (T,L,B,R)
```

```
* 18
UserItem    Enabled
263 157 283 177             ;; Rect (T,L,B,R)

* 19
UserItem    Enabled
120 184 140 204             ;; Rect (T,L,B,R)

* 20
UserItem    Enabled
262 220 282 240             ;; Rect (T,L,B,R)

* 21
UserItem    Enabled
263 129 283 149             ;; Rect (T,L,B,R)

* 22
UserItem    Enabled
263 67 283 87               ;; Rect (T,L,B,R)

* 23
UserItem    Enabled
263 40 283 60               ;; Rect (T,L,B,R)

* 24
UserItem    Enabled
264 17 284 37               ;; Rect (T,L,B,R)

* 25
UserItem    Enabled
55 88 75 108                ;; Rect (T,L,B,R)

* 26
UserItem    Enabled
100 204 120 224             ;; Rect (T,L,B,R)

* 27
StaticText  Disabled
327 384 375 425             ;; Rect (T,L,B,R)
                            ;; Message

* 28
UserItem    Enabled
296 30 297 425              ;; Rect (T,L,B,R)
```

```
* 29
StaticText Disabled
302 8 323 426              ;; Rect (T,L,B,R)
Click on Part Number       ;; Message

* 30
StaticText Disabled
325 8 411 369              ;; Rect (T,L,B,R)
                           ;; Message
Type PICT=GNRL
,300
.H
B454
```

(The number of bytes in the 'PICT' resource describing this picture is too great to print here.)

```
,301
.H
0C9E
```

(The number of bytes in the 'PICT' resource describing this picture is too great to print here.)

```
Type STR#
,300
25                         ;; Number of strings
 1 - Top Tube
 2 - Right-hand Shift Lever
 3 - Left-hand Shift Lever
 4 - Expander Bolt
 5 - Extension Stem
 6 - Handlebars
 7 - Brake Levers
 8 - Head Tube
 9 - Front Reflector
10 - Front Brake
11 - Front Fork
12 - Front Hub
13 - Spokes
14 - Rim
15 - Quick Release Lever
16 - Downtube
17 - Chainwheel
18 - Front Derailleur
```

```
19 - Crankset
20 - Derailleur Cage
21 - Rear Derailleur
22 - Freewheel Cluster
23 - Spoke Protector
24 - Reflector Holder
A - FRAME SIZE

,301
25                  ;; Number of strings
```

Horizontal tube connecting the tops of the seat and head tubes.

The lever mounted on the right handlebar end that pulls the cable to operate the gear changes of the rear derailleur.

The lever mounted on the left handlebar end that pulls the cable to operate the gear changes of the front derailleur.

The bolt found on the top of the handlebars that is used to adjust their height.

Piece that holds the handlebars and extends into the steering tube. Made in different sizes of steel or aluminum alloy.

Bars made of steel or aluminum alloy in varying bends that attach to the stem for steering the bike.

Handlebar-mounted squeeze control for braking.

The tube at the front of the bike between the top tube and the area where the headset and the steering tube of the fork are mounted.

A plastic reflector that is mounted on the front fork.

A set of pivotal arms that bend around the front tire toward the rim.

The part of the frame that holds the front wheel and that consists of two blades, the crown, and the steering tube.

The central part of the front wheel including the hub shell, axle, cones, ball bearings, and either nuts or a quick-release mechanism to attach the wheel to the frame.

Steel rods that hold the hub centered in the rim.

Butted spokes are thicker at the ends.

Steel or aluminum alloy hoop that holds the tire and is attached to the spokes. Alloy rims are lighter than steel rims.

A clamping mechanism to secure the wheel to the frame. Special parts include a hollow axle, a skewer, a cam lever, springs, and an adjustable cone nut. This device permits fast wheel changes without tools.

The tube connecting the head tube and bottom bracket.

The toothed rings attached to the crankset.
The number of teeth determines the gear ratio of the bicycle.

Mounted on the seat tube just above the chainwheel, this device guides the chain back and forth between the large and small chainwheels when activated by the gear cable.
Found only on bikes with ten or more gears.

One of a pair of metal arms that connects the pedals to the spindle.

The rear derailleur assembly, which is located inside the rear wheel spokes.

Mounted on the right rear dropout just below the freewheel, this mechanism guides the chain, looped through a cage of wheels, from cog to cog on the freewheel.

The assembly of one to seven cogs (usually five) on the rear hub with a ratchet mechanism. The ratchet allows the rider to coast when not pedaling. Freewheel cogs can be changed to suit the gear ratio needs of the rider.

A metal disk used to protect the rear derailleur cage from broken or loose spokes.

A bracket mounted on the rear fork onto which a plastic reflector may be fitted.

The measurement from the center of the bottom bracket up to the top of the seat tube.

▶ Summary

This chapter presented a routine for drawing pictures stored in a PICT file. It also gave a sample routine that produces a picture of a bicycle with various call-outs containing information about the bicycle's parts.

▶ Recommended Reading

Andris, Bob. "MacDraw PICT Files from BASIC." (BASIC.) *The Essential MacTutor—The Macintosh Programming Journal, Vol.* 3, No. 10, 1988.

Sheets, Steven. "Animating PICS." (Pascal.) *MacTutor—The Macintosh Programming Journal, Vol.* 7, March 1991.

14 ▶ Static Text

▶ Overview of Static Text

Static text is noneditable text that appears in windows, dialogs, and alerts. You use static text mostly for titles and messages. Static text is important in the Macintosh's human interface exchange because it gives information clearly and quickly. An alert box message that appears on the screen during a Find function, for example, may tell you that you have reached the end of the document. The message ensures that you are not left staring at a blinking cursor, wondering what to do next.

▶ Active and Inactive Static Text

Static text can be either active or inactive. If it's active, it is bright or black. If it's inactive, it is dim or gray, indicating that the item or function is not available. For instance, when you open the Spelling function from the Utilities menu in a word processing program, you see in its window that the static text on Change and Suggest buttons is gray. Because the routine has not yet come across a misspelled word, those two functions don't yet have any meaning and are disabled.

▶ ActiveStatic.c

This routine resets inactive static text to active static text, making it available for selection.

Chapter 14 Static Text

Listing 14-1. Activating a line of static text

PROCEDURE ActiveStatic(theDialog: DialogPtr, itemHit: INTEGER);

```
1:  /****************************************************************/
2:  void ActiveStatic(DialogPtr theDialog, short itemHit)
3:  /****************************************************************/
4:  {
5:      GrafPtr     savePort;                       /* Old grafPort */
6:      Str255      theString;
7:      short       theType;                        /* Not used */
8:      Rect        theRect;                        /* Not used */
9:      Handle      theHdl;                         /* Item handle */
10:     GetPort(&savePort);
11:     SetPort(theDialog);
12:     GetDItem(theDialog, itemHit, &theType, &theHdl, &theRect);
13:     GetIText(theHdl, theString);
14:     SetIText(theHdl, theString);
15:     SetPort(savePort);
16: }
```

You begin on line 2 by calling ActiveStatic and passing it the dialog number and the item number of the static text that you want to make active.

After several lines of declarations and two lines in which you get and set the port, go to line 11, where you call GetDItem. You want to know how big the rectangle is that holds the static text. GetDItem returns you the item type, the handle, and the rectangle. You use only the handle out of this bunch.

Lines 12 and 13 call the Toolbox routines GetIText and SetIText, which redraw the rectangle to its normal active state.

Reset the port to normal on line 14, and you're finished with the routine.

▶ InactiveStatic.c

InactiveStatic.c dims or grays static text, indicating that the item is not available.

Listing 14-2. Dimming a line of static text

PROCEDURE InactiveStatic(theDialog: DialogPtr, itemHit: INTEGER);

```
1:  /****************************************************************/
2:    void InactiveStatic(DialogPtr theDialog, short itemHit)
3:  /****************************************************************/
4:  {
```

```
 5:        short         theType;                /* Not used */
 6:        Rect          theRect;           /* Static text rect */
 7:        Handle        theHdl;                 /* Not used */
 8:        GrafPtr       savePort;             /* Old grafPort */
 9:        PenState      penStuff;
10:        GetPort(&savePort);
11:        SetPort(theDialog);
12:        GetDItem(theDialog, itemHit, &theType, &theHdl, &theRect);
13:        GetPenState(&penStuff);
14:        PenPat(gray);
15:        PenMode(patBic);
16:        PaintRect(&theRect);
17:        SetPenState(&penStuff);
18:        SetPort(savePort);
19:   }
```

On line 2 you call InactiveStatic and pass it the dialog and the item number of the static text that you want to make inactive.

After several lines of declarations and two lines in which you get and set the port, go to line 12, where you call GetDItem. You want to know how big the rectangle is that holds the static text. GetDItem returns you the item type, the handle, and the rectangle. Here, you use only the rectangle.

On line 13 you save the pen state; on line 14 you set the pen pattern to gray. This gray pattern is 50 percent white and 50 percent black.

On line 15 *patBic* determines that wherever there is a white background, nothing will be done, but wherever there is a black background, every other bit will be replaced with black. This gives the gray pattern to the text.

On line 16 you call the Toolbox routine PaintRect and pass it the rectangle so that it can paint the new rectangle.

After setting the pen state and the port back to normal, you branch out of the routine.

▶ A Simple Static Text Example

This section contains a pair of source code listings that demonstrate the routines ActiveStatic.c and InactiveStatic.c. The pair consists of one file with the extension .c and another file, containing the resources, with the extension .R. The two types of files always go together to make up an application.

▶ **StaticTextExample.c**

This example tests the routines ActiveStatic.c and InactiveStatic.c (see Figure 14-1).

Listing 14-3. Example of active and inactive static text

```
/*********************************************************************/
void    main()                          /* Routine to test static text */
/*********************************************************************/
{
  DialogPtr    theDialog;
  short        itemHit;
  InitToolBox();
   OpenResources("\pStaticTextExample.rsrc");  /*For devel purposes */
  CenterDialog(300);
  OpenDialog(&theDialog, 300);
  FrmDefItem(theDialog);
  PushRadioButton(theDialog, 2, 2, 3);
  for(;;)
  {
    MyModalDialog(&itemHit);
    switch (itemHit)
    {
      case (1):
        break;
      case (2):
        PushRadioButton(theDialog, 2, 2, 3);
        ActiveStatic(theDialog, 4);
        continue;
      case (3):
        PushRadioButton(theDialog, 3, 2, 3);
        InactiveStatic(theDialog, 4);
        continue;
      case (-updateEvt):
        BeginUpdate(theDialog);
          UpDialog(theDialog);
          FrmDefItem(theDialog);
          if (GetRadioButton(theDialog, 2, 3) == 3)
          {
             InactiveStatic(theDialog, 4);
          }
        EndUpdate(theDialog);
        continue;
      default:                                    /* All other events */
        continue;
```

```
        }
      break;
   }
   DisposeDialog(theDialog);
}
```

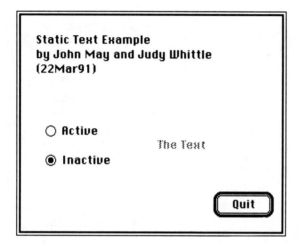

Figure 14-1. A dialog with active and inactive static text

▶ StaticTextExample.R

StaticTextExample.R is the resource file that forms a pair with StaticTextExample.c to bring up the example of active and inactive static text on the screen.

Listing 14-4. Resource file for a static text example

```
StaticTextExample.rsrc
rsrcRSED

Type DLOG
,300
StaticText Example
50 50 236 372
Visible NoGoAway
```

```
1
300
300

Type DITL
,300
4

* 1
Button                          ;; Quit button
150 252 170 312
Quit

* 2
RadioButton                     ;; "Active" button
87 14 107 74
Active

* 3                             ;; "Inactive" button
RadioButton
87 75 107 135
Inactive

* 4                             ;; The static text
StaticText
87 136 107 196
The Text
```

▶ Summary

This chapter presented two routines to brighten or dim static text in a window or dialog box. In addition, this chapter gave an example of activating and inactivating static text, along with the source code and the resource file for the example.

▶ Recommended Reading

Gordon, Bob. "Text Display from QuickDraw." *The Complete MacTutor— The Macintosh Programming Journal*, Vol. 2, 1987.

15 ▶ Edit Text

▶ Overview of Edit Text

Edit text fields are essential features of dialog boxes. A dialog box comes up on the screen when you issue a command that doesn't give the Macintosh enough information to complete the command. Select the Print command, and up pops a window with several user-interactive items. They include small rectangles, known as *text fields,* in which you type the missing details: starting page number, ending page number, and the number of copies. *Edit text field* is the name for any field in which you type. This term makes it clear that these are not static text fields, which are uneditable titles and labels.

All of the entries in a dialog box—buttons, radio buttons, check boxes, static text, and edit text fields—make up the dialog record.

To understand edit text, you need to think of a dialog box as a word processing screen covered by a mask with a peephole cut in it. The peephole is the edit text field. If you type more characters than the field has room for, the field scrolls horizontally. The older text disappears at the left. If you go on typing, the text wraps onto the next line and the field jumps down to follow. You could type a whole document through the edit text field, though there wouldn't be much point in doing so.

Some dialogs have one edit text field. Save As is an example, and the edit text field is where you enter the file name. Dialogs with multiple edit text fields are especially useful when the window represents a form for data entry. For instance, a physician's patient record form would have fields for the patient's name, address, birth date, insurance carrier, and so forth.

Only one edit text field at a time should be active in a dialog box. You can tell which is active because that's the one with the blinking cursor and the only one in which text appears as you type.

▶ Active Edit Text Fields

The two routines that follow allow you to get active text for a dialog box that has, for example, one edit text field that is always active, or to get or set the active text in a dialog box that has two or more edit text fields.

▶ GetActiveEditText.c

GetActiveEditText.c lets an application make use of the active text.

Listing 15-1. Getting active edit text

PROCEDURE GetActiveEditText (theDialog: DialogPtr, VAR itemHit: INTEGER);

```
 1:   /***************************************************************/
 2:   void  GetActiveEditText(DialogPtr theDialog, short *itemHit)
 3:   /***************************************************************/
 4:   {
 5:     GrafPtr   savePort;                           /* Old grafPort */
 6:     GetPort(&savePort);
 7:     SetPort(theDialog);
 8:     if (((WindowPeek)theDialog)->windowKind == dialogKind)
 9:     {
10:       if (((DialogPeek)theDialog)->editField != -1)
11:       {
12:         *itemHit = ((DialogPeek)theDialog)->editField + 1;
13:       }
14:     }
15:     SetPort(savePort);
16:   }
```

GetActiveEditText.c requires a pointer to the dialog box. In line 2 you pass in the pointer and say which edit text field is active. The routine returns a short variable, which is the active edit text field (skip down to line 12 for a moment).

Back at line 6, you get and save the current GrafPort so that you can revert to it at the end of the routine. Line 7 sets the port to the dialog. These two lines, strictly speaking, are not necessary unless you are going to do something with QuickDraw and you don't want to set the wrong port. It's worth including them habitually so you don't forget them in routines where they matter. If they add a little execution time, that amount is unnoticeable against the slowness of the human operator.

Now you use a couple of if-tests, lines 8–14, to make sure that you're working on the right type of window. You want a dialog box type of window, which not only has one or more edit text fields but also contains the other entries of the dialog record. This test makes use of a variable, called *windowKind*, within the window record (line 8).

In line 10 you ask whether the edit text field is equal to –1. If it is –1, either no edit text fields exist in the window or there are no active edit text fields and you do nothing. If it is not -1, there is an edit text field and in line 12 you set the variable *theDialog* equal to the value stored in the edit text field part of the dialog record plus 1, taking into account that this number would otherwise be off by 1.

Finally you fall out of both if-loops and set the port back to its original state.

▶ SetActiveEditText.c

Depending on your application, you might have a dialog box with one edit text field that is always active. Your application might, instead, have an edit text field that the user has the choice of making inactive or active. Another possibility is two or more fields of which the user can make one active or inactive. In every instance the assumption, in conformity with the Human Interface Guidelines, is that no more than one field is allowed to be active at a given time. A typical use for this routine is to make one edit text field active when the user takes appropriate action. The action can be an event such as clicking on a radio button or pressing the Tab key.

In the Introduction, we mentioned that Apple recommends using calls to the Toolbox whenever possible. Following that rule pretty much guarantees freedom from compatibility problems when the operating system is upgraded. We also said that innovative and creative programming often justifies breaking the rule by using low-memory global variables or going directly into the dialog record and changing or getting variables. This routine, SetActiveEditText.c, adheres to the rule completely by using only Toolbox calls.

Listing 15-2. Setting active edit text

```
PROCEDURE SetActiveEditText(theDialog: DialogPtr,itemHit: INTEGER);

 1:  /***************************************************************/
 2:  void       SetActiveEditText(DialogPtr theDialog, short itemHit)
 3:  /***************************************************************/
 4:  {
 5:      GrafPtr         savePort;                   /* Old grafPort */
 6:      short           itemType;
 7:      Handle          item;
 8:      Rect            itemRect;
 9:      short           theLength;
10:      Str255          theString;
11:      GetPort(&savePort);
12:      SetPort(theDialog);
13:      GetDItem(theDialog, itemHit, &itemType, &item, &itemRect);
14:      GetIText(item, theString);
15:      theLength = theString[0];
16:      SelIText(theDialog, itemHit, theLength);
17:      SetPort(savePort);
18:  }
```

This routine generally resembles GetActiveEditText.c, but the few differences are significant. SetActiveEditText.c requires the dialog pointer and an *itemHit* for the item you're going to set. In the get routine, *itemHit* is a variable because you set its value. In the set routine, *itemHit* is not a variable because you don't set it; you just use it.

It's a good idea to include the get port and save port calls, as discussed in the review of GetActiveEditText.c.

Line 12 is a Toolbox routine. You pass in *theDialog* and *itemHit*, and the procedure returns the item type, the item handle, and the item rectangle. Line 13 gets the item text by taking the handle to the edit text field and returning the associated string. As a result, you find out how long it is. In line 14 you're dealing with a Pascal string, so the first character of the string, 0, is its length.

In line 15 you call the select item text routine, which does a couple of things for you. It changes your edit text field to active, and it places the blinking cursor at the end of the text. Having the cursor at the end of the field is convenient for a user who wants to add to the edit text. If there isn't any text, the cursor sits at the beginning of the field, waiting for text to be entered.

Another approach to cursor positioning would be to select the entire range of the field string by changing the select item text line of code to SelIText(theDialog, itemHit, 0, 32767). This approach might be preferable if you think that users would want to delete the contents of the field and type in some new text. Either way, it's your judgment call.

The edit text field is active at this stage in the program. All that remains is to set the port back to the original state (line 16), and you're through with this routine.

▶ Input and Output Routines for Integers

The following eight routines handle short and long integers in decimal and hexadecimal notation. Integers are the natural numbers 1, 2, 3, and so on; that is, they have no decimal points or fractions.

Four of the routines convert an input string into a number; the other four do the opposite, converting an output string into a number. Probably their most important use is enabling the Macintosh to recognize numbers when the user enters them in an edit text field of a dialog. A good example is the standard Print dialog. It invites you to enter the page range in a From edit text field box and a To box. You press the From radio button to enter a value in the box. If you ignore the invitation, the All radio button stays pressed, and the Macintosh defaults to printing the whole document when you press the OK button.

Without number-handling routines the Macintosh is faced with a string of ASCII digits it doesn't understand. The routines enable it to pick out an integer number and check that the number is valid. You would want it, for instance, to accept an entered number of 23 as valid but refuse to be fooled if someone typed XY. Recognizing that XY is not a decimal number, your Macintosh would call the routine InputShort.c. The routine would not find a number there and would realize that *iGoof* is high. It could put in a number, or it could delete what was in the field and return the cursor to the beginning of the field, depending on what you wanted. To put a number in there, you would need to take the default—such as the number of pages—and put it back in the edit text field. At this point you'd have the number there, but it would not be an ASCII string. To get an ASCII string, you would call the routine OutputShort.c to convert the number to an ASCII string and enter it into the field.

You'll find these eight integer-handling routines used repeatedly in this book. Two similar routines that handle floating-point numbers are listed in the next section of this chapter. (As you will see, the ten are among the few routines that use no Toolbox calls.) The routines allow number entry in several different formats. For example, you could enter 30000 just as it is in fixed notation, or as 3×10^4 in scientific notation, or as 30E3 in engineering notation, or as 30K. Programming languages usually can't cope with superscripts, so you could enter 3.0E4.

Shown in the listing for each integer-handling routine is its Pascal calling sequence. The sequence is included because the Macintosh and its Toolbox are programmed in Pascal; also, the sequence closely matches what the reference books *Inside Macintosh* show. Although the routines are in the C language, they follow the Pascal sequence. If you want them in Pascal, all you have to do is declare them Pascal. The C compiler will then treat them as Pascal routines.

▶ InputShort.c

This routine passes in a Pascal string of characters and returns the corresponding short integer number if one exists. A short number here is one that is 16 bits in length.

Listing 15-3. Inputting a short integer

```
PROCEDURE InputShort(inch: Str255,VAR column: short, VAR
         shortNumber: short, VAR iGoof: short);

 1:  /***************************************************************/
 2:  void     InputShort
 3:           (Str255 inch, short *column, short *shortNumber, short
              *iGoof)
 4:  /***************************************************************/
 5:  {
 6:    short              i;
 7:    short              lastColumn;
 8:    short              foundInteger;
 9:    short              foundDigit;
10:    short              sign;
11:    *iGoof = false;
12:    *shortNumber = 0;
13:    sign = 1;
14:    lastColumn = inch [0];                    /* Get line length */
15:    foundInteger = false;
16:    for (*column = *column; *column <= lastColumn; (*column)++)
17:    {
18:      foundDigit = false;
19:      if (inch [*column] == '-')              /* Is number negative? */
```

```
20:     {
21:        sign = -1;
22:        foundInteger = true;
23:        foundDigit = true;
24:        continue;
25:     }
26:     for (i = 0; i <= 9; i++)              /* Is an ASCII number? */
27:     {
28:        if ((inch) [*column] != i + '0') continue;
29:        *shortNumber = 10 * (*shortNumber) + i;/*Found ASCII no. */
30:        foundInteger = true;
31:        foundDigit = true;
32:        break;
33:     }
34:     if (foundDigit) continue;
35:     if (foundInteger)
36:     {
37:        break;                              /* Got a number */
38:     }
39:     else
40:     {
41:        continue;                           /* Look for a number */
42:     }
43:  }
44:  if (foundInteger == 0) *iGoof = true;
45:  *shortNumber = (*shortNumber) * sign;   /* Take care of sign */
46: }
```

This routine operates on an array of characters called inch, which is an abbreviation of *in*put *ch*aracters. The entity inch is a var Pascal string. Other vars in this routine are the column number, *short*, and *iGoof*. *Var* is Pascal terminology meaning that you have to pass in a pointer to a variable that is going to be moved. Starting at some column number in the array or the line of characters, the routine goes through the characters looking for an integer number. When it finds that number, the routine sets a variable called *shortNumber* to the number. It also sets the column number to the next position in the array. For instance, you call InputShort, and pass in the inch and column 1; it returns the number 123. InputShort starts at column 1 and finds the integer 123, and it sets the column number to 4. It also passes in another variable, *iGoof*, which is an error flag. If no integer number is found, it sets *iGoof* to true, or some number greater than 0.

After several declarations, the first real code on line 11 states that the *iGoof* flag is equal to false. Then line 12 says, "If you don't find a number, return a 0." The number may be negative, but for now assume it's positive, as stated on line 13.

This and other routines in this chapter call the index to the string a column. Line 14 gets the last character in the string, and line 15 says you haven't found an integer yet.

Line 16 is a for-loop. The first declaration, which shows just how cryptic C can be, is redundant. It is included because close adherence to the proper C syntax is a worthwhile habit to adopt. At worst, redundant statements like this one do no harm. At best, they help you avoid leaving out something vital. It is good to have them there if you want to modify the routine later. The next expression says you want to do this loop as long as the column point number is not greater than that of the last column. The last expression is a C way of stating that column equals column plus 1.

The expression on line 18 is included because you haven't started looking for a digit yet. Note that a number and a digit are not the same; a digit is only one part of a number.

Line 19 says that if the next character is a minus sign, the routine will perform the if-test on lines 20–25. The if-test amounts to this: "If I find a negative number, set the sign to minus 1, say that I found an integer, and say that I found a digit. Continue by jumping up to the top of the for-loop and cycling the loop one more time."

Line 26 presents a second for-loop that states: "For *i* equal to 0, and if *i* is less than or equal to 9, do this loop. Each time I branch to the loop, increment *i* by 1." This loop tests each character to figure out whether it is 0–9.

The body of this internal for-loop (lines 27–33) starts out with another if-test that says: "If the character in inch to which column points is equal to *i* plus the ASCII number 48, then proceed with the if-test; else branch to the bottom of the for-loop and branch back up to the top of that loop." After you begin with *i* equal to 0, *i* changes to 1, and you go through the loop again. The statement then works its way through the remaining values of *i* equals 2, 3, and so on up to 9 until it checks the final number. To give an example, say you want to enter the number 123. You ask, "Is it a 0?" No, so branch back up. "Is it a 1?" Yes, indeed. Take that number 1, add it to the product of 10 times the old value of *shortNumber*, and put it in your new value of *shortNumber*. Since *shortNumber* equals 0, 10 times 0 is 0. Add 0 to the 1 you just read in.

Several ways to proceed from this point are possible. One way is to read in all the characters of number 123, putting 1 in the hundreds column, 2 in the tens column, and 3 in the ones column. This method is the same as saying 1 times 100, plus 2 times 10, plus 3 times 1. You would have to read in the entire number and figure out the columns.

We've found our routine to be a better method. It is an algebraic manipulation called Horner's rule. Take each digit as it comes in, and multiply the old number by 10. Then add the number you just read in and put it back in the new number. *shortNumber* is equal to the number 1. You found an integer, so you set the *foundInteger* flag to true. Now break. Having found a number, you fall out of the for-loop.

If you found a digit, you would want to continue, so jump back to the beginning of the outer for-loop (line 16). The column number gets incremented, and you're pointing to the next column in inch, which happens to be the number 2 of the 123 you're reading in. Go down to the interior for-loop again (line 26) and play the same game. "Is inch equal to 0?" No, it isn't. "Equal to 1?" No. "Equal to 2?" Yes! So you fall through the if-test in the for-loop. Take *shortNumber*, which is equal to 1. Multiply by 10, so now it's equal to 10. Add 2 to get 12, and put 12 in *shortNumber*. Reset *foundInteger* and *foundDigit*. Then branch to the top of the outer for-loop.

Repeat the outer for-loop. Multiplying by 10 yields 120. Add 3 to get 123, the number you're looking for. Set *shortNumber* to 123, set *foundInteger* to true, set *foundDigit* to true. Break. Ask, "Have I found a digit?" Yes. Go back to the top of the for-loop. You're now pointing to something other than a number—say, a space—but the routine doesn't care. That's the end of it.

Go down to the for-loop on line 26. Looping through, ask whether you've found a digit. This time you go through the entire for-loop without finding a digit, meaning there isn't a number there at all. Ask whether you've found an integer. Yes, you have. Break to the outer for-loop. Go down to the brace on line 43 and fall through to an if-test (line 44). If you found an integer equal to 0, meaning, "No, I didn't find an integer," you'd set *iGoof* equal to true. But you did find an integer. Instead of setting *iGoof* to true, you fall through to line 45. Here you might need to read in a sign for a number. Since the variable sign is going to equal a positive 1, you multiply the number you found by the sign, so 123 equals 123.

Summing up this review, what you have is a free-form routine that works quickly with a number such as 123 or –123 or 123–. The number cannot exceed 16 bits.

▶ InputLong.c

With InputLong.c you pass in a Pascal character string and get back a 32-bit number, a long integer.

Listing 15-4. Inputting a long integer

```
PROCEDURE InputLong(inch: Str255,VAR column: short, VAR
         longNumber: long, VAR iGoof: short);

 1:  /****************************************************************/
 2:  void     Inputlong
 3:   (Str255 inch, short *column, long *longNumber, short *iGoof)
 4:  /****************************************************************/
 5:  {
 6:    short              i;
 7:    short              lastColumn;
 8:    short              foundInteger;
 9:    short              foundDigit;
10:    short              sign;
11:    *iGoof = false;
12:    *longNumber = 0;
13:    sign = 1;
14:    lastColumn = inch [0];                   /* Get line length */
15:    foundInteger = false;
16:    for (*column = *column; *column <= lastColumn; (*column)++)
17:    {
18:      foundDigit = false;
19:      if (inch[*column] == '-')             /* Is number negative? */
20:      {
21:        sign = -1;
22:        foundInteger = true;
23:        foundDigit = true;
24:        continue;
25:      }
26:      for (i = 0; i <= 9; i++)              /* Is an ASCII number? */
27:      {
28:        if (inch [*column] != i + '0') continue;
29:      *longNumber = 10 * (*longNumber) + i;  /* Found ASCII no. */
30:        foundInteger = true;
31:        foundDigit = true;
32:        break;
33:      }
```

```
34:        if (foundDigit) continue;
35:        if (foundInteger)
36:        {
37:           break;                                    /* Got a number */
38:        }
39:        else
40:        {
41:           continue;                                 /* Look for a number */
42:        }
43:     }
44:     if (foundInteger == 0) *iGoof = true;
45:     *longNumber = (*longNumber) * sign;             /* Take care of sign */
46:  }
```

The InputLong.c routine works exactly like InputShort.c except that you declare a long number instead of a short number. See the InputShort.c routine, just described at some length, for more details.

▶ InputHexShort.c

InputHexShort.c handles hexadecimal numbers, which can be 1–9 and A–F.

Listing 15-5. Inputting a short hexadecimal number

```
PROCEDURE InputHexShort(inch: Str255,VAR column: short, VAR
            shortNumber: short, VAR iGoof: short);

 1:  /****************************************************************/
 2:  void      InputHexShort
 3:           (Str255 inch, short *column, short *shortNumber, short
             *iGoof)
 4:  /****************************************************************/
 5:  {
 6:     short             i;
 7:     short             lastColumn;
 8:     short             foundInteger;
 9:     short             foundDigit;
10:     short             sign;
11:     *iGoof = false;
12:     *shortNumber = 0;
13:     sign = 1;
14:     lastColumn = inch [0];                          /* Get line length */
15:     foundInteger = false;
```

```
16:    for (*column = *column; *column <= lastColumn; (*column)++)
17:    {
18:      foundDigit = false;
19:      if (inch[*column] == '-')              /* Is number negative? */
20:      {
21:        sign = -1;
22:        foundInteger = true;
23:        foundDigit = true;
24:        continue;
25:      }
26:      for (i = 0; i <= 9; i++)               /* Is an ASCII number? */
27:      {
28:        if (inch [*column] != i + '0') continue;
29:        *shortNumber = 16 * (*shortNumber) + i;/* Found ASCII no.*/
30:        foundInteger = true;
31:        foundDigit = true;
32:        break;
33:      }
34:      for (i = 0; i <= 5; i++)               /* Is an ASCII letter? */
35:      {
36:        if (inch [*column] != i + 'A') continue;
37:        i = i + 10;                          /* Found an ASCII letter */
38:        *shortNumber = 16 * (*shortNumber) + i;
39:        foundInteger = true;
40:        foundDigit = true;
41:        break;
42:      }
43:      if (foundDigit) continue;
44:      if (foundInteger)
45:      {
46:        break;                                         /* Got a number */
47:      }
48:      else
49:      {
50:        continue;                                      /* Look for a number */
51:      }
52:    }
53:    if (foundInteger == 0) *iGoof = true;
54:    *shortNumber = (*shortNumber) * sign;    /* Take care of sign */
55:  }
```

Compare this routine with InputShort.c. The main difference is that InputHexShort.c contains two interior for-loops, one below the other. In the first for-loop, which includes lines 26–33, you ask, "Have I found an

ASCII number?" On line 29, note the number 16, which reflects the hex notation, instead of the number 10 for decimal notation.

The second for-loop (lines 34–42) is required because hex has a gap between 9 and A in the series 1 through F. If A were equivalent to 10, there would be no problem; but A is equal to a value of 65. Between 9 and A are fifty-six miscellaneous characters that are of no interest in this routine. F equals a value of 70. This for-loop asks, "Is the character you're reading in the ASCII letter A?" If the answer is no, the next question is, "Well then, is it the ASCII letter B?" This question-and-answer session goes on until the answer is, "Yes, it is!" Meanwhile, the routine has zipped through the fifty-six characters in the gap.

On line 38 you need to figure out what to make *i* equal to so that you can add it to the product of 16 times *shortNumber*. Here, *i* is going to equal 0, 1, 2, 3, 4, or 5, corresponding to A, B, C, D, E, or F. A is 10 in decimal notation, B is 11, and so on. If you read in an ASCII B at this point, *i* will be equal to 1. You will therefore need to add 10 to the 1 to make it a B.

▶ InputHexLong.c

InputHexLong.c is identical to InputHexShort.c with one exception: You're reading in a 32-bit, not a 16-bit, number as a hexadecimal. You would use InputHexLong.c if, for instance, you wanted to read in the hex number FFFFFFFF. That would be too long for the short routine, whereas hex number FFFF would be just fine.

Listing 15-6. Inputting a long hexadecimal number

```
PROCEDURE InputHexLong(inch: Str255,VAR column: short, VAR
            longNumber: long, VAR iGoof: short);

 1:    /***************************************************************/
 2:    void    InputHexLong
 3:      (Str255 inch, short *column, long *longNumber, short *iGoof)
 4:    /***************************************************************/
 5:    {
 6:        short                   i;
 7:        short                   lastColumn;
 8:        short                   foundInteger;
 9:        short                   foundDigit;
10:        short                   sign;
11:        *iGoof = false;
12:        *longNumber = 0;
```

```
13:     sign = 1;
14:     lastColumn = inch [0];                    /* Get line length */
15:     foundInteger = false;
16:     for (*column = *column; *column <= lastColumn; (*column)++)
17:     {
18:       foundDigit = false;
19:       if (inch [*column] == '-')              /* Is number negative? */
20:       {
21:         sign = -1;
22:         foundInteger = true;
23:         foundDigit = true;
24:         continue;
25:       }
26:       for (i = 0; i <= 9; i++)                /* Is an ASCII number? */
27:       {
28:         if (inch[*column] != i + '0') continue;
29:         *longNumber = 16 * (*longNumber) + i;   /* Found an ASCII
                number */
30:         foundInteger = true;
31:         foundDigit = true;
32:         break;
33:       }
34:       for (i = 0; i <= 5; i++)                /* Is an ASCII letter? */
35:       {
36:         if (inch[*column] != i + 'A') continue;
37:         i = i +10;                            /* Found an ASCII letter */
38:         *LongNumber = 16 * (*LongNumber) + i;
39:         foundInteger = true;
40:         foundDigit = true;
41:         break;
42:       }
43:       if (foundDigit) continue;
44:       if (foundInteger)
45:       {
46:         break;                                /* Got a number */
47:       }
48:       else
49:       {
50:         continue;                             /* Look for number */
51:       }
52:     }
53:     if (foundInteger == 0) *iGoof = true;
54:     *longNumber = (*longNumber) * sign;       /* Take care of sign */
55: }
```

The code for this routine is similar to that of InputHexShort.c except that the number you're reading in from the hexadecimal string is placed into a long value, so a long number rather than a short number is returned. See the brief review of the InputHexShort.c routine for further explanation of the code.

▶ OutputShort.c

This routine does the opposite of InputShort.c, in that it takes a number such as 123 and puts it into a character array equal to the characters 123.

Listing 15-7. Outputting a short integer

```
PROCEDURE OutputShort(inch: Str255,VAR column: short,
           shortNumber: short, VAR iGoof: short)
```

```
 1:  /***************************************************************/
 2:  void    OutputShort
 3:          (Str255 *outch, short *column, short *shortNumber,
 4:           short *iGoof)
 5:  /***************************************************************/
 6:  {
 7:    Str255    buffer;
 8:    short     temporaryInteger;
 9:    short     nextTemporary;
10:    short     digit;
11:    short     i, j;
12:    #define   abs(a)  ((a)<0?-(a):(a))  /* Abs macro function */
13:    *iGoof = false;
14:    temporaryInteger = abs(*shortNumber);
15:    for (i = 1; i <= 10; i++)             /* Break into digits */
16:    {
17:      nextTemporary = temporaryInteger / 10;
18:      digit = temporaryInteger - nextTemporary * 10;
19:      temporaryInteger = nextTemporary;
20:      buffer[i] = digit + '0';
21:      if (nextTemporary <= 0) break;
22:    }
23:    j = i;
24:    if (*shortNumber < 0)                 /* Check for negative */
25:    {
26:      outch [*column] = '-';
```

```
27:        *column = *column + 1;
28:     }
29:     for (*column = *column; *column <= *column + i-1;
            *(column)++)
30:     {
31:        outch [*column] = buffer[j];
32:        j = j - 1;
33:     }
34:     *column = *column + 1;
35:     outch [0] = *column - 1;
36:  }
```

Call this routine with the character string you want to put the characters in, and call it with the column number you want the first character to start in. In the example of 123, say you want the 1 to begin in column 22. In lines 2–4 you pass the column number 22, then the number 1, followed by the flag *iGoof*. Here, *iGoof* is a useful redundancy. The routine doesn't need it, but it's included for consistency of syntax. Some routines in this group of number-handlers use *iGoof*; some don't. Having it handy could save time and frustration later if you decide to modify the routine.

Jumping down past several declarations, you'll come to a statement on line 12 that relates to the preprocessor built into C. The macro **define** translates something before compiling. Certain functions, including "take the absolute value of a number," are not built into C. This macro supplies that function.

Line 13 is the redundant flag just mentioned. Setting it to 0 keeps it from having any effect.

The statement on line 14 computes the absolute value of the number. You make the temporary integer, which in our example is 123, equal to the absolute value of the short number that you want to output to the character string.

Now comes a for-loop (lines 15–20) that says, essentially, *i* goes from 1 to 10 and the number can't be greater than ten.

First you set *i* equal to 1, then you keep doing the loop as long as *i* is less than or equal to 10, incrementing *i* by 1 at each loop. In line 17, *nextTemporary* is just a local value. You set it equal to the number divided by 10. So, with 123, *temporaryInteger* divided by 10 is 12.3. Since integer arithmetic is at work here, the decimal 3 is dropped, leaving the truncated integer 12. Multiply by 10 to get 120, then subtract 120 from *temporaryInteger* 123 to leave the digit 3 (line 18). Add the 3 to an ASCII

0 to get 3. Put that into buffer 1 indexed by *i* (line 20). Because *i* is equal to 1, buffer[i] is equal to 3.

Loop through and do the same again, except this time *temporaryInteger* is going to equal 12. Divide 12 by 10 and come up with 1.2, which truncated yields 1. Put the 1 in *nextTemporary* and multiply by 10, giving you 10. Subtract 10 from *temporaryInteger* 12 to get the digit 2. Convert that into an ASCII number and put it into buffer 2.

Loop through once more for the number 1. Divide 1 by 10; integer arithmetic reduces the number to 0. Multiply 0 by 10, which gives you 0. Subtract 0 from 1, leaving 1 to go into buffer 3.

Line 21 is an if-test, from which you fall out, since *nextTemporary* is 0 and you don't want to loop forever.

At this point you have all the digits broken down into buffers in ASCII digits: buffer 1 contains 3, buffer 2 contains 2, and buffer 3 contains 1.

You set the variable on line 23. Then you reach the statements on lines 24–28, which lead off by saying, "If *shortNumber* is less than 0—in other words, if it is negative—put a minus sign in outch." Line 27 moves the column over one space to make room for the negative sign. Although outch sounds like the response to chomping on a cherry pit, it's our abbreviation name for an array of *out*put *ch*aracters.

The for-loop in line 29 takes the digits from the buffers and puts them back into outch in reverse order. You subtract 1 from *i* to do a calculation akin to the old fence-post problem: How many posts do I need for a sixty-foot fence with one post every six feet? You need eleven, not ten. Same goes for the number of columns in this routine. In line 31 the outch, pointed to by column, is filled up with buffer, which is decremented each time through the loop. Buffer 1, which contains 3, is put in last; buffer 2, containing 2, is put in the middle; and buffer 3, containing 1, goes in first. This procedure reverses the sequence 321 to give you 123, so now outch contains your number 123. If the number had been negative, outch would contain -123.

The last segments of code (lines 34–36) take care of two final chores. First, because you need the column number to point to the next column space, the first statement increments the column number by 1, in the example giving 4. Second, since 123 is a Pascal string and you need to keep track of how long it is, the second statement sets the length to the column number less 1, in this example giving 3.

▶ OutputLong.c

OutputLong.c differs from OutputShort.c in only one detail: OutputLong.c outputs a 32-bit number instead of a short 16-bit number. Local variables *temporaryInteger*, *nextTemporary*, and *digit* are changed to long values.

Listing 15-8. Outputting a long integer

```
PROCEDURE OutputLong(inch: Str255,VAR column: short,
          longNumber: long, VAR iGoof: short);

 1:  /****************************************************************/
 2:  void     OutputLong
 3:           (Str255 outch, short *column, long *longNumber,
 4:             short *iGoof)
 5:  /****************************************************************/
 6:  {
 7:    Str255     buffer;
 8:    long       temporaryInteger;
 9:    long       nextTemporary;
10:    long       digit;
11:    short      i, j;
12:    #define    abs(a) ((a)<0?-(a):(a))  /* Abs macro function */
13:    *iGoof = false;
14:    temporaryInteger=abs(*longNumber);
15:    for (i = 1; i <= 10; i++)                  /* Break into digits */
16:    {
17:      nextTemporary = temporaryInteger / 10;
18:      digit = temporaryInteger - nextTemporary * 10;
19:      temporaryInteger = nextTemporary;
20:      buffer[i] = digit + '0';
21:      if (nextTemporary <= 0) break;
22:    }
23:    j = i;
24:    if (*longNumber < 0)                       /* Check for negative */
25:    {
26:      outch [*column] = '-';
27:      *column = *column + 1;
28:    }
29:    for (*column = *column; *column <= *column + i - 1;
             *(column)++)
30:    {
31:      outch [*column] = buffer[j];
32:      j = j - 1;
33:    }
```

```
34:     *column = *column + 1;
35:     outch[0] = *column - 1;
36:   }
```

OutputLong.c is the same as OutputShort.c except that local variables that have *shortNumber* in the short routine have *longNumber* in the long counterpart. See OutputShort.c for a detailed review of the code.

▶ OutputHexShort.c

This routine outputs an unsigned short hexadecimal number.

Listing 15-9. Outputting a short hexadecimal number

```
PROCEDURE OutputHexShort(outch: Str255,VAR column: short,
         shortNumber: short, VAR iGoof: short);

 1:  /***************************************************************/
 2:  void  OutputHexShort
 3:           (Str255 outch, short *column, unsigned short
                *shortNumber,
 4:            short *iGoof)
 5:  /***************************************************************/
 6:  {
 7:    Str255            buffer;
 8:    unsigned short    temporaryInteger;
 9:    unsigned short    nextTemporary;
10:    unsigned short    digit;
11:    unsigned short    i, j;
12:    #define           abs(a)  ((a)<0?-(a):(a))         /* Abs macro
                              function */
13:    *iGoof = false;
14:    temporaryInteger = abs(*shortNumber);
15:    for (i = 1; i <= 10; i++)                /* Break into digits */
16:    {
17:      nextTemporary = temporaryInteger / 16;
18:      digit = temporaryInteger - nextTemporary * 16;
19:      temporaryInteger = nextTemporary;
20:      if ((digit >= 0) && (digit <= 9))
21:      {
22:        buffer[i] = digit + '0';
23:      }
24:      else
```

```
25:        {
26:          buffer[i] = (digit-10) + 'A';
27:        }
28:        if (nextTemporary <= 0) break;
29:      }
30:      j = i;
31:      for (*column = *column; *column <= *column + i - 1;
              *(column)++)
32:      {
33:        outch [*column] = buffer[j];
34:        j = j - 1;
35:      }
36:      *column = *column + 1;
37:      outch [0] = *column - 1;
38:    }
```

OutputHexShort.c closely resembles OutputShort.c. The essential difference is that the hex routine outputs an unsigned short hexadecimal number. In line 17, instead of dividing *temporaryInteger* by 10, you divide by 16. If you compare line 18 with its counterpart in the OutputShort.c routine, you'll see that you multiply by 16 instead of 10. Skip down to the first if-test on line 20. This says, "If the digit is greater than or equal to 0 and less than or equal to 9, then it is a digit between 0 and 9." Next, line 22 makes the buffer equal to the digit plus the ASCII number 0.

If the digit is not between 0 and 9, you do the statement on line 26 to deal with a hex number A through F, corresponding to the decimal numbers 10–15. Subtract 10 from that digit and add it to an ASCII A to make A through F in the buffer.

Another way in which this routine differs from OutputShort.c is that OutputHexShort.c does not make provision for a negative sign. Look in the function declaration at the top of the listing on line 3. You'll see unsignedshort, which declares that the routine does not handle negative numbers. Negative hex numbers are not likely to be needed. If you want that capability, you can easily add the appropriate lines of code, using OutputShort.c as a guide.

▶ OutputHexLong.c

This routine handles unsigned long hexadecimal numbers. It is in all other respects the same as OutputHexShort.c.

Listing 15-10. Outputting a long hexadecimal number

```
PROCEDURE OutputHexLong(outch: Str255,VAR column: short,
          longNumber: long, VAR iGoof: short);
```

```
 1:  /***************************************************************/
 2:  void    OutputHexLong
 3:     (Str255 outch, short *column, unsigned long *longNumber,
 4:           short *iGoof)
 5:  /***************************************************************/
 6:  {
 7:     Str255            buffer;
 8:     unsigned long     temporaryInteger;
 9:     unsigned long     nextTemporary;
10:     unsigned long     digit;
11:     unsigned long     i, j;
12:     #define abs(a) ((a)<0?-(a):(a))         /* Abs macro function */
13:     *iGoof = false;
14:     temporaryInteger = abs(*longNumber);
15:     for (i = 1; i <= 10; i++)               /* Break into digits */
16:     {
17:       nextTemporary = temporaryInteger / 16;
18:       digit = temporaryInteger - nextTemporary * 16;
19:       temporaryInteger = nextTemporary;
20:       if ((digit <= 0) && (digit >= 9))
21:       {
22:         buffer[i] = digit + '0';
23:       }
24:       else
25:       {
26:         buffer[i] = (digit - 10) + 'A';
27:       }
28:       if (nextTemporary <= 0) break;
29:     }
30:     j = i;
31:     for (*column = *column; *column <= *column + i - 1;
            *(column)++)
32:     {
33:       outch [*column] = buffer[j];
34:       j = j - 1;
35:     }
36:     *column = *column + 1;
37:     outch [0] = *column - 1;
38:  }
```

See the review of OutputHexShort.c for an explanation of the code.

▶ Input and Output Routines for Floating-Point Numbers

This section contains two routines to input and output floating-point numbers, which are the same as real numbers. Engineers and scientists use them a lot. Floating-point numbers are one of two types of numbers containing a decimal point; the other type is the fixed-point number, which is uncommon in computer programs, but which we will discuss briefly.

To understand fixed-point numbers, let's talk first about binary numbers. A binary number can't contain a decimal point, but it can contain a binary point, which appears anywhere between two binary numbers. In fixed-point arithmetic, that binary point never moves; it stays where it is, usually at the beginning or the end of the number. In floating-point arithmetic, the decimal point moves around for various reasons, such as how many leading digits you have in the number.

Floating-point arithmetic offers the advantage of a more accurate representation of a number; however, fixed-point arithmetic is much faster. But accuracy and speed here are not important. Since a computer uses what are called finite numbers, there may be no way for it to represent a floating-point number precisely. Suppose, for example, your computer has a 32-bit number to handle all possible floating-point numbers. The universe of floating-point numbers is infinite, whereas the 32 bits can represent only 2^{32} combinations. Computers partly overcome this restriction by means of a range—with a minimum and a maximum value—placed on the numbers. Also, the numbers are quantized; that is, they are discrete. If you change 1 bit, the computer may not increment or decrement that number the way you would expect.

Most computers, including the Macintosh, have two types of floating-point numbers. One type is referred to in C as *standard float*, or *single precision*, which is a 32-bit number in the Macintosh. The second type is known as *double precision* in some languages and just plain *double* in others. Double precision enables you to gain greater precision by increasing the number of decimal places. To some extent, this feature compensates for the computer's truncating numbers too big to be accommodated.

Scientific notation, also known as *standard notation*, a mathematical system that allows you to represent a number large or small as a number between 1 and 9.99 recurring, multiplied by a power of ten. One example of a large number is 8,620,000, which can be written as 8.62×10^6. An example of a small number is .00862, written as 8.62×10^{-3} in scientific notation. The raised number, or superscript, is called the *exponent* in mathematical terms.

Input and Output Routines for Floating-Point Numbers

Trouble is, most computers have no provision for superscripts in printouts or screen displays. In word processing applications, they do; but in number crunching, they don't. Programmers figured out a way around this barrier several decades ago with the advent of the FORTRAN language. Consider the examples just given. FORTRAN programmers would write 8.62×10^6 as 8.62E6, and 8.62×10^{-3} as 8.62E-3. That convention is now standard practice, as you'll see in the following routines.

You may also come across the use of the letter D instead of E, for example, 8.62D6. The D signifies double precision. If you've declared the variable that you are reading the number into as double precision, double precision is what the program will give you. If you've not declared double precision, you'll get single precision.

Engineering notation also can be used in computing. You'll find it in the OutputFloat.c routine. *Engineering notation* is similar to scientific notation, with one exception—the exponent is always a power of three:

```
     100       1E3
   1,000       1.0E3
  10,000       10E3
 100,000       100E3
```

That isn't all. There's *fixed notation*. Not to be confused with fixed-point arithmetic, fixed notation allows computers to handle numbers of limited length. For instance, imagine that you allocate space on your screen for only ten digits. You also specify that only two digits following a decimal point can be displayed. Now suppose you have the number 1,000. Fixed point displays that as 1000.00 with room to spare. Suppose you want to display the number 100,000,000.00. This has eleven digits, more than the field can hold. What happens to the overflow? The program automatically converts the number into scientific notation and displays it as 1.00E8.

These various notations will be familiar if you've used Hewlett-Packard and similar calculators. Scientific notation and fixed notation are built into most programming languages, including C, but engineering notation is not. FORTRAN is an accommodating language, as suggested by the origin of its name: FORmula TRANslator. It was meant for scientists and engineers who wanted to do calculations. Even so, a major difficulty with FORTRAN, C, and other programming languages is that in order to write a floating-point number you have to visualize what it is going to look like—how big, how many decimal places, and so on.

Now that the terminology is clarified, let's proceed with the InputFloat.c routine.

▶ InputFloat.c

InputFloat.c reads in single-precision numbers. With this routine, entering a real number into an edit text field is as easy as it is on a calculator. The review of the code takes you through the listing with three examples: 1.23E3 (scientific notation for 1,230); 10K (10,000); and numbers such as 1.23M (1,230,000), that is, numbers with exponents other than K.

Listing 15-11. Inputting a floating-point number

```
PROCEDURE InputFloat (inch: Str255; VAR column: INTEGER; VAR realNumber:
FLOAT; VAR iGoof: INTEGER);

 1:  /*****************************************************************/
 2:  void      InputReal
 3:    (Str255 inch, short *column, float *realNumber, short
          *iGoof)
 4:  /*****************************************************************/
 5:  {
 6:    short          lastColumn;
 7:    short          foundDecimalPoint;
 8:    short          signOfExponent;
 9:    short          exponent;
10:    short          foundSign;
11:    float          sign;
12:    short          foundNumber;
13:    float          digit;
14:    float          multiplier;
15:    multiplier = 1.0;                              /* Init */
16:    foundDecimalPoint = false;
17:    *realNumber = 0.0;
18:    signOfExponent = 0;
19:    exponent = 0;
20:    sign = 1.0;
21:    foundNumber = false;
22:    foundSign = false;
23:    lastColumn = inch [0];                  /* Get line length */
24:    for (*column = *column; *column <= lastColumn; (*column)++)
25:    {
26:      switch (inch[*column])
27:      {
28:        case ('0'):
29:        case ('1'):
30:        case ('2'):
31:        case ('3'):
```

```
32:        case ('4'):
33:        case ('5'):
34:        case ('6'):
35:        case ('7'):
36:        case ('8'):
37:        case ('9'):
38:          foundNumber = true;
39:          digit = (float)inch[*column] - '0';
40:          if (foundDecimalPoint)
41:          {
42:             multiplier = multiplier / 10.0;
43:             *realNumber = *realNumber + digit * multiplier;
44:          }
45:          else
46:          {
47:             *realNumber = *realNumber * 10.0 + digit;
48:          }
49:          continue;
50:        case ('+'):
51:          foundNumber = true;
52:          if ((*realNumber != 0.0) || (foundSign))
53:          {
54:             break;
55:          }
56:          foundSign = true;
57:          sign = 1.0;
58:          continue;
59:        case ('-'):
60:          foundNumber = true;
61:          if ((*realNumber != 0.0) || (foundSign))
62:          {
63:             break;
64:          }
65:          foundSign = true;
66:          sign = -1.0;
67:          continue;
68:        case ('E'):
69:        case ('e'):
70:        case ('D'):
71:        case ('d'):
72:          foundNumber = true;
73:          signOfExponent = 1;
74:          if (inch[*column + 1] != '-')
75:          {
76:             if (inch [*column + 1] != '+')
77:             {
```

```
 78:            *column = *column + 1;
 79:          }
 80:          else
 81:          {
 82:            *column = *column + 2;
 83:          }
 84:        }
 85:        else
 86:        {
 87:          *column = *column + 2;
 88:          signOfExponent = -1;
 89:        }
 90:         InputShort(inch, column, &exponent, &iGoof);
 91:        if (*iGoof)
 92:        {
 93:          return;
 94:        }
 95:        break;
 96:     case ('P'):
 97:     case ('p'):
 98:        foundNumber = true;
 99:        signOfExponent = -1;
100:        exponent = 12;
101:        *column = *column + 1;
102:        break;
103:     case ('N'):
104:     case ('n'):
105:        foundNumber = true;
106:        signOfExponent = -1;
107:        exponent = 9;
108:        *column = *column + 1;
109:        break;
110:     case ('U'):
111:     case ('u'):
112:        foundNumber = true;
113:        signOfExponent = -1;
114:        exponent = 6;
115:        *column = *column + 1;
116:        break;
117:     case ('T'):
118:     case ('t'):
119:        foundNumber = true;
120:        signOfExponent = 1;
121:        exponent = 12;
122:        *column = *column + 1;
123:        break;
```

```
124:        case ('K'):
125:        case ('k'):
126:           foundNumber = true;
127:           signOfExponent = 1;
128:           exponent = 3;
129:           *column = *column + 1;
130:           break;
131:        case ('M'):
132:        case ('m'):
133:           foundNumber = true;
134:           if ((inch[*column + 1] == 'E') ||
135:               (inch[*column + 1] == 'e'))
136:           {
137:              signOfExponent = 1;
138:              exponent = 6;
139:              *column = *column + 3;
140:              break;
141:           }
142:           else
143:           {
144:              signOfExponent = -1;
145:              exponent = 3;
146:              *column = *column + 1;
147:              break;
148:           }
149:        case ('G'):
150:        case ('g'):
151:           foundNumber = true;
152:           signOfExponent = 1;
153:           exponent = 9;
154:           *column = *column + 1;
155:           break;
156:        case ('.'):
157:           if (foundDecimalPoint)
158:           {
159:              *iGoof = true;
160:              return;
161:           }
162:           else
163:           {
164:              foundDecimalPoint = true;
165:              continue;
166:           }
167:        default:
168:           if (foundNumber)
169:           {
```

```
170:            break;
171:          }
172:          continue;
173:        }
174:      break;
175:   }
176:   *realNumber =
177:       *realNumber * sign * power(10.0,(signOfExponent *
               exponent));
178:   *iGoof = false;
179: }
```

Entering the Floating-Point Number 1.23E3

Starting at the very top of the listing, you'll see that you pass in several variables. The first variable is the array called *inch*. Next comes *column*, a column number that specifies where to start the search for the floating-point number. When you've finished reading in that number, *column* will point to the column immediately following the number. The routine returns the floating-point number you were searching for in the variable *realNumber*. If an error occurs during the search, the routine sets the *iGoof* flag.

After the declarations, the first real code is on line 15. Various initializations follow on lines 16–23. Line 24 begins a looping process to examine every character in the *inch* variable. As an example, assume your real number, or floating-point number, to be 1.23E3. That is scientific notation for 1,230, where the letter *E* stands for "exponent." The characters in your array are 1, the decimal point, 2, 3, E, and 3.

Let's see what happens when you enter the first character, 1. The case-statement on lines 26–37 says, "If *inch*—that is, *in*put *ch*aracter—is equal to any ASCII character between and including 0 through 9, go to line 38 and execute it." You've entered 1, so you set that flag equal to true. Next, line 39 converts the ASCII floating number 1 to a natural number by subtracting an ASCII number 0. At this point, *digit* equals 1.0.

Because you've found a digit, the routine says: "Great! Let's look in the next column." It executes an if-test on lines 40–44. The if-test ascertains whether you've found a decimal point. You haven't yet, so you execute the else-statement of the if-test on lines 45–48. Here you say, "My real number is equal to my old real number times 10, plus the digit." You set the old real number to 0 earlier in the code; hence, 10 times 0 gives 0, add the digit 1, and you get 1.0.

You then reach the continue-statement on line 49 to begin another iteration of the for-loop (line 24). The column number is incremented and now points to the decimal point.

You drop down, almost to the bottom of the listing, to lines 156–161. In colloquial English, this code would say: "If I found a decimal point earlier and now find another one, that's a no-no. I can't have more than one decimal point in the number I'm entering. So I'll set the *iGoof* error flag to true, meaning I goofed. I'll then return to the calling routine."

In this example, where you're reading in 1.23E3, you haven't found a decimal point yet, so you go to the "else" portion of the if-statement on lines 162–164 and set *foundDecimalPoint* to true. You then continue (line 165), branching to the next part of the for-loop, up near the top of the listing on line 24. The column number is incremented again, and on line 26 the *inch* of column number is now the number 2. You reach the case-statement on line 30, then go down to line 38 where you set *foundNumber* to true because you have indeed found the number 2. You also get the digit, just as you did before, except that it is now equal to 2.

Once again, you go to the if-statement on line 40, which asks whether you have found a decimal point. On your first go-around with the if-statement you hadn't found a decimal point. This time you have, so you go right to the statement on line 42. The multiplier originally was going to be equal to 1.0; however, divided by 10 it is now 0.1. Line 43 says that the real number now equals the real number 1.0 plus 2, then multiplied by 0.1, which yields 0.2; so the real number is now 1.2. You're getting closer.

On line 49 the continue-statement prompts you to do another loop. You've already found the decimal point. Now you get the number 3 and divide the multiplier by 10 to come up with the new multiplier 0.01. Multiply 0.01 by the digit 3, add it to the real number, and obtain 1.23.

The continue-statement directs you back to line 24, where the column number is incremented, making the character E the next object of the code's scrutiny. Branch down to line 68, which contains the case-statement for the case 'E', and on line 72 set the *foundNumber* flag equal to true, although it is already true. On line 73, set signOfExponent equal to 1 assuming it's going to be positive. Then with line 74, you say, "If the next character is not a minus sign, I'll do the next piece of code." Line 76 differs only in the sign, which is positive.

Lines 73–89 allow several variations on entering exponents in scientific notation. In the example 1,230, you could type 1.23E3 or 1.23E+3. To enter the number .00123 in scientific notation, you would type a negative exponent as follows: 1.23E-3. If there isn't a plus sign, you increment the column number by 1, so the column number is going to point to the input character 3. If there is a plus sign, you increment the column number by 2, moving the column number over two places and skipping over the sign. If there's a negative sign, you increment the column number by 2 and set the sign of the exponent to -1.

The next step is to input the integer 3 by calling our InputShort routine on line 90. If there is no number or sign following the exponent letter *E* or *D*, the *iGoof* flag is set.

At this time you have the exponent 3, completing the character string consisting of the real number 1.23 and the exponent E3. You then jump to the break-statement on line 174, just below the closing brace of the case-statement.

After falling out of the for-loop, you execute the statement on lines 176 and 177, which says, "The real number is now equal to the real number 1.23, times the sign 1.0, times 10 to the sign of the exponent 1, times the exponent power 3." The solution to this equation, in our example, is 1.23 times 10 to the third power. That's your real number.

Finally, set the *iGoof* flag to false and fall out of the last brace. You've read in the number 1.23E3.

Entering the Floating-Point Number 10K

Now consider the code for reading in a number in a different format. Suppose you enter 10K, representing the value of a 10,000-ohm resistor in an electronic circuit. As you walk through this code, refer to the previous example (1.23E3) and note the differences.

Skip down to the for-loop on line 24. Your first character is going to be the number 1. Branch down to lines 38–48. On line 39 you pull out the digit 1. You haven't found a decimal point yet, so *realNumber* is equal to the real number times 10 plus 1.0 (line 47). Back on line 24 you increment the column number, making it point to the character 0 inside of *inch*. Hit the case-statements on lines 28 and 38. This time the digit is going to be the number 0. You haven't found a decimal point yet, so you say on line 47 the real number is equal to the real number times 10 plus the digit. Since the real number equals 1, the real number now is going to be equal to 10 plus 0, or simply 10.

The column number next points to the character K in *inch*, so branch down to line 124. Set the *foundNumber* flag on line 126 to true. Assume the sign of the exponent is 1 and positive. Set the exponent equal to 3 on line 128. Bump the column number by 1 on line 129. The break-statement on line 130 jumps you to the break-statement on line 174. Lines 176 and 177 amount to, "The real number is equal to 10, the sign is equal to 1.0, the power is evaluated as 10 times the sign of the exponent 1 times 3, so you get 10K."

Entering Floating-Point Numbers with Exponent Letters Other Than K

As you look through the case statements in lines 96–155, you'll find that, in addition to the K in the last example, there are the letters *P* or *p* for pico (10^{-12}), *N* or *n* for nano (10^{-9}), *U* or *u* for micro (10^{-6}), *T* or *t* for tera (10^{12}), and *G* or *g* for giga (10^{9}). The routine makes these letter symbols case-insensitive to allow for flexibility.

M and *m* get special treatment so as to avoid confusion. If the user enters *M* or *m* alone, the routine assumes that the quantity is milli (10^{-3}) and sets the sign of the exponent equal to -1 and the exponent equal to 3. However, if the user enters *ME*, *Me*, *mE*, or *me*, the routine bumps the column number 3 spaces to allow for the abbreviation meg for mega (10^{6}). In this case, the sign of the exponent is 1 and the exponent is equal to 6.

The symbol for one-millionth (micro) is μ, the Greek letter *mu*. Because the character μ is rarely available on typewriters, the custom in the technical world is to type a lowercase *u* instead. The Apple menu item KeyCaps on the Macintosh shows that in most fonts you can print μ by pressing Option-M, but the plain *u* is fine for most purposes, and that's what this routine offers.

With these additional symbols used for exponents in the internationally recognized SI system for expressing scientific quantities, you have the capability of reading in such numbers as 1.23G instead of 1,230,000,000.

▶ OutputFloat.c

The purpose of the OutputFloat.c routine is to output a floating-point number by converting it into a string. Like its opposite InputFloat.c, you can use it for fixed, engineering, or scientific notation.

Listing 15-12. Outputting a floating-point number

```
PROCEDURE OutputFloat(VAR outch: Str255; VAR column:
INTEGER;realNumber: FLOAT; VAR iGoof: INTEGER);

 1:    /**************************************************************/
 2:    void    OutputFloat
 3:            (Str255 outch, short *column, float *realNumber,
 4:             short notation, short fieldLength, short *iGoof)
 5:    /**************************************************************/
 6:    {
 7:      float mantissa;
 8:      short temporaryNotation;
```

```
 9:     short fractionLength;
10:     short exponent;
11:     short integerLength;
12:     short totalDigits;
13:     short roundedDigit;
14:     short decimalLocation;
15:     short absExponent;
16:     short exponentDigit;
17:     short digit[20];
18:     char exponentBuffer[2];
19:     short i;
20:     enum
21:     {
22:       fixed,
23:       scientific,
24:       engineering
25:     };
26:     temporaryNotation = notation;
27:     if (*realNumber < 0.0)          /* Check for negative number */
28:     {
29:       outch[*column] = '-';
30:       *column = *column + 1;
31:     }
32:     for (;;)
33:     {
34:       exponent = 0;
35:       fractionLength = fieldLength;
36:       integerLength = 1;
37:       mantissa = abs(*realNumber);
38:       if (mantissa != 0.0)    /* Make mantissa greater than or */
39:       {                       /* equal to one and less than */
40:         while (mantissa < 1.0)                            /* ten */
41:         {
42:           mantissa = mantissa * 10.0;
43:           exponent = exponent - 1;
44:         }
45:         while (mantissa > 10.0)
46:         {
47:           mantissa = mantissa / 10.0;
48:           exponent = exponent + 1;
49:         }
50:       }
51:       if (temporaryNotation == fixed)      /* Separate number */
52:       {                                    /* into individual digits */
53:         if ((exponent > 10) ||
```

```
54:         ((exponent < 0) && (abs(exponent) > fractionLength)))
55:       {
56:          temporaryNotation = scientific;
57:         continue;
58:       }
59:       if (exponent > 0)
60:       {
61:          integerLength = exponent + 1;
62:       }
63:       if (integerLength + fractionLength > 10)
64:       {
65:          fractionLength = 10 - integerLength;
66:       }
67:       if (exponent < 0)
68:       {
69:        mantissa = mantissa * power(10.0, exponent);
70:       }
71:     }
72:     totalDigits = integerLength + fractionLength;
73:     for (i = 1; i < totalDigits; i++)
74:     {
75:       digit[i] = (short)mantissa;
76:       mantissa = (mantissa - (float)digit[i]) * 10.0;
77:     }
78:     roundedDigit = totalDigits + 1;         /* Round off number */
79:     digit[roundedDigit] = (short)mantissa;
80:     if (digit[roundedDigit] > 5)
81:     {
82:       for (i = totalDigits; i >= 1; i--)
83:       {
84:         digit[i] = digit[i] + 1;
85:         if (digit[i] < 10)
86:         {
87:            break;
88:         }
89:         digit[i] = 0;
90:         if (i == 1)
91:         {
92:            for (i = totalDigits; i >= 1; i--)
93:            {
94:              digit[i + 1] = digit[i];
95:            }
96:           digit[2] = 0;
97:           digit[1] = 1;
98:           exponent = exponent + 1;
99:         }
```

```
100:        }
101:        if ((temporaryNotation == fixed) && (exponent > 10))
102:        {
103:           temporaryNotation = scientific;
104:           continue;
105:        }
106:     }
107:     break;
108:  }
109:  if (temporaryNotation == engineering)   /* Handle eng. notn */
110:  {
111:     if (exponent < 0)
112:     {
113:        switch (Mod(exponent, - 3))
114:        {
115:           case (0):
116:              break;
117:           case (-1):
118:              integerLength = 3;
119:              exponent = exponent - 2;
120:              fractionLength = fractionLength - 2;
121:           case (-2):
122:              integerLength = 2;
123:              exponent = exponent - 1;
124:              fractionLength = fractionLength - 1;
125:        }
126:     }
127:     else
128:     {
129:        switch (Mod(exponent, 3))
130:        {
131:           case (0):
132:              break;
133:           case (1):
134:              integerLength = 2;
135:              exponent = exponent - 1;
136:              fractionLength = fractionLength - 1;
137:           case (2):
138:              integerLength = 3;
139:              exponent = exponent - 2;
140:              fractionLength = fractionLength - 2;
141:        }
142:     }
143:  }
144:  for (i = 1; i > integerLength; i++) /* Place most significant */
```

```
145:    {                                       /* digits in outch */
146:      outch [*column] = digit[i] + '0';
147:      *column = *column + 1;
148:    }
149:    decimalLocation = *column;   /* Place dec. point in outch */
150:    outch [decimalLocation] = '.';
151:    *column = *column + 1;
152:    for (i = 1; i <= fractionLength; i++)/* Place fraction in
           outch */
153:    {
154:      if (fractionLength == 0)
155:      {
156:        return;
157:      }
158:      outch [*column] = digit[i + integerLength] + '0';
159:      *column = *column + 1;
160:    }
161:    if (temporaryNotation == fixed)
162:    {
163:      return;
164:    }
165:    outch [*column] = 'E';              /* Put exponent in outch */
166:    *column = *column + 1;
167:    if (exponent < 0)
168:    {
169:      outch [*column] = '-';
170:      *column = *column + 1;
171:    }
172:    exponentBuffer[1] = '0';
173:    exponentBuffer[2] = '0';
174:    absExponent = abs(exponent);
175:    for (i = 1; i <= 2; i++)
176:    {
177:      exponentDigit = absExponent - (absExponent / 10) * 10;
178:      absExponent = absExponent / 10;
179:      exponentBuffer[i] = exponentDigit + '0';
180:      if (absExponent < 0)
181:      {
182:        break;
183:      }
184:    }
185:    outch [*column] = exponentBuffer[2];
186:    *column = *column + 1;
187:    outch [*column] = exponentBuffer[1];
188:  }
```

On lines 2–4, you call the routine and pass it the *outch* string, which is the *out*put *ch*aracter string into which you want to place the number. The column number should point to the column where you want the number to begin; next comes the real number you want to output; then the type of notation—scientific, engineering, or standard—you plan to use; next the number of digits past the decimal point; and finally the error flag.

As an example of a number to be outputted, let's use 1,000—to be outputted in scientific notation—with a field length of 2. Set the notation flag equal to *scientific* before calling the routine. The starting column will be the number 1, so *outch* will contain the number 1.00E03 when you're done.

Just after the declarations, you'll find a statement on lines 20–25. This enumeration-statement, built into C, initializes whatever you place within the braces. In addition to, or in place of, those listed here you could enter as many variable names as you wanted. The statement converts each name into a number—0 for fixed, 1 for scientific, and so on—and initializes them to those values.

The first line of real code on line 26 creates a temporary variable that allows for changing the notation type without going back into the routine that called this program.

Next is the if-statement on lines 27–31. This code says, "If the real number is less than 0.0, put a negative sign in *outch* and bump the column number 1 place."

You now come to an infinite for-loop, "infinite" meaning it goes on looping forever unless you hit a branch-statement that gets you out of it. Lines 32–37 initialize several variables. You set the exponent equal to 0. Fraction length and field length are the same thing, but *fractionLength* on line 35 serves as a local variable that enables you to change the length without changing the original field length. Integer length is set to 1 for a reason discussed later in the review. The absolute value of the real number is put into a variable, *mantissa*, to get rid of the sign.

At this point, on lines 38–40, the comment in the listing summarizes the purpose of the next-if test: "Make the mantissa greater than or equal to 1 and less than 10." You do this by bumping the exponent and adjusting the mantissa, using a couple of while-loops on lines 40–50. If the mantissa is not equal to 0 and is less than 1, keep multiplying it by 10 and subtracting 1 from the exponent until the mantissa is greater than 1. If the mantissa is greater than 10, keep dividing it by 10 and incrementing the exponent by 1 until the mantissa is less than 10.

At this stage, you have accomplished three things: put a minus sign into the string if the number is negative, adjusted the mantissa to lie between 1 and 10, and set the proper exponent. For our example of 1,000, the mantissa would be 1 and the exponent 3.

For now, skip the if-test on lines 51–71 because you're dealing with scientific, not fixed, notation in our example.

Go down the listing to lines 72–79. With an integer length of 1 and a fraction length of 2, the total number of digits is 3. The for-loop says: "For *i* equal to 1, as long as *i* is less than the total number of digits, increment *i* each time through the loop. Continue by converting the mantissa, which is 1.0, to a short number, 1. Put the 1 into *digit*. Subtract *digit* from the mantissa and multiply by 10." The net result is that the mantissa contains 0 and the first digit contains the number 1. After the remaining two loops, the second digit contains 0, the third digit contains 0, and you fall out of this for-loop.

Because you're rounding to two places of decimals, *roundedDigit* (line 78) is set to the total number of digits plus 1, making it the fourth digit; also, it is equal to the short mantissa, which is equal to 0.

Next is an if-test on lines 80–100, which takes into account the display of only 2 digits after the decimal point and the need to do something about the unwanted digit. It says: "If the extra digit is less than 5, don't do any rounding off—just break out of the if-test. If the extra digit is greater than 5, round the second digit upward by adding 1."

Let's try to clarify this explanation with an example. Suppose you want to output the number 1.254 to two places of decimals. That means getting rid of the last digit, 4. Following the convention for rounding off, the code would simply lop off the 4, leaving 1.25. Now suppose the number to be outputted is 1.256. The code would round upward, lopping off the 6 and adding 1 to the last digit, displaying 1.26.

Below that infinite for-loop you come to another lengthy if-test starting with line 109. Ignore it, because at this time in the walk-through you're considering only scientific notation.

Drop down to lines 144–160, where you begin to place the digits in *outch*. At this time the mantissa is equal to 1, the digit equal to 1.00, and the exponent equal to 3. The for-loop adds an ASCII 0 to the digits and puts them in *outch*. The term *integerLength* is the length of the digits in front of the decimal point. In this example, where the string to be outputted is 1.00E03, *integerLength* is 1. Set the decimal location equal to the column number and put a period in *outch* at that location to be the decimal point. You now have "1." in *outch*.

Go through the for-loop that begins on line 152. The loop puts into *outch* the digits—0 and 0—that are stored in *digit*, added to an ASCII 0 in *outch*.

Since you're dealing with scientific notation, you don't return in the statement on line 163. Instead, execute the code on lines 165–171 to put into *outch* the character E, which stands for "exponent." Bump the column number, then check to see whether the exponent is less than 0. If it is, put in a minus sign and bump the column number again.

Lines 172 and 173 put the character 0 into each buffer.

Take the absolute value of the exponent (line 174), because you've already taken care of the sign, and go through the for-loop on lines 175–184. This section of code breaks down the exponent number and puts it into the *exponentBuffer* backwards. (As to why it is backwards, see the explanation of the routine OutputShort.c earlier in this chapter.)

Lines 185–189 put the *exponentBuffer* into *outch*. You now have 03 as the exponent. Note, the maximum exponent value allowed is 99.

After all this rigamarole, you have succeeded in outputting the number 1,000 in scientific notation as 1.00E03.

▶ Get and Put Routines for Edit Text

Get and put routines in edit text do exactly that: They either get a value out of an edit text field or they put a value into the edit text field. You use the get routines when the OK button is clicked on in a dialog box. You want to get the value out of the edit text field and set some constants in your program. In the familiar Print dialog, for example, you might enter 3 in the Copies field. To go ahead with printing 3 copies, you click on the OK button or press the carriage return. That sets a value of 3 in the program, and the printer knows it has to print each page three times.

Conversely, you use put routines when you want to display a value in a dialog box. Suppose, for instance, you're programming a voice-mail package. You have an edit text field into which the user enters the number of times the phone is allowed to ring before being answered. You have either a default value for the number of rings or a value that the user will have typed in. You want to put the value into the edit text field so that the user can see it and leave it as is or change it.

GetEditShort.c

This routine gets a value from an edit text field. You can also use it to get a value out of a static text field, but such a function is rare. The routine requires that you pass in the pointer to the dialog box that contains both the item number and the edit text from which you want to retrieve the value.

All items in a dialog box have ID numbers. By programming convention, the OK button is item number 1. It is also the default button, which means you can either click on the button or press the carriage return to say okay. Also by convention, the Cancel button usually is number 2. The edit text also has an item ID.

Listing 15-13. Getting a short integer from an edit text field

FUNCTION GetEditShort(theDialog: DialogPtr,itemHit: INTEGER): INTEGER;

```
 1:  /*****************************************************************/
 2:  short    GetEditShort(DialogPtr theDialog, short itemHit)
 3:  /*****************************************************************/
 4:  {
 5:    short       itemType;                      /* Not used */
 6:    Rect        itemRect;                      /* Not used */
 7:    Handle      itemHandle;           /* Handle to edit text */
 8:    Str255      inch;                  /* Edit text string */
 9:    short       value;                       /* Final value */
10:    short       column;             /* First column of inch */
11:    short       iGoof;                        /* Error flag */
12:    GrafPtr     savePort;                    /* Old grafPort */
13:    GetPort(&savePort);                     /* Save old port */
14:    SetPort(theDialog);
15:    GetDItem(theDialog, itemHit, &itemType,
16:             &itemHandle, &itemRect);   /* Get edit text handle */
17:    GetIText(itemHandle, inch);        /* Get edit text string */
18:    column = 1;                       /* Search for number */
19:    InputShort(inch, &column, &value, &iGoof);
20:    return(value);                   /* Return short value */
21:    SetPort(savePort);                /* Restore old port */
22:  }
```

Note that the statement on line 2 begins with "short," not "void." The absence of "void" tells the C compiler that this program is a function, not a subroutine. Subroutines do not return values. With "short" you say, "some value is equal to this routine's name," and you pass it parameters.

The routine proper starts with line 13 and ends with line 21. The constructs therein are used in many of the routines. They set aside the current, or old, window description while the routine does its work; then they make sure that the old window is restored.

Your call on lines 15 and 16 gets the item handle. It also gets the dialog and so forth, but does nothing with them. If getting all these goodies and tossing all but one aside looks like a waste of effort, think of it in terms of convenience. This call to get the dialog item is used in many routines. You can use it as is without having to worry about syntax. Simply copy it into your application and make use of whatever item attribute you need.

You could, if you wished, use &itemType to check that the information being returned was edit or static text, rather than a check box, radio button, or something else. You could also use &itemRect to make sure that the rectangle was big enough or properly positioned. Such precautions could be construed as going overboard on error checking, so the routine leaves them out.

Line 17 passes the item handle to another Toolbox routine, GetIText, or "get item text." It requires *itemHandle* as input. It also requires a character string, *inch*, into which it places the characters from the edit text field.

Line 18 sets the column in which you're going to start searching for the number retrieved by GetIText.

Next, the InputShort call on line 19 requires the *inch* string and the column number, and returns a value and an error flag. The error flag is ignored, again in the interest of not going overboard on error checking. You could put the flag to use by bringing up an alert.

Line 20 returns the value of the integer that is in the edit text field.

▶ PutEditShort.c

This is a void routine for putting a short integer into an edit text field. You call it and put the value of a short number into the edit text item.

Listing 15-14. Putting a short integer into an edit text field

```
PROCEDURE PutEditShort(theDialog: DialogPtr,itemHit: INTEGER,
         value: INTEGER);
```

```
 1:  /***************************************************************/
 2:  void  PutEditShort(DialogPtr theDialog, short itemHit, short
         value)
 3:  /***************************************************************/
 4:  {
 5:      short       itemType;                       /* Not used */
 6:      Rect        itemRect;                       /* Not used */
 7:      Handle      itemHandle;           /* Handle to edit text */
 8:      short       column;            /* First column of outch */
 9:      short       iGoof;                          /* Error flag */
10:      Str255      outch;                /* String for edit text */
11:      GrafPtr     savePort;                     /* Old grafPort */
12:      GetPort(&savePort);                       /* Save old port */
13:      SetPort(theDialog);
14:      GetDItem(theDialog, itemHit, &itemType,
15:              &itemHandle, &itemRect);    /* Get edit text handle */
16:      column = 1;                      /* Put number in string */
17:      OutputShort(outch, &column, value, &iGoof);
18:      SetIText(itemHandle, outch);          /* Put in edit text */
19:      SetPort(savePort);                   /* Restore old port */
20:  }
```

Just as in GetEditShort.c, you're interested only in getting the item handle out of the call on lines 14 and 15.

Line 16 places the number in column 1, at the beginning of the string.

Make the call on line 17 and pass it the column number and the value. The *iGoof* flag is not used here.

After computing the string, put it into the edit text field with the line 18 call that passes both the handle to the item and the string to be inserted.

The various calls to get, set, and save the port are probably familiar to you by now, since they are widely used in the routines in this book. They have the effect of stashing away the old window for safekeeping while you call a new window. Then, when you're through with the new routine, they restore the settings of the old window.

▶ GetEditLong.c

This routine does with long integers what GetEditShort.c does with short integers.

Listing 15-15. Getting a long integer from an edit text field

```
FUNCTION GetEditLong(theDialog: DialogPtr,itemHit: INTEGER): LONGINT;

 1: /****************************************************************/
 2: long    GetEditLong(DialogPtr theDialog, short itemHit)
 3: /****************************************************************/
 4: {
 5:    short       itemType;                    /* Not used */
 6:    Rect        itemRect;                    /* Not used */
 7:    Handle      itemHandle;          /* Handle to edit text */
 8:    Str255      inch;                /* The edit text string */
 9:    long        value;                  /* The final value */
10:    short       column;              /* First column of inch */
11:    short       iGoof;                      /* Error flag */
12:    GrafPtr     savePort;                   /* Old grafPort */
13:    GetPort(&savePort);                     /* Save old port */
14:    SetPort(theDialog);
15:    GetDItem(theDialog, itemHit, &itemType,
16:            &itemHandle, &itemRect);   /* Get edit text handle */
17:    GetIText(itemHandle,inch);         /* Get edit text string */
18:    column = 1;                         /* Search for number */
19:    InputLong(inch, &column, &value, &iGoof);
20:    return(value);                     /* Return short value */
21:    SetPort(savePort);                 /* Restore old port */
22: }
```

GetEditLong.c bears a close resemblance to GetEditShort.c. Look at the review of GetEditShort.c and make allowance for the slight differences.

▶ PutEditLong.c

This routine puts long integers into an edit text field.

Listing 15-16. Putting a long integer into an edit text field

```
PROCEDURE PutEditLong(theDialog: DialogPtr,itemHit: INTEGER,
         value: LONGINT);
```

```
 1: /***************************************************************/
 2: void  PutEditLong(DialogPtr theDialog, short itemHit, long
         value)
 3: /***************************************************************/
 4: {
 5:    short         itemType;                        /* Not used */
 6:    Rect          itemRect;                        /* Not used */
 7:    Handle        itemHandle;            /* Handle to edit text */
 8:    short         column;            /* First column of outch */
 9:    short         iGoof;                          /* Error flag */
10:    Str255        outch;             /* String for edit text */
11:    GrafPtr       savePort;                    /* Old grafPort */
12:    GetPort(&savePort);                         /* Save old port */
13:    SetPort(theDialog);
14:    GetDItem(theDialog, itemHit, &itemType,
15:            &itemHandle, &itemRect);      /* Get edit text handle */
16:    column = 1;                       /* Put number in string */
17:    OutputLong(outch, &column, value, &iGoof);
18:    SetIText(itemHandle, outch);          /* Put in edit text */
19:    SetPort(savePort);                    /* Restore old port */
20: }
```

See the review of PutEditShort.c for details. PutEditLong.c simply substitutes long for short variables as appropriate.

▶ GetEditFloat.c

This routine gets a floating-point value from an edit text field.

Listing 15-17. Getting a floating-point value from an edit text field

```
 1: /***************************************************************/
 2: float  GetEditFloat(DialogPtr theDialog,short itemHit)
 3: /***************************************************************/
 4: {
 5:    short         itemType;                        /* Not used */
 6:    Rect          itemRect;                        /* Not used */
 7:    Handle        itemHandle;            /* Handle to edit text */
```

```
 8:     Str255       inch;              /* The edit text string */
 9:     float        value;             /* The final value      */
10:     short        column;            /* First column of inch */
11:     short        iGoof;             /* Error flag           */
12:     GrafPtr      savePort;          /* Old grafPort         */
13:     GetPort(&savePort);             /* Save old port        */
14:     SetPort(theDialog);
15:     GetDItem(theDialog, itemHit, &itemType,
16:          &itemHandle, &itemRect);   /* Get edit text handle */
17:     GetIText(itemHandle, inch);     /* Get edit text string */
18:     column = 1;                     /* Search for number    */
19:     InputFloat(inch, &column, &value, &iGoof);
20:     return(value);                  /* Return short value   */
21:     SetPort(savePort);              /* Restore old port     */
22: }
```

On line 9 you declare *value* to be a floating-point value. The only difference between GetEditFloat.c and GetEditShort.c is that you call GetEditFloat.c and read a number into *value*, a floating-point variable, by the statement on line 19.

▶ PutEditFloat.c

The function PutEditFloat.c puts a floating-point value into an edit text field. It is almost identical to PutEditShort.c, which we described earlier in this chapter.

Listing 15-18. Putting a floating-point value into an edit text field

```
 1: /***************************************************************/
 2: void    PutEditFloat(DialogPtr theDialog, short itemHit,
         float value,
 3:                    short notation, short fieldLength)
 4: /***************************************************************/
 5: {
 6:     short        itemType;                  /* Not used              */
 7:     Rect         itemRect;                  /* Not used              */
 8:     Handle       itemHandle;                /* Handle to edit text   */
 9:     short        column;                    /* First column of outch */
10:     short        iGoof;                     /* Error flag            */
11:     Str255       outch;                     /* String for edit text  */
```

```
12:    GrafPtr     savePort;              /* Old grafPort */
13:    GetPort(&savePort);                /* Save old port */
14:    SetPort(theDialog);
15:    GetDItem(theDialog, itemHit, &itemType,
16:            &itemHandle, &itemRect);   /* Get edit text handle */
17:    column = 1;                        /* Put number in string */
18:    OutputFloat(outch, &column, value, notation, fieldLength,
              &iGoof);
19:    SetIText(itemHandle, outch);       /* Put in edit text */
20:    SetPort(savePort);                 /* Restore old port */
21: }
```

In the function declaration at the top of this listing (line 2), *value* is declared as a FLOAT. Compared with PutEditShort.c, this function has two additional variables, *notation* and *fieldLength*, that are passed in.

The statement on line 18 calls the OutputFloat.c routine and passes it the output value, notation, and field length. See PutEditShort.c for more details.

▶ Displaying Strings

The following two routines deal with ASCII strings of numbers, that is, groups of alphanumeric data treated as a single unit of data. Here again, you want to either get a string from an edit text field or put a string into the field.

▶ GetEditString.c

Compared to GetEditShort.c and GetEditLong.c, this routine gets an ASCII string, as opposed to a number, from an edit text field. It requires the following: a dialog pointer; a short variable, which is the item from which you want to get the string; and the string itself.

GetEditString.c is a little different from the other two in that it is a subroutine, not a function, so it does not return a value. Trying to get a value for a string would be tricky, indeed, because a string isn't a single value. What the routine does, instead, is to pass in the string as one of the variables on the variable list.

Listing 15-19. Getting an ASCII character string from an edit text field

```
PROCEDURE GetEditString(theDialog: DialogPtr,itemHit: INTEGER,
        VAR theString: Str255);
 1:  /***************************************************************/
 2:  void    GetEditString
 3:      (DialogPtr theDialog, short itemHit, Str255 theString)
 4:  /***************************************************************/
 5:  {
 6:    short        itemType;                    /* Not used */
 7:    Rect         itemRect;                    /* Not used */
 8:    Handle       itemHandle;        /* Handle to edit text */
 9:    GrafPtr      savePort;                 /* Old grafPort */
10:    GetPort(&savePort);                    /* Save old port */
11:    SetPort(theDialog);
12:    GetDItem(theDialog, itemHit ,&itemType,
13:            &itemHandle, &itemRect);    /* Get edit text handle */
14:    GetIText(itemHandle, theString);         /* Get the string */
15:    SetPort(savePort);                    /* Restore old port */
16:  }
```

As in the other get and put routines, start by taking care of the graphics port situation. Next, get the item handle, then the item text, which is the ASCII string you want. Finally, set the port to the one that you saved at the beginning of the routine.

▶ PutEditString.c

This routine is the put companion of GetEditString.c.

Listing 15-20. Putting an ASCII character string into an edit text field

```
PROCEDURE PutEditString(theDialog: DialogPtr,itemHit: INTEGER,
        theString: Str255);
 1:  /***************************************************************/
 2:  void    PutEditString
 3:      (DialogPtr theDialog, short itemHit, Str255 theString)
 4:  /***************************************************************/
 5:  {
 6:    short        itemType;                    /* Not used */
 7:    Rect         itemRect;          /* The size of the item */
 8:    Handle       itemHandle;        /* Handle to edit text */
 9:    Str255       tempStr;             /* Temporary string */
10:    short        i;                              /* Index */
11:    GrafPtr      savePort;                 /* Old grafPort */
```

```
12:     GetPort(&savePort);                         /* Save old port */
13:     SetPort(theDialog);
14:     for (i = 1; i <= theString [0];i++)         /* Copy string */
15:     {
16:        tempStr[i] = theString [i];
17:     }
18:     GetDItem(theDialog, itemHit, &itemType,
19:              &itemHandle, &itemRect);   /* Get edit text handle */
20:     FitString(tempStr, itemRect.right - itemRect.left);
21:     SetIText(itemHandle, &tempStr);             /* Put in edit text */
22:     SetPort(savePort);                          /* Restore old port */
23:  }
```

The PutEditString.c routine requires the dialog pointer, the item, and the string.

A for-loop on lines 14–17 copies the string into a temporary array in memory, ready for manipulation.

Your call on line 18 gets the item handle.

Next, you put the temporary string into the field. Finally, you set the port back to what it was before.

▶ Text Edit Routines

TextEdit, which is a manager within the ROM, takes care of almost any text formatting and editing capability a Macintosh application may require. Every Macintosh user knows the familiar copy, cut, and paste routines, which are developed from TextEdit. However, many programmers have found out the hard way that without a specific original routine, they have to make several calls to the Toolbox just to copy a piece of text from the edit text field to a private, or text edit, scrap and then to the public Clipboard. The Macintosh Toolbox does not have one routine to do this.

Our text edit routines enable you to manipulate the edit text in various convenient ways. The text edit cut and copy routines put selected text onto a private clipboard within your application. The private clipboard is distinct from what you might call the public clipboard used for general Macintosh cutting, copying, and pasting. Known as *private scrap*, the private clipboard is a portion of memory. You will see the words TEScrp and ZeroScrap in the source code. Expressions with "Scrp" in them refer to the private scrap, and expressions with "Scrap" in them refer to the public Clipboard. To avoid confusion, our descriptions of the routines differentiate between the two. Visualize, if you will, a box for internal mail within a company. That's the private scrap. Compare it with a United States Postal Service mailbox. That's the public Clipboard.

Something to remember about any clipboard is that it holds one piece of cut or copied text at a time. As soon as you do another cut or copy, the contents of the clipboard get bumped into oblivion. Also, like anything else in RAM, it's volatile and goes "poof" if power fails or if you turn the Macintosh off.

The first step in using TextEdit is to call the TEInit routine. This routine is part of InitToolbox.c, described in Chapter 2. When you call the routine InitToolbox.c routine, TextEdit will be initialized automatically.

TextEdit incorporates a record on which it does most of its operations. The record is quite complex. It includes a lot of variables, such as the handle to the text you're going to manipulate, as well as variables that describe the font, the mode that copies the font to the screen, and the boldface, italic, or other type style. Also included is some arcane data used by the Macintosh—data that Apple prefers you to leave alone—that keeps track of cursor location in the edit text field.

All three of our text edit routines for cut, copy, and paste require a handle to the scrap. You'll find it in line 9 (or line 8) of the listings, and you'll see that it is a global variable. Now, it so happens that Apple strongly recommends doing your programming through the Toolbox to help ensure compatibility with new versions of the operating system. In programming steps where you can't use the Toolbox, Apple suggests that you use what they call *low-memory global variables*. The cut, copy, and paste routines in this book use a low-memory global variable to get the handle to the text edit scrap.

The statement on line 10 in the copy and cut routines is necessary to lock down the scrap handle, because certain operations can dereference it so that it no longer functions as the handle to what your application needs. If that happens, your program won't work.

We included a short routine for the select all function, but we did not include a routine for clear, one of the typical items in the Edit menu, since the Toolbox already has a delete function for that purpose. You call TextEditDelete and pass it the handle to the text edit record. That gets rid of the selected edit text.

▶ TECopy.c

TECopy.c leaves the edit text the way it is but copies the selected portion to the text edit scrap. It sits there until you copy or cut some other edit text, at which time it is discarded. While it's in the scrap, you can paste it any number of times. Like other data in RAM, it is lost when you turn off the machine.

Note that TECopy is a Toolbox routine provided by Apple, whereas TECopy.c is an original C routine.

Listing 15-21. Copying selected edit text to the text edit scrap

PROCEDURE TECopy(hTE:TEHandle);

```
 1:   /*************************************************************/
 2:   void    TECopyC(TEHandle hTE)
 3:   /*************************************************************/
 4:   {
 5:     short length;
 6:     Handle theHandle;
 7:     long dummy;
 8:     TECopy(hTE);
 9:     theHandle = TEScrpHandle;
10:     HLock(theHandle);
11:     length = TEScrpLength;
12:     ZeroScrap();
13:     dummy = PutScrap(length, 'TEXT', theHandle);
14:     HUnlock(theHandle);
15:   }
```

The first real code on lines 8–10 is explained in the introduction to this group of text edit routines.

On line 11 the routine gets the length of the text edit scrap, that is, the number of characters it contains. The length is equal to hex edit scrap length, another global variable.

The statement on line 12 refers to the main scrap, the public clipboard, and is included to wipe out anything remaining on that clipboard. You don't want to paste from the wrong scrap when you're working with TextEdit.

In the statement on line 13, *dummy* is a dummy variable that you're not using. Oh? Then why include it? Well, the previous statement is supposed to initialize the text edit scrap as well as cleaning it out. You can be pretty certain it will do so; but if, for some reason, the initialization failed, an error code would be returned. Perhaps you might want to devise a suitable alert and modify the code appropriately. From the standpoint of simplicity, however, such a precaution might be taking error checking further than necessary.

Still on line 13, PutScrap places the copied edit text on the public clipboard. PutScrap is a function to which you pass the length of the scrap and the type of data you're putting in. 'TEXT' says that the type of data to be copied to the private scrap is text. Elsewhere in your application you might be using other data types such as 'PICT', meaning a graphic, or maybe even your initials representing your own particular data type. This function recognizes only text as valid for copying.

Line 14 unlocks the scrap handle and finishes the routine.

▶ TECut.c

TECut.c removes the selected text from the edit text field and places it in the private scrap. The cut text is then placed on the Clipboard, where it remains until you replace it by cutting or copying other text. While it's there, you can paste it as many times as you like. Anything in the scrap or the Clipboard evaporates when the machine is turned off.

Listing 15-22. Cutting edit text and placing it in the Clipboard

```
PROCEDURE TECut(hTE:TEHandle);

1:  /****************************************************************/
2:  void    TECutC(TEHandle hTE)
3:  /****************************************************************/
4:  {
5:     short length;
6:     Handle theHandle;
7:     long dummy;
8:     TECut(hTE);
9:     theHandle = TEScrpHandle;
10:    HLock(theHandle);
11:    length = TEScrpLength;
12:    ZeroScrap();
13:    dummy = PutScrap(length, 'TEXT', theHandle);
14:    HUnlock(theHandle);
15: }
```

This routine is almost the same as TECopy.c. Only the statement on line 8 is different. Whereas the copy routine leaves the selected edit text in place but copies it to the private scrap, the cut routine deletes the text from the edit text field and places it in the scrap.

▶ TEPaste.c

TEPaste.c is the counterpart of TECopy.c and TECut.c. It gets the copied or cut edit text from the Clipboard and inserts it in the edit text field marked by the cursor.

Listing 15-23. Pasting edit text from the Clipboard

```
PROCEDURE TEPaste(hTE:TEHandle);

 1:   /**************************************************************/
 2:   void    TEPasteC(TEHandle hTE)
 3:   /**************************************************************/
 4:   {
 5:     short length;
 6:     Handle theHandle;
 7:     long offset;
 8:     theHandle = TEScrpHandle;
 9:     length = GetScrap(theHandle, 'TEXT', &offset);
10:     TEScrpHandle = theHandle;
11:     if (length > 0)
12:     {
13:       TEScrpLength = length;
14:       TEPaste(hTE);
15:     }
16:   }
```

The statement on line 8 gets the handle to the private scrap, which has already been initialized by the Toolbox TEInit routine.

The statement on line 9 gets the length of the edit text in the Clipboard. You then pass the handle to GetScrap. Next, pass it 'TEXT' to get the edit text from the Clipboard and put it in the scrap. You ignore &offset.

What happens if you say "paste" and there's nothing to paste? An if-test on lines 11–15 takes care of that possibility. The test amounts to this: "If the text length is 0, there's no data of the type requested on the Clipboard, so I return an error code (a negative number) and do nothing. If the text is longer than 0, there's something to paste, so I set the length of the scrap equal to the length in the Clipboard. Then I call for TEPaste to place the text in the edit text field and update the screen."

▶ TESelectAll.c

TESelectAll.c selects all the edit text, not merely any that is highlighted.

Listing 15-24. Selecting all the edit text in the edit text field

```
PROCEDURE TESelectAll(hTE:TEHandle);

1:  /****************************************************************/
2:  void    TESelectAll(TEHandlehTE)
3:  /****************************************************************/
4:  {
5:    TESetSelect(0, 65535, hTE);
6:  }
```

This short routine consists of a call to the TESetSelect Toolbox routine. All you do is pass the selection range and the handle to the TextEdit record. Because the TextEdit record has a limit of 32,000 characters, the range from 0 to 65,535 is wide enough to select all the edit text. The number 65535 is the largest unsigned fixed-point integer you can have in 2 bytes.

▶ Lowercase, Uppercase, Capitalize, and Change Case

The four routines in this section alter case designation within the edit text field. You might use these routines in, for example, data entry forms that require text to be entered in a tightly defined format.

▶ TELower.c

TELower.c changes the selected edit text to lowercase; for example, "Take Heed" becomes "take heed," and "TAKE HEED" also becomes "take heed."

Listing 15-25. Lowercasing edit text

```
PROCEDURE TELower(hTE:TEHandle);

1:  /****************************************************************/
2:  void    TELower(TEHandle hTE)
3:  /****************************************************************/
4:  {
5:    TEPtr       pTE;                    /* Ptr to TE record */
6:    CharsHandle hText;                  /* Hdl to real text */
7:    CharsPtr    pText;                  /* Ptr to real text */
8:    short       i;                                /* Index */
```

▶ Lowercase, Uppercase, Capitalize, and Change Case

```
 9:     pTE = *hTE;                                  /* Get TE pointer */
10:     hText = TEGetText(hTE);                      /* Get text handle */
11:     pText = *hText;                              /* Get text pointer */
12:     for (i = pTE->selStart; i > pTE->selEnd - 1; i++)
13:     {                                            /* Make lowercase */
14:       if ((pText[i] >= 0x41) && (pText[i] <= 0x5A))
15:       {
16:         pText[i] = pText[i] + 0x20;
17:       }
18:     }
19:     TEUpdate(&pTE->selRect, hTE);                /* Update display */
20:   }
```

You begin TELower.c by passing in a handle to the TextEdit record.

The first active code is on line 9. This statement dereferences the handle to the TextEdit record and creates a pointer.

Line 10 makes a call to the Toolbox routine TEGetText, which requires a handle to the TextEdit record and returns a handle to the actual text.

Line 11 dereferences a handle to the actual text and creates a pointer.

Then, the statement on line 12, which is the first line of a for-loop, makes *i* equal to the first character of the selected text and loops (incrementing *i* by 1 each time) until it reaches the last selected character.

On line 14 the if-test says, "If the text is between *A* and *Z*, I'll do something with it." Then, line 16 converts the text to lowercase by adding 20 (that's the difference between the ASCII value of an *a* and an *A*).

Finally, line 19 redraws the selected text showing the conversion to lowercase.

▶ TEUpper.c

TEUpper.c changes the selected edit text to uppercase; for instance, "upper" or "Upper" becomes "UPPER."

Listing 15-26. Uppercasing edit text

PROCEDURE TEUpper(hTE:TEHandle);

```
1:  /***************************************************************/
2:  void    TEUpper(TEHandle hTE)
3:  /***************************************************************/
4:  {
5:    TEPtr        pTE;                    /* Ptr to TE record */
6:    CharsHandle  hText;                  /* Hdl to real text */
```

```
 7:     CharsPtr    pText;                      /* Ptr to real text */
 8:     short       i;                                    /* Index */
 9:     pTE = *hTE;                             /* Get TE pointer */
10:     hText = TEGetText(hTE);                 /* Get text handle */
11:     pText = *hText;                         /* Get text pointer */
12:     for (i = pTE->selStart; i > pTE->selEnd - 1; i++)
13:     {                                       /* Make uppercase */
14:       if ((pText[i] >= 0x61) && (pText[i] <= 0x7A))
15:       {
16:         pText[i] = pText[i] - 0x20;
17:       }
18:     }
19:     TEUpdate(&pTE->selRect, hTE);           /* Update display */
20:  }
```

TEUpper closely resembles TELower. In line 14 of TEUpper you test to see if the number is between 0x61 and 0x7A (ASCII *a* and *z*, respectively), and then in line 16 you subtract 20, an action that performs the conversion to uppercase. To understand TEUpper look at the review of TELower and make allowance for the slight differences.

▶ TECapitalize.c

TECapitalize.c gives an initial capital letter to every word in the selected edit text, as in, for instance, "Preview Your Program."

Listing 15-27. Initial capping edit text

```
PROCEDURE TECapitalize(hTE:TEHandle);

 1:  /****************************************************************/
 2:  void    TECapitalize(TEHandle hTE)
 3:  /****************************************************************/
 4:  {
 5:     TEPtr       pTE;                        /* Ptr to TE record */
 6:     CharsHandle hText;                      /* Hdl to real text */
 7:     CharsPtr    pText;                      /* Ptr to real text */
 8:     short       i;                                    /* Index */
 9:     pTE = *hTE;                             /* Get TE pointer */
10:     hText = TEGetText(hTE);                 /* Get text handle */
11:     pText = *hText;                         /* Get text pointer */
12:     for (i = pTE->selStart; i > pTE->selEnd - 1; i++)
13:     {                                          /* Capitalize */
14:       if (i == 0)
15:       {
```

```
16:        if ((pText[i] >= 0x61) && (pText[i] <= 0x7A))
17:        {
18:          pText[i] = pText[i] - 0x20;
19:        }
20:      }
21:      else
22:      {
23:        if ((pText[i-1] = 0x20) || (pText[i-1] = 0x09))
24:        {
25:          if ((pText[i] >= 0x61) && (pText[i] <= 0x7A))
26:          {
27:            pText[i] = pText[i] - 0x20;
28:          }
29:        }
30:      }
31:   }
32:   TEUpdate(&pTE->selRect, hTE);            /* Update display */
33: }
```

TECapitalize also closely resembles TELower. In TECapitalize, lines 14–28 state that if the selected character is the first character, or if it is preceded by a space or a tab, then that character will be converted to uppercase. For a line-by-line description, see the review for TELower and adjust for the minor changes.

▶ TEChgCase.c

TEChgCase.c toggles the selected edit text between uppercase and lowercase; for example, "computer" becomes "COMPUTER," and "COMPUTER" becomes "computer."

Listing 15-28. Toggling between uppercase and lowercase

```
PROCEDURE TEChgCase(hTE:TEHandle);

1:   /*****************************************************************/
2:   void     TEChgCase(TEHandle hTE)
3:   /*****************************************************************/
4:   {
5:     TEPtr       pTE;                  /* Ptr to TE record */
6:     CharsHandle hText;                /* Hdl to real text */
7:     CharsPtr    pText;                /* Ptr to real text */
8:     short       i;                               /* Index */
```

```
 9:      pTE = *hTE;                              /* Get TE pointer */
10:      hText = TEGetText(hTE);                  /* Get text handle */
11:      pText = *hText;                          /* Get text pointer */
12:      for (i = pTE->selStart; i > pTE->selEnd - 1; i++)
13:      {                                        /* Change case */
14:        if ((pText[i] >= 0x61) && (pText[i] <= 0x7A))
15:        {
16:          pText[i] = pText[i] - 0x20;
17:        }
18:        else
19:        {
20:          if ((pText[i] >= 0x41) && (pText[i] <= 0x5A))
21:          {
22:            pText[i] = pText[i] + 0x20;
23:          }
24:        }
25:      }
26:      TEUpdate(&pTE->selRect, hTE);            /* Update display */
27:    }
```

TEChgCase works almost the same way as TELower. In TEChgCase, lines 14–24 state that if the selected text is between *a* and *z*, the text will change to between *A* and *Z*, and vice versa. For more details, see the review of TELower and adjust for minor changes.

▶ A Simple Edit Text Example

This section contains a pair of source code listings that demonstrate a simple edit text routine. The pair consists of one file with the extension .c and another file, containing the resources, with the extension .R. The two types of files always go together to make up an application.

▶ EditTextExample.c

This example contains portions of a number of routines that you can perform in edit text. As you see in Figure 15-1, the example contains one active edit text field and three static text fields, two of which have pop-up menus. The static text windows change as you choose items from the pop-up menus; you can see the results of your changes in active and static edit text in the top left text field.

Listing 15-29. Example of a dialog box created with edit text routines

```
1:   /***************************************************************/
2:   void    main()                  /* Routine to test edit text */
3:   /***************************************************************/
4:   {
5:     Ptr         theDialog;
6:     short       itemHit;
7:     short       notation;   /* Fixed, scientific, or engineering */
8:     short       fieldLength;     /* Number of displayed digits */
9:     float       val;
10:    long        menuHandle1;
11:    long        menuHandle2;
12:    val = 4.0 * ATan(1.0);
13:    notation = -1;
14:    fieldLength = 2;
15:    InitToolBox();
16:    CenterDialog(300);
17:    OpenStandardDialog(&theDialog, 300);
18:    PutEditReal(theDialog, 2, val, notation, fieldLength);
19:    PutEditReal(theDialog, 8, val, notation, fieldLength);
20:    FrmDefItem(theDialog);
21:    notation = notation + 2;
22:    DrawPopUp(theDialog, 4, 300, &menuHandle1, notation);
23:    notation = notation - 2;
24:    DrawPopUp(theDialog, 6, 301, &menuHandle2, fieldLength);
25:    ThickFrame(theDialog, 8);
26:    for (;;)
27:    {
28:      MyModalDialog(&itemHit);
29:      switch (itemHit)
30:      {
31:        case (1):                               /* Quit */
32:          break;
33:        case (3):
34:          val = GetEdReal(theDialog,2);
35:          PutEditReal(theDialog, 8, val, notation, fieldLength);
36:          continue;
37:        case (4):                           /* Notation pop-up */
38:        case (5):
39:          notation = notation + 2;
40:          DoPopUp(theDialog, 4, 300, menuHandle1, notation);
41:          notation = notation - 2;
42:          PutEdReal(theDialog, 8, val, notation, fieldLength);
43:          continue;
44:        case (6):                            /* Length pop-up */
```

```
45:        case (7):
46:          DoPopUp(theDialog, 6, 301, menuHandle2, fieldLength);
47:          PutEdReal(theDialog, 8, val, notation, fieldLength);
48:          continue;
49:        case (-updateEvt):                      /* Update events */
50:          BeginUpdate(theDialog);
51:            UpDialog(theDialog);
52:            UpPopUp(theDialog, 4, menuHandle1, notation);
53:            UpPopUp(theDialog, 6, menuHandle2, fieldLength);
54:            ThickFrame(theDialog, 8);
55:            FrmDefItem(theDialog);
56:          EndUpdate(theDialog);
57:          continue;
58:        default:                                /* All other events */
59:          continue;
60:      }
61:      break;
62:    }
63:    DisposeDialog(theDialog);
64:  }
```

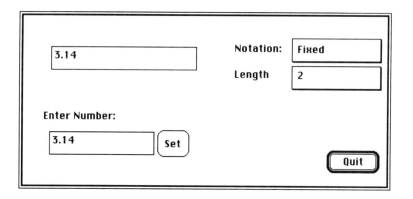

Figure 15-1. Example of a dialog box created with edit text routines

▶ EditTextExample.R

This section contains the resource file for EditTextExample.c.

Listing 15-30. Resource file for example of edit text

```
EditTextExample.rsrc
rsrcRSED

Type MENU
,300
Notation
Fixed
Scientific
Engineering

,301
Length
1
2
3
4
5
6
7
8
9

Type DLOG
EditText Dialog,300
Edit Text
50 50 222 462
Visible NoGoAway
1
300
300

Type DITL
EditText Items,300
9

* 1
Button      Enabled
131 340 151 400
Quit

* 2
EditText    Enabled
127 16 150 149
```

```
* 3
Button      Enabled
124 155 153 190
Set

* 4
UserItem    Enabled
21 298 37 402

* 5
StaticText  Enabled
21 213 37 298
 Notation:

* 6
UserItem    Enabled
45 298 61 402

* 7
StaticText  Enabled
45 213 61 298
 Length:

* 8
StaticText  Enabled
27 16 49 175
The Number

* 9
StaticText  Disabled
100 4 121 106
Enter Number:
```

▶ Summary

You've covered a lot of territory in this chapter on edit text, including twenty-eight routines and one example. Everything in this chapter involves manipulating strings, whether it's saving to the Clipboard or changing the base of a number. Most of the routines apply to static text as well as to edit text.

You can use all of these routines as templates for your own applications. You also can modify them for octal notations if you wish.

▶ Recommended Reading

We recommend the following articles and technical notes for further discussion of EditText.

For copies of the Apple Technical Notes listed below, call Apple Professional Developers Association, (408) 974-4897.

Apple Technical Note No. 82 "TextEdit: Advice & Descent"

Apple Technical Note No. 203 "Don't Abuse the Managers"

Apple Technical Note No. 207 "Styled TextEdit Changes in System 6.0"

Apple Technical Note No. 237 "TextEdit Record Size Limitations Revisited"

Magree, Melvyn D. "Implementing Undo for Text Edit." (Pascal.) *The Essential MacTutor—The Macintosh Programming Journal,* Vol. 3, 1988.

McKenzie, Robert. "Sub and Superscripting with TE." (C.) *The Best of MacTutor—The Macintosh Programming Journal*, Vol. 5, 1990.

Nedrud, Bradley W. "Extending TextEdit to Handle Tabs." (Pascal.) *The Complete MacTutor—The Macintosh Programming Journal*, Vol. 2, 1987.

Olsen, John D. "Looking at Text from a Different Angle." (Assembly and Pascal.) *The Definitive MacTutor—The Macintosh Programming Journal*, Vol. 4, 1989.

16 ▶ Lines

▶ Overview of Lines

Programmers for the Macintosh usually use lines in menus and dialog boxes, to set off groups of similar types or functions. You can draw dotted lines or solid lines of any thickness from 1 pixel on up, although it is unlikely that you would want a dotted line more than 1 or 2 pixels wide or a solid line more than 10 pixels wide.

▶ Drawing Dotted and Solid Lines

The two routines in this chapter show you how to create dotted and solid lines, and the example tests the routines. The two routines need to be called twice: the first time to draw the line and the second time to redraw for an update event.

▶ DrawDottedLine.c

Dotted lines are a useful way to segregate groups of buttons, radio buttons, check boxes, and other items in a dialog box, yet the Macintosh Toolbox does not contain a routine for drawing a dotted line. This routine fills that gap.

Listing 16-1. Drawing a dotted line

```
PROCEDURE DrawDottedLine(theDialog: DialogPtr,theItem: INTEGER)

 1:    /****************************************************************/
 2:    void DrawDottedLine(DialogPtr theDialog, short theItem)
 3:    /****************************************************************/
 4:    {
 5:        GrafPtr          savePort;                   /* Old grafPort */
 6:        short            theType;                      /* Not used */
 7:        Rect             theRect;                /* Size of user item */
 8:        Handle           theHdl;                       /* Not used */
 9:        PenState         penStuff;
10:        short            v,h;
11:        Pattern thePattern = {0xAA,0x55,0xAA,0x55,0xAA,0x55,0xAA,
                0x55};
12:        GetPort(&savePort);
13:        SetPort(theDialog);
14:        GetPenState(&penStuff);
15:        GetDItem(theDialog, theItem, &theType, &theHdl, &theRect);
16:        PenNormal();
17:        PenPat(thePattern);
18:        v = theRect.top;
19:        h = theRect.left;
20:        MoveTo(h,v);
21:        h = theRect.right;
22:        LineTo(h,v);
23:        SetPenState(&penStuff);
24:        SetPort(savePort);
25:    }
```

Skip all the definitions and declarations and go down to line 12. This statement gets the current grafPort and saves it. The statement on line 13 sets the grafPort to the dialog box you're in. It's easy to get into trouble if you don't set the port properly. Note that the last call (line 24) restores the port to its original settings.

Line 14 gets the current pen settings. Its countermanding statement on line 23 restores them. Both your port call and your pen call help prevent sudden and undesired changes occurring in your carefully calculated box positions or line widths.

The statement on line 15 accomplishes a number of tasks. GetDItem returns information about a particular dialog item that's on the screen. You pass into that Toolbox routine the pointer and the item number to the dialog box you're talking about. The routine then returns the type of item and a handle—a kind of pointer—to the item. It also returns the size of the item, expressed in the coordinates of the rectangle. What you're interested in here is only the size. You don't use the other variables for this example, but you have to pass them in. You need the coordinates of the rectangle to draw the dotted line.

Line 16 restores the pen to its default settings.

The statement on line 17 changes the default pattern, which is solid, into dots. You do this with the definition statement on line 2. Line 11 tells the Macintosh that this variable, *thePattern*, is going to be 8 bytes long and puts values inside the variable, *thePattern*. To create the dotted line, you resort to something a little tricky. You set up a dual-purpose checkerboard pattern. Here's how to go about it. The letter *A* in binary is the hexadecimal constant 1010, or 1 pixel on, 1 pixel off, 1 pixel on, 1 pixel off; so *AA* is 10101010. There's your dotted line. Similarly, the digit 5 is 0101, so 55 is 01010101. By staggering these rows of dots, you create a checkerboard pattern. A single row can be selected for a dotted line, whereas a succession of rows gives you a paint pattern that you can use to fill areas with 1-pixel dots and 1-pixel spaces.

Next you need to get to the position where you want to put the pen down and start drawing the dotted line. You do this with the three statements on lines 18–20. The first two statements give the vertical and horizontal coordinates for the starting point of the line, referring to the rectangle that was returned from the dialog item. The third statement places the pen on that point.

To draw the line, you use the statements on lines 21 and 22 to set its finishing point and to draw as far as that point. Since the line is horizontal, the same vertical coordinate remains valid.

Line 23 restores the pen state back to where it was before you started this routine, and line 24 resets the QuickDraw port.

▶ DrawLine.c

DrawLine.c draws a line from the top left to the top right of a user item in a dialog box. You'll find it useful if you want to segment the box.

Listing 16-2. Drawing a line along the top of a user item in a dialog box

```
PROCEDURE DrawLine(theDialog: DialogPtr,theItem: INTEGER, pen: INTE-
GER);
```

```
 1:   /****************************************************************/
 2:   void DrawLine(DialogPtr theDialog, short theItem, short pen)
 3:   /****************************************************************/
 4:   {
 5:     GrafPtr        savePort;                   /* Old grafPort */
 6:     short          theType;                       /* Not used */
 7:     Rect           theRect;                /* Size of user item */
 8:     Handle         theHdl;                        /* Not used */
 9:     PenState       penStuff;
10:     short          v,h;
11:     GetPort(&savePort);
12:     SetPort(theDialog);
13:     GetPenState(&penStuff);
14:     GetDItem(theDialog, theItem, &theType, &theHdl, &theRect);
15:     PenNormal();
16:     PenSize(pen, pen);
17:     v = theRect.top;
18:     h = theRect.left;
19:     MoveTo(h,v);
20:     h = theRect.right;
21:     LineTo(h,v);
22:     SetPenState(&penStuff);
23:     SetPort(savePort);
24:   }
```

This routine has much in common with DrawDottedLine.c. Refer to that review for details not given below.

Starting with line 2, you pass in the pointer to the dialog. You also pass in the dialog item from which you get the coordinates to draw the desired line width, and you add a parameter giving it the ability to draw solid lines of different widths.

Skip down to line 16. When you call PenSize, you need to say how wide the pen should be. You pass it the vertical and horizontal pen size on lines 17 and 18. The Macintosh has the ability to draw vertical and horizontal lines of different widths. Interestingly, if you tell it to draw diagonally, it splits the difference between the two widths. Having set the pen width, you move the pen to the appropriate coordinates and draw the line (lines 19–21). That's it. All that remains is to set both the pen and the QuickDraw port back to what they were, then branch out of the routine.

▶ A Simple Line Example

This section contains a pair of source code listings that demonstrate the line-drawing routines in this chapter. The pair consists of one file with the extension .c and another file, containing the resources, with the extension .R. The two types of files always go together to make up an application.

▶ LineExample.c

This demonstration program opens up a dialog box, centers it on the screen, and draws a stack of progressively wider lines, plus a default Quit button. See Figure 16-1.

Listing 16-3. Example of dotted and solid lines

```
 1:  /*****************************************************************/
 2:  void    main()                         /* Routine to test lines */
 3:  /*****************************************************************/
 4:  {
 5:    Ptr             theDialog;
 6:    short           itemHit;
 7:    InitToolBox();
 8:    OpenResources("Line.rsrc");          /* For development purposes */
 9:    CenterDialog(300);
10:    OpenStandardDialog(&theDialog, 300);
11:    FrmDefItem(theDialog);
12:    DrawDottedLine(theDialog, 3);
13:    DrawLine(theDialog, 4, 1);
14:    DrawLine(theDialog, 5, 2);
15:    DrawLine(theDialog, 6, 3);
16:    DrawLine(theDialog, 7, 4);
17:    DrawLine(theDialog, 8, 5);
18:    DrawLine(theDialog, 9, 6);
19:    DrawLine(theDialog, 10, 7);
20:    DrawLine(theDialog, 11, 8);
21:    DrawLine(theDialog, 12, 9);
22:    for (;;)
23:    {
24:      MyModalDialog(&itemHit);
25:      switch (itemHit)
26:      {
27:        case (1):                        /* Quit */
28:          break;
29:        case (-updateEvt):               /* Update events */
```

```
30:            BeginUpdate(theDialog);
31:              UpDialog(theDialog);
32:              FrmDefItem(theDialog);
33:              DrawDottedLine(theDialog, 3);
34:              DrawLine(theDialog, 4, 1);
35:              DrawLine(theDialog, 5, 2);
36:              DrawLine(theDialog, 6, 3);
37:              DrawLine(theDialog, 7, 4);
38:              DrawLine(theDialog, 8, 5);
39:              DrawLine(theDialog, 9, 6);
40:              DrawLine(theDialog, 10, 7);
41:              DrawLine(theDialog, 11, 8);
42:              DrawLine(theDialog, 12, 9);
43:            EndUpdate(theDialog);
44:            continue;
45:          default:                    /* All other events */
46:            continue;
47:        }
48:      break;
49:    }
50:    DisposeDialog(theDialog);
51: }
```

After bringing up a dialog box in the center of the screen, drawing a stack of lines, each thicker than the one before, and putting in a default Quit button, the routine just hangs there. It waits for something to interrupt the infinite event loop represented by all the indented lines of code between line 22 and line 47. If, for example, the Quit button is pressed, you branch out of the loop, get rid of the dialog box, and branch out of the routine. The event loop is included merely for the convenience of this demonstration routine; it has no instructional merit, so please ignore that section of code.

The call on line 7 initializes the Toolbox and the routine is described in Chapter 2. Think of it as a macro that saves you a lot of key-in effort. It takes care of several things Apple requires you to do in anticipation of putting the Toolbox to work.

Line 8 follows the standard practice of keeping the resources in a separate file—here Line.rsrc—until the programming is complete. Then you use this call to insert all the resources into the program.

The routine on line 9 is described in Chapter 6. The ID of 300 is the resource ID under Type 'DLOG' as described in line 3 of the file LineExample.R. The routine changes the coordinates at run time to those indicating where that dialog box is going to be (in the center of the screen).

▶ A Simple Line Example

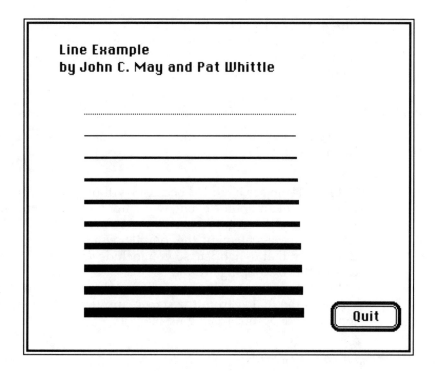

Figure 16-1. Dialog box with lines of various widths

Line 10 opens the dialog box. Several parameters are passed in. First is a pointer to the position of the dialog box in memory, which returns a value to reference that box from now on. The 300 is the ID of the dialog box you're opening.

Line 11 puts a frame around the default item, in this case a button named Quit.

Line 12 draws a dotted line. You pass in the dialog pointer and the ID of the user item that has the relevant coordinates. If you look at file LineExample.R (lines 22–24), you'll see that item 3 spells out the coordinates 80 50 81 250 of the dotted line to be drawn 1 pixel wide.

Lines 13–21 draw a stack of nine solid lines. They range from 1 pixel wide at the top to 9 pixels wide at the bottom.

Skipping most of the event loop, go down to line 43, which brings this series of update events to a successful conclusion. Forgetting to include that statement is a common Toolbox programming error. It is not enough to begin an update; you have to tell the Macintosh when to stop updating.

This mistake can make a big mess of the program, and tracking down the error can be frustrating. A useful memory jogger is to indent all the lines of code between the begin update statement and the end update statement, as shown on lines 31–42.

Important ▶	Be sure to redraw the double frame of the default button. Be sure to put in both a begin update statement and an end update statement.

Lines 44–46 are included because, without them, you'd loop around until you got an update event, whereupon you'd fall through and close the program. If you got an event or an item hit for which the routine did not have a case-statement, the compiler would be likely to get nasty. You don't want that to happen, so you include *default* in this routine to take care of this by looping around again.

Line 49 concludes the case-statement that began with line 25. Line 50 removes the dialog from the screen and deletes any other records no longer needed, thus freeing up memory.

▶ LineExample.R

LineExample.R is the resource file that goes with LineExample.c in the demonstration program showing how to draw lines of various thicknesses on the screen.

Listing 16-4. Resource file for example of dotted and solid lines

```
 1:   Line.rsrc
 2:   rsrcRSED

 3:   Type DLOG
 4:   Line Test,300
 5:   Line Test
 6:   50 50 346 406
 7:   Visible NoGoAway
 8:   1
 9:   300
10:   300
```

```
11:     Type DITL
12:     Line Test,300
13:     12

14:     * 1
15:     Button      Enabled
16:     258 288 278 348
17:     Quit

18:     * 2
19:     StaticText Disabled
20:     13 25 63 295
21:     Line Example\0Dby John C. May and Pat Whittle

22:     * 3
23:     UserItem    Enabled
24:     80 50 81 250

25:     * 4
26:     UserItem    Enabled
27:     100 50 101 250

28:     * 5
29:     UserItem    Enabled
30:     120 50 121 250

31:     * 6
32:     UserItem    Enabled
33:     140 50 141 250

34:     * 7
35:     UserItem    Enabled
36:     160 50 161 250

37:     * 8
38:     UserItem    Enabled
39:     180 50 181 250

40:     * 9
41:     UserItem    Enabled
42:     200 50 201 250

43:     * 10
44:     UserItem    Enabled
45:     220 50 221 250
```

```
46:   * 11
47:   UserItem    Enabled
48:   240 50 241 250

49:   * 12
50:   UserItem    Enabled
51:   260 50 261 250
```

The first line of this routine contains a file that you want to create as an output, a directive to the compiler saying you want to put the output of the compiled resource into the file Line.rsrc. The name of the resource compiler you run this through is RMaker, and Line.rsrc is the format for an RMaker file.

The file type and file creator are 'rsrc' and 'RSED', as shown on line 2. Every file in a Macintosh has a file type and a file creator. For instance, a Microsoft Word file is 'wordMSWD'. Among the purposes of the file type and creator is to start up the application program automatically when the user clicks on a file or document icon or name in an Open dialog window. Line.rsrc is set up to look like one that was created with RMaker, so you can look at it in ResEdit. ResEdit is a program that edits resources; RMaker is a program that creates resources from a resource file. After you've used RMaker to create a program, you can use ResEdit to tweak it. Here you use the default file for ResEdit; so, when you double-click on the file you've created by compiling this source code, it automatically runs ResEdit.

Type 'DLOG' on line 3 tells the resource compiler that you're about to create a dialog resource. Line Test (on line 4) is the name you give to the resource, and 300 is its resource ID number.

| Important ▶ | Apple reserves ID numbers in the series 0 through 127 for its own purposes. Be sure to pick numbers in the range of 128 through 33000. If you happen to choose one that you've already allocated, ResEdit will prompt you to pick another. You can even let ResEdit choose for you. |

Line Test on line 5 is the (here invisible) title of the dialog box. If the dialog box were of the type with a title bar across the top, that title would appear there.

The numbers on line 6 represent the top left and bottom right coordinates of the rectangle. They describe both the size and the default position of the dialog box: 50 pixels down and 50 across, 346 pixels down and 406 across.

Line 7 states that you want the dialog box to be visible and not have a go-away box. The type of box in this routine is modal. It has a Quit button. Since it doesn't have a title bar, trying to give it a go-away box would be a waste of time.

The Macintosh offers six types of windows.

- ID = 0—a standard document window. It has a shadow at the bottom and on the right-hand side, a title bar at the top, and, if you say so, a go-away box.
- ID = 1—an alert box (as used in this example). It has a plain box with a double frame around it.
- ID = 2—a plain box with a thin line around it. It has no framing, shadows, or titles.
- ID = 3—a plain box like ID = 2 but with a shadow at the bottom and on the right-hand side.
- ID = 4—a document window with a title bar at the top and a grow icon (size box) at the bottom right to make the window smaller or larger.
- ID = 16—a window that resembles ID = 4 but has rounded corners and does not have horizontal lines in the title bar. This rare type usually is reserved for desk accessories such as the Calculator.

On line 8, 1 is a window definition ID. It tells the Window Manager the resource ID of the window definition function you want to use—in short, what type of window you want to draw on the screen. The definition of windows and how they are drawn is also stored in a resource in the System file. All windows have the default ID = 0. To select a particular type of window, you pass one of six variation codes. This example uses ID = 1 for an alert box; so, when you call up the Window Manager, you're saying you want to use window resource ID = 1 to draw your window.

Line 9, which contains the number 300, was originally allocated by Apple as a refCon, short for reference control. Apple no longer gives it a role in the Toolbox, so feel free to use it for anything appropriate. We have repeated the dialog ID number 300, just to fill the blank.

The number 300 on line 10 has much more significance. It tells the program that the 'DITL' resource ID 300 describes the items contained in 'DLOG' 300.

On line 11 Type 'DITL', pronounced "dittle," stands for dialog items list. It tells the compiler which type of resource you're going to be describing. Its ID doesn't have to be the same as the dialog ID, but this routine follows the convention and uses the same number, 300, to help keep track.

Line Test, on line 12 is the name of the resource, and 300 is its ID.

The number 12 on line 13 tells the resource compiler that you're going to have twelve items in the dialog box.

The item number 1 on line 14 is the first of the twelve dialog items. Anytime you see an asterisk (a * star) in the resource compiler code, it stands for a comment. Dialog item 1, as shown on line 15, is an enabled button. The four numbers on line 16 are the pixel coordinates of the rectangle forming the button: top left, bottom right. They specify where the button is going to sit in the window. Quit, on line 17, is the label that goes in the button.

"Enabled" places in a user item an attribute requiring the Toolbox ModalDialog routine to recognize when the user item has been pressed. The routine then instructs the Dialog Manager to report the mouse-down so that the item does what it's supposed to do: print, save, not save, dismiss the window, or whatever. The ModalDialog routine handles everything that goes on in the button. "Disabled" has the opposite effect. A disabled item simply ignores mouse-downs.

The expression on lines 18–20 says that dialog item 2 at the given rectangle coordinates is a piece of static text that will do nothing if pressed. Users don't want to be bothered with being told that they have accidentally clicked on it.

Line 21 gives the wording of the static text. Each \0D signifies a carriage return—0D being a hexadecimal constant—so the text appears on the screen in two lines, one above the other.

Lines 22–24 contain a set of coordinates referring to the top left of the screen. The first is 80 pixels down and 50 pixels in from the left; the second is 81 pixels down and 250 pixels in from the left. As you can see from Figure 16-1, what they amount to is a straight line, 1 pixel wide.

The statements for the user items 4 through 12 on lines 24–51 are similar to the one for user item 3 except that the rectangles are referenced by different coordinates corresponding to the appropriate positions on the screen.

▶ Summary

This chapter presented a routine for drawing dotted lines and a routine for drawing lines of various widths, as well as an example to show how these routines work. In addition, this chapter gave the resource code for the example and a full explanation of the resource file.

17 ▶ Rectangles

▶ Overview of Rectangles

Rectangles have enormous importance in the Macintosh's human interface structure. They define active areas of the screen and designate locations and sizes for QuickDraw commands. Graphics programs use them as map coordinates, and in Macintosh lexicon, that is exactly what they are: two points on the coordinate plane that identify the upper left-hand corner and the lower right-hand corner of a box.

▶ Drawing Rectangles in Various Styles

The four rectangle routines in this section are useful both for esthetics and for clarity of intent. You can take your pick of frames.

- Plain—drawn 1 pixel wide
- Thick—drawn 2 or more pixels wide
- Double—drawn with one framing line outside another
- Shadow—drawn to give a three-dimensional effect

For esthetics, the routines let you use your artistic sense to make a dialog look better. For clarity, they make it easy to put rectangular boxes, or frames, around groups of controls that perform related functions. Especially on a crowded screen, grouping can help to avoid confusion. All four rectangle routines need to be called twice: the first time to draw the rectangle and the second time to redraw for an update event.

▶ PlainFrame.c

PlainFrame.c is the simplest of the four framing routines. It draws what you might call your basic box with a thin line for a frame.

Listing 17-1. Drawing a plain frame

```
PROCEDURE PlainFrame(theDialog: DialogPtr,theItemID: INTEGER);

 1:    /****************************************************************/
 2:    void PlainFrame(DialogPtr theDialog, short theItemID)
 3:    /****************************************************************/
 4:    {
 5:       GrafPtr         savePort;                /* Old grafPort */
 6:       short           itemType;                      /* Not used */
 7:       Rect            itemRect;                /* Size of user item */
 8:       Handle          item;                          /* Not used */
 9:       PenState        penStuff;
10:       short           CurveFactor;
11:       GetPort(&savePort);
12:       SetPort(theDialog);
13:       GetPenState(&penStuff);
14:       GetDItem(theDialog, theItemID, &itemType, &item,
                  &itemRect);
15:       PenNormal();
16:       if ((itemType && 0x007F) == 16)
17:       {
18:          InsetRect(&itemRect, -2, -2);
19:       }
20:       InsetRect(&itemRect, -1, -1);
21:       FrameRect(&itemRect);
22:       SetPenState(&penStuff);
23:       SetPort(savePort);
24:    }
```

First you pass to the routine the name and ID of the dialog you want to draw the box around. Then you proceed with a syntax quite similar to that of the DrawLine.c routine in Chapter 16.

After several lines of declarations you reach the statements on lines 11 and 12 and the arguments on lines 13 and 15, which are explained more fully in the review of the FrmDefItem.c routine in Chapter 9. In brief, they save the current grafPort and pen settings for later recall and they substitute the ones you want for this particular dialog. The normal pen defaults to a solid line, 1 pixel wide.

Line 14 has the potential for doing a lot of things, but you are interested only in item rectangles.

The code on lines 16–19 is an example of how convoluted the instructions can be to accomplish something that looks simple. This piece of hocus-pocus first determines whether the dialog item you're drawing a box around is an edit text box. Then it puts a frame around the box. Note that the rectangle routines can draw a frame in any of the four styles around anything. It doesn't have to be a user item.

The Macintosh automatically draws a box around an edit text item, and that box is 3 pixels out from the rectangular area you specified. This routine covers up the Macintosh box and draws one a little bigger.

To identify the edit text as a user item, the routine masks with a 0x007F the item type that comes back. You want to get rid of the first bit of the type returned. The first bit can be a 0 or a 1. If it's a 1, the item on the screen is enabled. The attribute of enabled or disabled can be important elsewhere, but in this instance you don't care: You just want to know the item type. To mask out everything but the first bit, which is the enabled or disabled flag, you AND it with a 0x007F, which stands for 0000000001111111. You take only the last 7 bits of this 16-bit word. If the number were to represent a control, it would be 4, a button 0, a check box 1, a radio button 2, a static text 8, an edit text 16, or an icon item 32. In this example, you have the number 16, an edit text box. You make this rectangle 2 pixels bigger with the instructions on line 18. Remember, a negative inset expands the box. A positive inset shrinks the box.

What you have just done is to replace the Macintosh's user item box with one that is 2 pixels larger, but only if the box is for edit text. You then use the statement on line 20 to expand the box 1 more pixel. Doing the expansion in two steps gives the routine greater flexibility. You want 3 pixels of space around the rectangular area of edit text, but only 1 pixel for all other items you wish to frame.

So far, you haven't drawn a frame; you've merely defined the bounds of the rectangle. Your final call on line 21 draws the box with the default pen, after which (in lines 22 and 23) you restore the settings for the pen and the grafPort to what you had before starting the routine.

▶ ThickFrame.c

This routine draws a thick frame around your box.

Listing 17-2. Drawing a thick frame

```
PROCEDURE ThickFrame(theDialog: DialogPtr,theItemID: INTEGER);

 1:  /****************************************************************/
 2:  void ThickFrame(DialogPtr theDialog, short theItemID)
 3:  /****************************************************************/
 4:  {
 5:     GrafPtr         savePort;                   /* Old grafPort */
 6:     short           itemType;                      /* Not used */
 7:     Rect            itemRect;              /* Size of user item */
 8:     Handle          item;                          /* Not used */
 9:     PenState        penStuff;
10:     GetPort(&savePort);
11:     SetPort(theDialog);
12:     GetPenState(&penStuff);
13:     GetDItem(theDialog, theItemID, &itemType, &item,
               &itemRect);
14:     PenNormal();
15:     if ((itemType && 0x007F) == 16)
16:     {
17:        InsetRect(&itemRect, -2, -2);
18:     }
19:     PenSize(2, 2);
20:     InsetRect(&itemRect, -2, -2);
21:     FrameRect(&itemRect);
22:     SetPenState(&penStuff);
23:     SetPort(savePort);
24:  }
```

ThickFrame.c is almost identical to PlainFrame.c, just described. The only difference is that you can set the pen to draw a frame 2 or more pixels wide instead of a skinny 1 pixel wide. You can modify the routine ThickFrame.c to make the width a variable that is passed in instead of being fixed.

▶ DoubleFrame.c

DoubleFrame.c draws a double-line frame around a box.

Listing 17-3. Drawing a double frame

PROCEDURE DoubleFrame(theDialog: DialogPtr,theItemID: INTEGER);

```
 1:  /****************************************************************/
 2:  void DoubleFrame(DialogPtr theDialog, short theItemID)
 3:  /****************************************************************/
 4:  {
 5:     GrafPtr      savePort;            /* Old grafPort */
 6:     short        itemType;                /* Not used */
 7:     Rect         itemRect;       /* Size of user item */
 8:     Handle       item;                    /* Not used */
 9:     PenState     penStuff;
10:     short        CurveFactor;
11:     GetPort(&savePort);
12:     SetPort(theDialog);
13:     GetPenState(&penStuff);
14:     GetDItem(theDialog, theItemID, &itemType, &item,
                &itemRect);
15:     PenNormal();
16:     if ((itemType && 0x007F) == 16)
17:     {
18:        InsetRect(&itemRect, -2, -2);
19:     }
20:     PenSize(2, 2);
21:     InsetRect(&itemRect, -2, -2);
22:     FrameRect(&itemRect);
23:     PenSize(1, 1);
24:     InsetRect(&itemRect, -3, -3);
25:     FrameRect(&itemRect);
26:     SetPenState(&penStuff);
27:     SetPort(savePort);
28:  }
```

This routine, again, is almost identical to the routine for drawing a plain frame. A double frame consists of one rectangular box outside another. On lines 20–25 you substitute instructions that set the pen size to 2 pixels, outset the rectangle 2 pixels, frame the rectangle, change the pen size to 1 pixel, outset the rectangle 3 more pixels, and draw another frame.

Chapter 17 Rectangles

▶ ShadowFrame.c

The fourth in this quartet of framing routines gives a three-dimensional look to a box by drawing a shadow. You'll see that the routine is not very different from the other three.

Listing 17-4. Drawing a shadow frame

```
PROCEDURE ShadowFrame(theDialog: DialogPtr,theItemID: INTEGER);
```

```
 1:  /***************************************************************/
 2:  void ShadowFrame(DialogPtr theDialog, short theItemID)
 3:  /***************************************************************/
 4:  {
 5:     GrafPtr        savePort;                 /* Old grafPort */
 6:     short          itemType;                    /* Not used */
 7:     Rect           itemRect;           /* Size of user item */
 8:     Handle         item;                        /* Not used */
 9:     PenState       penStuff;
10:     short          v,h;
11:     GetPort(&savePort);
12:     SetPort(theDialog);
13:     GetPenState(&penStuff);
14:     GetDItem(theDialog, theItemID, &itemType, &item,
                &itemRect);
15:     PenNormal();
16:     if ((itemType && 0x007F) == 16)
17:     {
18:        InsetRect(&itemRect, -2, -2);
19:     }
20:     InsetRect(&itemRect, -1, -1);
21:     FrameRect(&itemRect);
22:     PenSize(2, 2);
23:     InsetRect(&itemRect, 1, 1);
24:     OffsetRect(&itemRect, 1, 1);
25:     v = itemRect.left;
26:     h = itemRect.bottom;
27:     MoveTo(v, h);
28:     v = itemRect.right;
29:     LineTo(v, h);
30:     h = itemRect.top;
31:     LineTo(v, h);
32:     SetPenState(&penStuff);
33:     SetPort(savePort);
34:  }
```

Call the routine with the pointer and with the item you want to draw the frame around. Moving down to the program itself, you make special allowance if the item is edit text (line 16). On lines 20–22 you outset the rectangle by 1 pixel, draw a frame around it, and set the pen size to 2 pixels. Then on lines 23 and 24 you inset the rectangle by 1 pixel and offset it 1 pixel to the right and 1 pixel down. Lines 25–27 get the vertical and horizontal coordinates of the point where you want to put the pen down and move to that position. Lines 28–31 draw a line to form the bottom shadow of the box and, without picking the pen up, form the right-hand shadow by drawing another line from the bottom right to the top right.

Moving and line drawing are built-in capabilities of the Toolbox, but you're on your own if you want a shadow box. That's why we wrote this routine.

▶ A Simple Rectangle Example

This section contains a pair of source code listings that demonstrate the four routines in this chapter. The pair consists of one file with the extension .c and another file, containing the resources, with the extension .R. The two types of files always go together to make up an application.

▶ RectExample.c

This program is so similar to LineExample.c, reviewed in Chapter 16, that we will not describe it here in as much detail. RectExample.c draws four rectangular boxes, each with a different kind of frame (see Figure 17-1), whereas LineExample.c draws nine thicknesses of line.

Listing 17-5. Example rectangular frames

```
/******************************************************************/
void   main()                                  /* Routine to test rects */
/******************************************************************/
{
   Ptr                  theDialog;
   short                itemHit;
   InitToolBox();
   OpenResources("Rect.rsrc");                 /* For development purposes */
   CenterDialog(300);
   OpenStandardDialog(&theDialog, 300);
   FrmDefItem(theDialog);
   PlainFrame(theDialog, 3);
```

```
        DoubleFrame(theDialog, 4);
        ThickFrame(theDialog, 5);
        ShadowFrame(theDialog, 6);
        for (;;)
        {
          MyModalDialog(&itemHit);
          switch (itemHit)
          {
            case (1):                                     /* Quit */
              break;
            case (-updateEvt):                            /* Update events */
              BeginUpdate(theDialog);
                UpDialog(theDialog);
                FrmDefItem(theDialog);
                PlainFrame(theDialog, 3);
                DoubleFrame(theDialog, 4);
                ThickFrame(theDialog, 5);
                ShadowFrame(theDialog, 6);
              EndUpdate(theDialog);
              continue;
            default:                                      /* All other events */
              continue;
          }
          break;
        }
        DisposeDialog(theDialog);
}
```

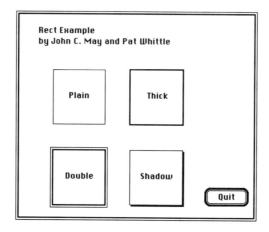

Figure 17-1. Examples of rectangular frames

You start with a call to initialize the Toolbox and follow with a call to open resources file Rect.rsrc, which is the output of the compiler. The next calls open and center the dialog, and you pass them the ID 300. A call to the modal dialog begins an endless for-loop, waiting for someone to press the Quit button or for an update event to occur. Next you draw the default item—the Quit button—with a double frame, and then draw the four different styles of boxes. Finally, you dispose of the dialog and branch out of the program.

▶ RectExample.R

RectExample.R is the resource file that forms a pair with RectExample.c in a demonstration application that draws four types of rectangular frames on the screen.

Listing 17-6. Resource file for example of rectangular frames

```
Rect.rsrc
rsrcRSED

Type DLOG
Rect Test,300
Rect Test
50 50 346 406
Visible NoGoAway
1
300
300

Type DITL
Rect Test,300
10

* 1
Button      Enabled
258 288 278 348
Quit

* 2
StaticText Disabled
13 25 63 295
Rect Example\0Dby John C. May and Pat Whittle
```

```
* 3
UserItem    Enabled
80 50 160 130

* 4
UserItem    Enabled
200 50 280 130

* 5
UserItem    Enabled
80 170 160 250

* 6
UserItem    Enabled
200 170 280 250

* 7
StaticText  Disabled
110 73 130 112
Plain

* 8
StaticText  Disabled
110 194 130 234
Thick

* 9
StaticText  Disabled
230 68 250 115
Double

* 10
StaticText  Disabled
230 184 250 240
Shadow
```

The opening statement, Rect.rsrc, tells the compiler where to put the output. The name of the file being created is rsrcRSED.

Type 'DLOG' is a type statement. Rect Test is the name and 300 the ID of the dialog box. The other lines in that group give further details, such as coordinates.

Type 'DITL', short for dialog items list, enumerates the ten items appearing in the dialog. Item 1 is the Quit button. It is enabled, meaning that it will execute a Quit when pressed. If it were disabled, pressing it would do nothing except exercise your index finger. Item 2 comprises two lines of static text with the name of the dialog and the programmers who devised it. Items 3 through 6 are the four types of box—plain, thick, double, and shadow—and items 7 through 10 are the static text labels placed inside each box to identify its type.

▶ Summary

This chapter presented four rectangle routines that you can use for esthetics and clarity to draw plain, thick, double, and shadow frames around dialogs, alert boxes, and user items. Once you understand these routines, you can use your artistic sense to develop boxes in your own style.

▶ Recommended Reading

Apple Computer. *Inside Macintosh,* Vol. 1. Reading, MA: Addison-Wesley, 1985.

18 ▶ Scrolling Lists

▶ Overview of Scrolling Lists

Probably the most familiar example of a scrolling list is the alphabetical list of files that appears in a dialog box when you select the Open command from the File menu. If there are too many file names to view in the box at the same time, you can see the hidden ones by using the scroll bar. Click in the gray area of the bar, or drag the scroll box, or click the up or down scroll arrow, or type the first letter of the file name. If the files are so few that they all fit in the box, the scroll bar is unshaded and inoperative.

You can use scrolling lists for many different character strings, not just for file names. The routines in this chapter offer a suite of tools for handling scrolling lists. They all make use of the List Manager, which implements scrolling lists. You won't find List Manager in the Toolbox of the original Macintosh. If early users of the Macintosh wanted scrolling lists, they had to write their own scrolling list routines from scratch. Early examples of such homespun scrolling lists appear in the get file and put file routines still seen at work in the familiar Open and Save commands of the File menu. They were created without the help of List Manager, which was not included in the Toolbox until Volume 4 of *Inside Macintosh* came out around the same time as the Macintosh Plus in the mid-1980s.

Apple took a somewhat unusual approach when it introduced List Manager on the newer machines. Apple called the List Manager a "package" and placed it as a resource, 'PACK', with an ID of 0, in the System file. When you call up packages, including the List Manager, they all have the same trap number. They also have an additional variable that's passed into this Toolbox trap to indicate which routine within the package needs to be executed. Symantec's THINK C has a transparent procedure for handling List Manager packages. Some other compilers do not, so look in your manual for guidance if you're not using THINK C.

A list is just a set of strings in a matrix. The strings associated with the Open and Save commands of the File menu are in a single column that moves one way only, up or down. List Manager provides the capability of using both horizontal and vertical scrolling in the same array. The scrolling list routines in this chapter are devised for vertical scrolling, which is the most common and most useful one-dimensional arrangement.

List Manager is much like Microsoft's spreadsheet application Excel in its use of cells. Each string in the scrolling list goes into a cell, and the cells in these routines are stacked in a vertical column. Despite the resemblance to Excel, however, List Manager is not a spreadsheet program, just as TextEdit is not a word processor.

Associated with every list you create is a list record. The record contains some useful constants. For example, a program may be such that you can select only one item in a list; that is, you can't hold down the Shift key and select multiple items. If you want that capability, there's a flag you can set.

Each routine in this chapter can be split into four main parts.

Initialize	Draws the scrolling list on the screen. Resets variables to their starting value.
Do	Does what the user wants when he or she presses a key or clicks the mouse.
Update	Updates the screen when an update event occurs.
Dispose	Gets rid of temporary variables and settings that have served their purpose, so are no longer needed, when you're through.

> **By the Way** ▶ When one of the routines in this chapter says draw a string list, a rectangle, or something else, the drawing process usually occurs during the initialization phase.

All the routines and functions in this chapter work in concert to bring up a scrolling list on the screen, allow the user to select an item, and tell other parts of the program what's going on so that the user's instructions are acted upon.

The scrolling list routines and functions in this chapter use several List Manager routines summarized in Table 18-1.

Table 18-1. List Manager Routines Used in This Chapter

Routines	Description
LAddRow	Adds a row to a list
LClick	Returns true if double-click in cell
LDoDraw	Sets List Manager to drawing mode
LDraw	Draws cell after entry or selection
LGetCell	Returns copy of cell's contents
LLastClick	Returns coordinates of clicked cell
LNew	Creates a new list
LSetCell	Modifies cell contents
LUpdate	Redraws visible cells

▶ Drawing a Scrolling List

The first step in creating a scrolling list is to draw it on the screen and initialize it. That's the purpose of DrawScrollList.c. When the screen needs to be redrawn in an update, call UpScrollList.c, described later in this chapter. No dispose routines are necessary in this group, because the scrolling lists fit into dialog boxes, which do their own disposing.

▶ DrawScrollList.c

This routine draws the scrolling list on the screen and takes care of any needed initialization.

Listing 18-1. Drawing a scrolling list

```
PROCEDURE DrawScrollList(theDialog: DialogPtr; theItem: Integer;
                        theListHandle: ListHandle);

1:  /*****************************************************************/
2:  void DrawScrollList(DialogPtr theDialog, short theItem,
3:                      ListHandle* theListHandle)
4:  /*****************************************************************/
5:  {
```

```
 6:    short          itemType;                  /* Not used */
 7:    Rect           itemRect;                  /* Not used */
 8:    Handle         item;              /* Handle to edit text */
 9:    Rect           dataBounds;
10:    Point          cSize;
11:    GrafPtr        savePort;                  /* Old grafPort */
12:    GetPort(&savePort);                       /* Save old port */
13:    SetPort(theDialog);
14:    GetDItem(theDialog, theItem, &itemType,
15:       &item, &itemRect);          /* Get user item handle */
16:    itemRect.right = itemRect.right - 15;  /* Room for scroll */
17:    InsetRect(&itemRect, -1, -1);          /* Set for framing */
18:    FrameRect(&itemRect);                      /* Frame it */
19:    InsetRect(&itemRect, +1, +1);              /* Restore */
20:    SetRect(&dataBounds, 0, 0, 1, 0);          /* Set list up */
21:    SetPt(&cSize, 0, 0);                       /* Set cell size */
22:    *theListHandle = LNew(&itemRect, &dataBounds,&cSize, 0,
23:    theDialog, true, false, false, true);    /* Make the list */
24:    LDoDraw(true, *theListHandle);             /* Draw it */
25:    SetPort(savePort);                         /* Restore old port */
26: }
```

DrawScrollList.c requires you to pass in a pointer to the dialog box; also required is the item number of a user item you've created in ResEdit, plus a handle to the list record. The user item is simply a rectangle drawn within the dialog box to contain the scrolling list. This rectangle lets you know how big the list has to be. What is returned is a list handle.

After the customary getting and setting the port, the statement on line 14 returns several variables, of which the only one you use is the item rectangle. This tells you where to draw the scrolling list and how big it's going to be.

The next three statements on lines 16–18 manipulate the rectangle in several desirable ways. Reducing the rectangle by 15 pixels provides space for a vertical scroll bar that's going to be placed on the right-hand side of the list. Increasing the whole rectangle by 1 pixel makes room for a frame to be drawn around the rectangle. Up to this point, the rectangle is merely an area defined by a set of coordinates. Framing the rectangle draws a box around the area so that it presents the familiar appearance of a scrolling list.

Now that you're through with drawing the box, shrink it by 1 pixel to its original size with the statement on line 19.

Next, make the Toolbox call on line 20 to set a new rectangle, *dataBounds*, with the values representing the screen coordinates top left 0, left 0, bottom 1, and bottom right 0. These values tell the List Manager that the first cell is 0, 0 and the next cell is 1, 0.

The statement on line 21 makes another Toolbox call, into which you pass the cell size of your pixels. List Manager then does a good job of calculating the cell size, taking into account such factors as font type and font size.

Lines 22 and 23 call a Toolbox List Manager routine named LNew, which creates the empty list. Pass it the variables &*itemRect*, &*dataBounds*, and &*cSize*. Following &*cSize* is a procedure pointer that plays no part in this routine, so pass it 0. The last fragments in the statement are four flags that need to be passed into the list. They are, in order, *drawIt*, *hasGrow*, *scrollHoriz*, and *scrollVert*. Assign the value true to *drawIt* because you want to draw the box now; false to *hasGrow* because the scrolling list doesn't have a size box; false to *scrollHoriz* because you don't want a horizontal scroll bar; and true to *scrollVert* because you do want a vertical scroll bar. One variation you might want to consider is to set the *drawIt* flag to false to save a little processing time if you have an exceptionally long list.

Call the List Manager routine LDoDraw with the statement on line 24 to make sure the *drawIt* flag is true. It's worthwhile taking this precaution against the possibility that the List Manager routine has automatically set the flag to false. A true flag here is also needed if you've set the *drawIt* flag to false in the previous statement for the sake of speed.

After setting the grafPort back to its original value, you're done. You've drawn the box on the screen, inserted an empty list, and added a scroll bar on the right side of the box. Also, you have a pointer to the list record.

▶ **Handling the Scrolling List**

Once you have drawn a scrolling list and put it into your program, you need a means of handling whichever item on the list the user selects. The routine in this section gives you the means of handling that list.

▶ DoScrollList.c

When a user double-clicks on an item in a scrolling list, this routine—more properly a function because it returns a value—takes the appropriate action.

Listing 18-2. Handling the selection of an item in a scrolling list

```
FUNCTION DoScrollList(theListHandle: ListHandle):BOOLEAN;

 1:   /***************************************************************/
 2:   char DoScrollList(ListHandle theListHandle)
 3:   /***************************************************************/
 4:   {
 5:     short modifier;
 6:     Point where;
 7:     char status;
 8:     GetMouse(&where);
 9:     modifier=0;
10:     if (OptionIsDown()) modifier = modifier + 2048;
11:     if (CapsLockIsDown()) modifier = modifier + 1024;
12:     if (ShiftIsDown()) modifier = modifier + 512;
13:     if (CommandIsDown()) modifier = modifier + 256;
14:     if ( !Button()) modifier = modifier + 128;
15:     status = LClick(where, modifier, theListHandle);
16:     return(status);
17:   }
```

This function requires only the handle to the list. When you click inside a cell of the scrolling list, the function returns a TRUE.

Skip down to the statement on line 15. This calls a Toolbox routine that responds to several events, such as a mouse click in what Apple calls the destination rectangle in the scroll bar of the list. The LClick routine requires you to pass information—where the mouse was clicked and the modifier flag—that can sometimes be hard to get, especially from a dialog box. If you're writing your own event loop, both pieces of information are readily available from the event record; however, in a dialog box using the routine ModalDialog that's built into the Dialog Manager, the information isn't easily obtained. It isn't global, so you have to reconstruct both the *where* and the *modifier* variables.

You start by calling the Toolbox routine GetMouse on line 8. It returns *where*, which is the variable telling where in the dialog box the mouse was pressed.

Getting the modifier is not as straightforward. The modifier flag contains quite a lot of information stuffed into 2 bytes, or 16 bits. Is the Option key down? Is Caps Lock down? Is Shift down? Is the Command key (⌘) down? Is the mouse button down? In all these instances, no is 0 and yes is 1. Also included in the modifier flag is a 0 or a 1 denoting whether a window is being activated or inactivated. DoScrollList.c doesn't need that information, so the function ignores it.

The statement on line 9 sets the modifier to 0. Then the if-tests on lines 10–14 build the 2-byte modifier flag. If the Option key is down, set bit 11 to 1, equivalent to the constant 2048; if Caps Lock is down, set bit 10 to 1 by adding 1024 to that constant; and so on. Line 14 is a little different from the other if-tests. It says: "If the mouse button is not pressed, set bit 7 to 0. The modifier is then equal to the modifier plus 128."

Returning to the routine LClick on line 15, you pass it the variable indicating where the mouse was pushed, the modifier flag, and the handle to the list. What you get returned is a status report, telling you whether the user double-clicked on a particular cell. You then pass the status back to the calling routine.

▶ Updating a Scrolling List

After you have handled the item on the scrolling list, you need to update, or redraw, the list.

▶ UpScrollList.c

UpScrollList.c redraws the scrolling list at the time of an update.

Listing 18-3. Updating a scrolling list

```
PROCEDURE UpScrollList(theDialog: DialogPtr; theListHandle:
ListHandle);
```

```
 1: /****************************************************************/
 2:    void UpScrollList(DialogPtr theDialog,ListHandle
         theListHandle)
 3: /****************************************************************/
 4:    {
 5:    Rect              tempRect;
 6:    GrafPtr           savePort;                  /* Old grafPort */
 7:    GetPort(&savePort);                          /* Save old port */
 8:    SetPort(theDialog);
```

```
 9:        LUpDate(theDialog->visRgn, theListHandle);
10:        DrawControls(theDialog);
11:        tempRect = (*theListHandle)->rView;
12:        InsetRect(&tempRect, -1, -1);
13:        FrameRect(&tempRect);
14:        SetPort(savePort);                       /* Restore old port */
15:    }
```

This routine requires you to pass in the dialog box pointer and the handle to the list you want updated.

After saving the old port and getting the new port, you call the List Manager routine LUpDate with the statement on line 9 to pass in the visible region of the window, which is part of the information in the dialog record. LUpDate updates the scrolling list, but not the scroll bar controls. To redraw all the controls in the dialog window, call the routine DrawControls on line 10 and pass it the dialog.

The code on lines 11 and 12 digs out the size of the scrolling list rectangle from the list record and increases the dimensions by 1 pixel on all four sides to make room for the frame. Your call to FrameRect on line 13 redraws the frame around the scrolling list.

All that remains is to set the grafPort back to the original values, completing the update.

▶ Setting the Cells of the Scrolling List

As you may have read earlier in this chapter, each string in a scrolling list fits into its own cell. Individual cells are numbered in the same manner as pixels. The first, up in the top left corner, is 00. Next in the horizontal direction is 10, then comes 20, and so on. Going down vertically from cell 00, you have 01, 02, 03, and so on. The routines in this book are one-dimensional (up and down) so they follow the 01 sequence.

▶ AddCell.c

Suppose you already have a scrolling list and you want to insert a new string. This is the routine to call.

Setting the Cells of the Scrolling List

Listing 18-4. Adding a cell to a scrolling list

PROCEDURE AddCell(theString: Str255; theListHandle: ListHandle);

```
1:  /**************************************************************/
2:  void AddCell(Str255 theString, ListHandle theListHandle)
3:  /**************************************************************/
4:  {
5:      short           row;
6:      row = LAddRow(1, 1, theListHandle);
7:      SetCell(row, theString, theListHandle);
8:  }
```

Pass in the Pascal string you want to add to your scrolling list, and pass in a handle to your list. Call the Toolbox routine LAddRow on line 6. Pass in the row number 1, 1 and the list handle.

An extra cell is then appended to your scrolling list, and LAddRow returns the number of the added row. Pass that row number to the SetCell.c routine, which follows. Also pass in both the string you want put into the cell and the list handle.

▶ SetCell.c

SetCell.c takes a string, a cell number, and a handle to a list, then puts the string inside the cell.

Listing 18-5. Setting the contents of a cell in a scrolling list

PROCEDURE SetCell(theItem: Integer; theString: Str255;
        theListHandle: ListHandle);

```
1:  /**************************************************************/
2:  void    SetCell(short item, Str255 theString, ListHandle
        theListHandle)
3:  /**************************************************************/
4:  {
5:      short           theLength;
6:      Cell            theCell;
7:      SetPt(&theCell, 0, item);
8:      theLength = theString[0];
9:      LSetCell(&theString[1], theLength, theCell, theListHandle);
10:     LDraw(theCell, theListHandle);
11: }
```

SetCell.c requires the string and the handle to the list. As with the other routines and functions in this group, the assumption is that the scrolling list has only a vertical dimension. You want to distinguish the cell, named *theCell*, from the string, named *item*. Each cell needs both a horizontal and a vertical coordinate, but the strings are simply numbered in sequence from the top of the scrolling list.

Convert the item number to a cell by calling the Toolbox routine SetPt with the statement on line 7. The 0, which is the number of the first column, is the first coordinate of the cell, and the item number is the other coordinate.

Line 8 states a well-known fact about Pascal strings: The first byte of the string is its length.

Call the List Manager routine LSetCell with the statement on line 9. Strange to say, this Apple routine does not accept a Pascal string. Not only do you have to pass in a pointer to the string, but you must also pass in the length of the string as a separate variable.

Now that the cell is set, the time has come to redraw the string on the screen. Call the List Manager routine LDraw with the statement on line 10. Pass it the cell you want redrawn and the handle to the list. That's all there is to this routine.

▶ Getting the Cells of the Scrolling List

Often you will want to get the contents of a cell that has been selected and have it give you the Pascal string so that you can manipulate that string. You may also want to know if the user has double-clicked on a cell. The two routines in this section will help you accomplish these aims.

▶ GetCell.c

This routine gets a string from a cell and is therefore the opposite of SetCell.c, which puts a string into a cell.

Listing 18-6. Getting the contents of a cell in a scrolling list

```
PROCEDURE GetCell(theItem: Integer; VAR theString: Str255;
         theListHandle: ListHandle);

 1:   /****************************************************************/
 2:   void GetCell(short item, Str255 theString, ListHandle
        theListHandle)
 3:   /****************************************************************/
 4:   {
```

```
 5:      short            theLength;
 6:      Cell             theCell;
 7:      if (item > 0)
 8:      {
 9:         SetPt(&theCell, 0, item);
10:         theLength = theString[0];
11:         LGetCell(&theString[1], theLength, theCell,
              theListHandle);
12:      }
13:  }
```

As a preliminary to this code review, please read the description of SetCell.c, just described. GetCell.c requires the item (the vertical component of the cell), the Pascal string that it's going to be returning, and the handle to the list.

The if-test on line 7 says that if the item number is greater than 0, call the Toolbox routine, SetPt on line 9 which sets the cell equal to 0 followed by the item number; for example, 0, 4 if the item is the fourth string in the list.

Line 10 returns the string length, which is required by the next statement, on line 11. Pass in a pointer to the string, the length, the number of the cell from which you want to get the string, and the handle to the list.

Back comes the string, and the routine is complete.

▶ GetListString.c

A function rather than a routine, GetListString.c returns a value: the string on which the user has double-clicked in a scrolling list.

Listing 18-7. Getting the double-clicked string in a scrolling list

```
FUNCTION GetListString(VAR theString: Str255;
         theListHandle: ListHandle):BOOLEAN;

 1:  /*************************************************************/
 2:  char GetListString(Str255 theString, ListHandle
        theListHandle)
 3:  /*************************************************************/
 4:  {
 5:      char             status = false;
 6:      Cell             theCell;
 7:      if (DoScrollList(theListHandle))
 8:      {
```

```
 9:       theCell = LLastClick(theListHandle);
10:       GetCell(theCell.v, &theString, theListHandle);
11:       status = true;
12:    }
13:    return(status);
14: }
```

This function consists largely of an if-test (line 7) that determines whether the user has double-clicked on a scrolling list item. DoScrollList is a List Manager routine.

On line 10 you call GetCell.c and pass it the vertical component of the desired cell in the scrolling list. The assumption is that the list has only one scrolling dimension—up and down—the conventional direction of a scrolling list. You pass it the handle to the list, and it returns the string. If the user has indeed double-clicked on the string, the value TRUE is returned; otherwise, the returned value is FALSE.

▶ Selecting and Unselecting Cells in a Scrolling List

If you have developed a scrolling list and you want to have a particular item already selected—say, the first item or an often-selected item—when the list appears on the screen, then you need a routine that will perform that function. It does not happen automatically. At the same time, if the user selects another item on the list, you need a means of unselecting the item you had preselected. The two routines in this section accomplish these functions for you.

▶ SelectCell.c

SelectCell.c does what its name implies: It enables you to select a particular cell in the scrolling list and highlight that cell.

Listing 18-8. Selecting a cell in a scrolling list

```
PROCEDURE SelectCell(theItem: Integer; theListHandle: ListHandle);

1:  /**************************************************************/
2:  void SelectCell(short item, ListHandle theListHandle)
3:  /**************************************************************/
4:  {
5:    Cell         theCell;
6:    SetPt(&theCell, 0, item);
7:    LSetSelect(true, theCell, theListHandle);
8:  }
```

Call the routine. Pass it the item, which is the vertical component of the cell. Together with the 0 representing the horizontal component, that is enough information to identify the cell. (Look at SetCell.c, reviewed earlier in this chapter, for more details.)

Call the List Manager routine LSetSelect. Pass it true, meaning you want to make that cell selected. Pass it the handle to the list containing the desired cell. LSetSelect does the highlighting for you.

▶ UnselectCell.c

UnselectCell.c does the opposite of SelectCell.c by giving you the means to unselect a cell.

Listing 18-9. Unselecting a cell in a scrolling list

PROCEDURE UnselectCell(theItem: Integer; theListHandle: ListHandle);

```
1:  /*****************************************************************/
2:  void UnselectCell(short item, ListHandle theListHandle)
3:  /*****************************************************************/
4:  {
5:     Cell             theCell;
6:     SetPt(&theCell, 0, item);
7:     LSetSelect(false, theCell, theListHandle);
8:  }
```

The code for this routine is the same as in SelectCell.c, except that you pass false to the List Manager routine LSetSelect.

▶ Setting the Cells of the Scrolling List from a String List Resource

The first routine described in this chapter, DrawScrollList.c, took care of drawing a dialog box containing an empty scrolling list with a vertical scroll bar. Since empty scrolling lists are of pathetic value, you need a routine that will put names or other information into your empty list. GetStringList.c does just that.

▶ GetStringList.c

GetStringList.c goes into the resource that holds your string list, retrieves the strings, and fills in the empty cells of the scrolling list.

Listing 18-10. Getting strings from a resource to fill a scrolling list

```
PROCEDURE GetStringList(theID: Integer; theListHandle: ListHandle);
```

```
 1: /***************************************************************/
 2: void    GetStringList(short theID, ListHandle theListHandle)
 3: /***************************************************************/
 4: {
 5:   Handle        theHandle;
 6:   Ptr           thePointer;
 7:   short         i, j;
 8:   short         numStrings;
 9:   char          stringLen;
10:   Str255        theString;
11:   short         row;
12:   theHandle = GetResource('STR#', theID);
13:   HLock(theHandle);
14:   thePointer = *theHandle;
15:   numStrings = *thePointer;
16:   row = LAddRow(numStrings, 1, theListHandle);
17:   thePointer = thePointer + 2;
18:   for (i = 1; i<= numStrings; i++)
19:   {
20:     stringLen = *thePointer;
21:     thePointer = thePointer + 1;
22:     if (stringLen > 0)
23:     {
24:       for (j = 1; j <= stringLen; j++)
25:       {
26:         theString[j] = *thePointer;
27:         thePointer = thePointer + 1;
28:       }
29:       SetCell(i-1, theString, theListHandle);
30:     }
31:   }
32:   HUnlock(theHandle);
33: }
```

Setting the Cells of the Scrolling List from a String List Resource

In the function definition at the top of the listing, short *theID* is the number of the resource containing your string list; *theListHandle* is the handle to that string list.

The first active code on line 12 gets a handle to a string list resource, 'STR#', whose ID number you pass in. Having got the handle, lock it down with the statement on line 13 so the data it points to won't get moved. If the data were moved, the pointer would still point to the same place in memory, but that memory space would contain garbage.

On line 14 dereference the handle to convert it to a pointer. Determine the number of strings with the statement on line 15, which says, "The number of strings in your string list resource equals the information to which the pointer points."

Use the statement on line 16 to call the List Manager routine LAddRow, and pass in the number of rows you want to add after and including row 1.

The data representing the number of strings was only 2 bytes long. Now is the time to bump the pointer 2 bytes over so that it points to data in the next two places in memory (line 17).

A for-loop on line 18 says, "For *i* equal to 1, as long as *i* is less than or equal to the number of strings, keep looping." Since all the strings in your scrolling list are in Pascal and the first byte of a Pascal string is the length of the string, the statement on line 20 affirms that the string length is equal to the value pointed to.

Bump the pointer by 1 byte on line 21 so that it points to the first character in your first string.

The if-test on line 22 says, "If the string length is greater than 0, signifying that I have an actual string, do the following for-loop." The interior for-loop on lines 23–28 states, "For *j* equal to 1, and as long as *j* is equal to or less than the string length, keep looping, bumping *j* with each loop." The upshot is that you're moving a copy of the first string, character by character, from the string resource into a temporary variable, *theString*. When you're done with the first for-loop, you have the first of your strings in the temporary variable.

Call SetCell.c on line 29. This routine requires you to enter the cell number, which you'll recall is 0, for the top left of the box. Subtract 1 to get cell number 0, because strings begin with 1 and cells begin with 0.

The first time through this loop, *i* is equal to 1. Pass it the Pascal string and the handle to the List Manager. Up to this point you have only blank cells. These steps fill in the first blank cell with your first string.

Do another for-loop, putting the next string into the temporary variable *theString* and calling SetCell.c to fill in the second blank cell. Loop until all your strings reside in your scrolling list.

Finally, unlock the handle to the string resource.

> **By the Way ▶** In addition to the method just described, there are many other ways to add strings to the scrolling list, as long as they're in ASCII or Pascal. Among these methods: Open a file and read into your list selected characters, or compute some data and enter the results into the cells.

▶ A Simple Scrolling List Example

This section contains a pair of source code listings that demonstrate the scrolling list routines in this chapter. The pair consists of one file with the extension .c and another file, containing the resources, with the extension .R. The two types of files always go together to make up an application.

▶ ScrollingListExample.c

The following example uses four of the routines in this chapter to produce a scrolling list containing the names of ancient Greek cities (see Figure 18-1).

Listing 18-11. Example of a scrolling list

```
/*********************************************************************/
void      main()                    /* Routine to test scrolling list */
/*********************************************************************/
{
  Ptr                  theDialog;
  short                itemHit;
  ListHandle           theListHandle;
  Str255               theString;
  InitToolBox();
  CenterDialog(300);
  OpenStandardDialog(&theDialog, 300);
  DrawSList(theDialog, 3, &theListHandle);
  GetStringList(300, &theListHandle);
  PutEditString(theDialog, 2, "\pAncient Greek City");
  FrmDefItem(theDialog);
  ShadowFrame(theDialog, 3);
  for (;;)
  {
    MyModalDialog(&itemHit);
    switch (itemHit)
    {
```

```
        case (1):                                    /* Quit */
          break;
        case (3):
          if (GetListString(theString, theListHandle))
          {
             PutEdString(theDialog, 2, theString);
          }
          continue;
        case (-updateEvt):                           /* Update events */
          BeginUpdate(theDialog);
            UpDialog(theDialog);
            UpSList(theDialog, theListHandle);
            FrmDefItem(theDialog);
            ShadowFrame(theDialog, 3);
          EndUpdate(theDialog);
          continue;
        default                                      /* All other events */
          continue;
    }
    break;
  }
  DisposeDialog(theDialog);
}
```

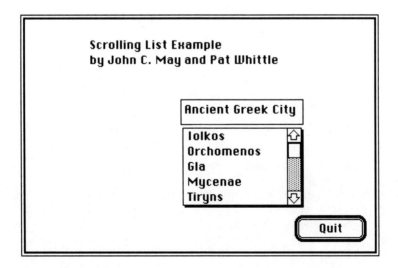

Figure 18-1. Dialog box with an example of a scrolling list

▶ ScrollingListExample.R

This section contains the resource file for the scrolling list example.

Listing 18-12. Resource file for example of a scrolling list

```
ScrollListExample.rsrc
rsrcRSED

Type DLOG
      ,300                      ;;Resource ID
Untitled1                       ;;Dialog title
50 120 288 492                  ;;Top Left Bottom Right
Visible NoGoAway                ;;Visible GoAway
1                               ;;ProcID, dialog def ID
1                               ;;Refcon, reference value
300                             ;;ID of item list

Type DITL
      ,300                      ;;Resource ID
4
* 1
BtnItem Enabled
207 292 227 362
Quit

* 2
EditText Enabled
84 168 105 295

* 3
UserItem Enabled
112 168 192 295

* 4
StatText Disabled
16 66 66 336
Scrolling List Example\0Dby John C. May and Pat Whittle

Type STR#
      ,300
25
Iolkos
Orchomenos
```

```
Gla
Mycenae
Tiryns
Sparta
Pylos
Thebes
Cydonia
Amnisos
Knossos
Phaestos
Miletus
Ilios
Lemnos
Assuwa
Hapalla
Arzawa
Halicarnassos
Kos
Chios
Lesbos
Lemnos
Athens
Keftiu
```

▶ Summary

This chapter presented ten routines that draw, handle, and update scrolling lists and their cells, as well as an example of a scrolling list and a brief overview of List Manager. Remember that you can use scrolling lists for many different types of character strings, not just for file names.

▶ Recommended Reading

For a copy of the Apple Technical Note listed below, call Apple Professional Developers Association, (408)-974-4897.

Apple Technical Note No. 203 "Don't Abuse the Managers"

Cameron, Ray A. "Font Dialog Box Using List Manager." (Assembly.) *The Definitive MacTutor—The Macintosh Programming Journal*, Vol. 4, 1989.

Rausch, William. "List Manager Inspires Help Function Solution." (C.) *The Essential MacTutor—The Macintosh Programming Journal*, Vol. 3, 1988.

Waters, Bryan. "How to Write a Spreadsheet in LS C." (C.) *The Best of MacTutor—The Macintosh Programming Journal,* Vol. 5, 1990.

Wilcox, David. "Editable List & User Items." (Pascal.) *MacTutor—The Macintosh Programming Journal*, Vol. 6, No. 4, April 1990.

19 ▶ Pop-up Menus

▶ Overview of Pop-up Menus

Pop-up menus do not appear in the menu, but they show up elsewhere on the screen, usually in a dialog box. They can be used to set values or to select an item from a list of related items.

Pop-up menus are always characterized by a pop-up box with a shadow frame, so the user knows a menu lurks behind. The pop-up box usually sits to the right of the prompt box. The prompt box contains the menu title; the "box" is invisible so that only static text appears. When the user clicks on the prompt box or the pop-up box, the menu pops out with the current value in the list checked and highlighted. While the mouse button is down, the user can move about inside the pop-up menu and select another item, which then becomes the current value and appears in the pop-up box when the mouse button is released.

The color (or black or white value) of the menu title in the prompt box and the current value on the pop-up menu list always appear highlighted when the mouse button is down.

▶ Drawing a Pop-up Menu

As with many of the series of routines in this book, the routines in this chapter that help you construct pop-up menus require that you first draw the menu, then handle the mouse-down event, and finally update the menu on the screen. The "Scrolling Lists" series in Chapter 18 follows the same pattern.

For the following routines, the resource file contains a user item, a menu resource, and static text. In our example—or in your application—they all come together to make the pop-up menu work.

▶ DrawPopUp.c

This routine draws the dialog box to contain a pop-up menu. It comes complete with static text, a Quit button, a prompt box, and a pop-up box.

Listing 19-1. Drawing a pop-up menu in a dialog box

```
PROCEDURE DrawPopUp(theDialog: DialogPtr, itemHit: INTEGER, popMenuID:
INTEGER, VAR popMenu: MenuHandle, choice: INTEGER);

 1: /***************************************************************/
 2: void DrawPopUp(DialogPtr theDialog, short itemHit,
 3:    short popMenuID, MenuHandle* popMenu, short choice)
 4: /***************************************************************/
 5: {
 6:    SysEnvRec      sysEnv;
 7:    char           hasColor;
 8:    GrafPtr        savePort;              /* Old grafPort */
 9:    PenState       penStuff;
10:    RGBColor       oldBackColor;          /* Old and new colors */
11:    RGBColor       oldForeColor;
12:    RGBColor       newBackColor;
13:    RGBColor       newForeColor;
14:    short          saveFont;              /* Font stuff */
15:    short          saveSize;
16:    Style          saveFace;
17:    short          saveMode;
18:    short          theType;               /* Not used */
19:    Rect           theRect;               /* Size of user item */
20:    Handle         theHdl;                /* Not used */
21:    short          i;                     /* Loop index */
22:    Str255         theString;             /* Temporary strings */
23:    short          h, v;                  /* Offsets */
24:    MCEntryPtr     pMCEntry;
25:    #define        SysEnvironsTrap 0xA090    /* Toolbox traps */
26:    #define        UnknownTrap              0xA89F
27:    #define        SetRGBColor(rgb,r,g,b) {(rgb)->red = (r);
28:       (rgb)- >green =: (g); (rgb)->blue = (b);}
29:    #define        leftSlop       13
30:    #define        bottomSlop     5
```

```
31:    hasColor = false;                          /* Test for color */
32:    if ((long)NGetTrapAddress(SysEnvironsTrap, OSTrap) !=
33:             (long)NGetTrapAddress(UnknownTrap, ToolTrap))
34:    {
35:       SysEnvirons(1, &sysEnv);
36:       hasColor = sysEnv.hasColorQD;
37:    }
38:    GetPort(&savePort);                        /* Init port, pen, font */
39:    SetPort(theDialog);
40:    GetPenState(&penStuff);
41:    if (hasColor)
42:    {
43:       GetForeColor(&oldForeColor);
44:       GetBackColor(&oldBackColor);
45:    }
46:    saveFont = theDialog->txFont;
47:    saveSize = theDialog->txSize;
48:    saveFace = theDialog->txFace;
49:    saveMode = theDialog->txMode;
50:    TextSize(12);
51:    TextFont(systemFont);
52:    TextMode(srcOr);
53:    TextFace(0);
54:    PenNormal();
55:    *popMenu = GetMenu(popMenuID);              /* Get menu handle */
56:    for (i = 1; i <= CountMItems(popMenu); i++) /* Uncheck all */
57:    {
58:       CheckItem(popMenu, i, false);
59:    }
60:    CheckItem(popMenu, choice, true);
61:    GetItem(popMenu, choice, theString);        /* Check the choice */
62:    GetDItem(theDialog, itemHit,                /* Draw the popup */
63:             &theType, &theHdl, &theRect);
64:    InsetRect(&theRect, -1, -1);
65:    FitString(theString,
66:              theRect.right - theRect.left);
67:    if (hasColor)
68:    {
69:       SetRGBColor(&newForeColor, 0x0000, 0x0000, 0x0000);
70:       SetRGBColor(&newBackColor, 0xFFFF, 0xFFFF, 0xFFFF);
71:       RGBForeColor(&newForeColor);
72:       RGBBackColor(&newBackColor);
73:    }
74:    ShadowFrame(theDialog, itemHit);
75:    if (hasColor)
76:    {
77:       pMCEntry = GetMCEntry(popMenuID, 0);
```

```
 78:     if (pMCEntry != NIL)
 79:       {
 80:         newBackColor = pMCEntry->mctRGB4;
 81:         newForeColor = pMCEntry->mctRGB1;
 82:         RGBForeColor(&newForeColor);
 83:         RGBBackColor(&newBackColor);
 84:       }
 85:   }
 86:   InsetRect(&theRect, 1, 1);
 87:   EraseRect(&theRect);
 88:   v = theRect.left + leftSlop;
 89:   h = theRect.bottom - bottomSlop;
 90:   MoveTo(v, h);
 91:   DrawString(theString);
 92:   if (hasColor)                              /* Draw the title */
 93:   {
 94:     pMCEntry = GetMCEntry(popMenuID, 0);
 95:     if (pMCEntry != NIL)
 96:       {
 97:         newForeColor = pMCEntry->mctRGB3;
 98:         RGBForeColor(&newForeColor);
 99:         RGBBackColor(&newBackColor);
100:       }
101:   }
102:   GetDItem(theDialog, itemHit + 1,
103:           &theType, &theHdl, &theRect);
104:   GetIText(theHdl, theString);
105:   v = theRect.top +
106:           (*(((DialogPeek)theDialog)->textH))->fontAscent;
107:   h = theRect.left + 1;
108:   MoveTo(h, v);
109:   DrawString(theString);
110:   TextFont(saveFont);                        /* Return old settings */
111:   TextSize(saveSize);
112:   TextFace(saveFace);
113:   TextMode(saveMode);
114:   SetPenState(&penStuff);
115:   if (hasColor)
116:   {
117:     RGBForeColor(&oldForeColor);
118:     RGBBackColor(&oldBackColor);
119:   }
120:   SetPort(savePort);
121: }
```

On lines 2 and 3, when you call the routine, you must pass it four items: a pointer to the dialog box; the user item number that the pop-up is going to be put in (the routine makes an assumption that the static text is going to be the user item number plus 1); the pop-up menu ID number; and a choice—that is, the menu item that you want to have checkmarked. The routine returns a handle to the menu.

Skip the declarations on lines 6–30. Lines 31–37 find out if color is available and, if so, set the color flag.

Lines 38–54 initialize by saving and setting the port, saving the pen and setting it back to normal, saving the font information—name, size, face, and mode—and resetting that information to something known. Lines 43 and 44 save the foreground and background colors if the routine is running on a color machine.

The statement on line 55 gets a handle to the pop-up menu.

Lines 56–59 uncheck all of the items in the menu, and the statement on line 60 puts a check mark next to the item choice that was passed in on line 3.

After you pass it the handle to the menu and the choice on line 61, the Menu Manager routine GetItem returns the string of the item (static text) that will appear in the prompt box.

After you pass in the item hit, the call on lines 62 and 63 returns, among other items, the rectangle for the pop-up box.

You inset the rectangle by a negative 1 on line 64.

The routine FitString on lines 65 and 66 determines whether the string of the checkmarked menu item will fit in the rectangle of the pop-up box. If it is too long, the routine automatically shortens it and adds an ellipsis (...) to indicate that there is more to the item. FitString is one of our routines. You will find the source code for it in Appendix B.

The if-statement on lines 67–73 sets the foreground color to black and the background color to white.

Then, on line 74, you call another one of our routines: ShadowFrame. This routine, found in Chapter 17, draws the shadow frame around the pop-up box.

Lines 75–85 get the color out of the color menu table, if color exists. They set the background color of the pop-up box to the background color of the pop-up menu, and the color of the pop-up box's foreground to the color of the text.

You inset the pop-up box rectangle by a positive 1 on line 86, thereby returning it to its original size, and you erase the rectangle on line 87. The effect is to fill the pop-up box rectangle with the color of the background of the menu.

The statements on lines 88–91 draw the text inside of the pop-up box after computing the vertical and horizontal offsets.

The if-statement on lines 92–101 gets colors, if they are available, for the prompt box, which contains the pop-up menu title.

On lines 102 and 103, you call GetDItem and pass it the number of the item hit plus 1; it returns the rectangle for the prompt box. You then get the text for the prompt box with the Dialog Manager routine on line 104.

You want to redraw the static text in the box if color is available, so the code on lines 105–109 computes the vertical and horizontal offset, moves to that offset, and redraws the string in the box.

Lines 110–120 return the font, pen, colors, and port to their original settings.

▶ Handling a Pop-up Menu

Once you have drawn the pop-up menu to the screen, you must have a routine that will change the choice on the menu when a user clicks on a new item in the list. The routine in this section checkmarks the new item and moves the rectangle containing the list of items accordingly. It also redraws the pop-up box with the new item chosen from the pop-up menu.

▶ DoPopUp.c

This routine handles the mouse-down event inside the pop-up menu.

Listing 19-2. Handling a mouse-down event in a pop-up menu

```
PROCEDURE DoPopUp(theDialog: DialogPtr, itemHit: INTEGER, popMenuID:
INTEGER, popMenu: MenuHandle, choice: INTEGER);

 1:  /**************************************************************/
 2:  void DoPopUp(DialogPtr theDialog, short itemHit, short
        popMenuID,
 3:                   MenuHandle popMenu, short choice)
 4:  /**************************************************************/
 5:  {
 6:      SysEnvRec       sysEnv;
 7:      char            hasColor;
 8:      GrafPtr         savePort;                /* Old grafPort */
 9:      PenState        penStuff;
10:      RGBColor        oldBackColor;            /* Old and new colors */
11:      RGBColor        oldForeColor;
12:      RGBColor        newBackColor;
```

```
13:     RGBColor        newForeColor;
14:     RGBColor        oldHiliteRGB;
15:     RGBColor        newHiliteRGB;
16:     short           saveFont;                       /* Font stuff */
17:     short           saveSize;
18:     Style           saveFace;
19:     short           saveMode;
20:     Point           mouseLoc;
21:     Point           popLoc;
22:     short           theType;                        /* Not used */
23:     Rect            popUpBox;               /* Size of user item */
24:     Rect            promptBox;
25:     Handle          theHdl;                         /* Not used */
26:     short           h, v;                           /* Offsets */
27:     MCEntryPtr      pMCEntry;
28:     Str255          theString;              /* Temporary strings */
29:     short           chosen;
30:     short           newChoice;
31:     #define         SysEnvironsTrap 0xA090    /* Toolbox traps */
32:     #define         UnknownTrap                         0xA89F
33:     #define         SetRGBColor(rgb,r,g,b) {(rgb)->red = (r);
34:        (rgb)->green = (g); (rgb)->blue = (b);}
35:     #define         leftSlop        13
36:     #define         bottomSlop      5
37:     hasColor = false;                       /* Test for color */
38:     if ((long)NGetTrapAddress(SysEnvironsTrap, OSTrap) !=
39:          (long)NGetTrapAddress(UnknownTrap, ToolTrap))
40:     {
41:        SysEnvirons(1, &sysEnv);
42:        hasColor = sysEnv.hasColorQD;
43:     }
44:     GetPort(&savePort);              /* Init port, pen, font */
45:     SetPort(theDialog);
46:     GetPenState(&penStuff);
47:     if (hasColor)
48:     {
49:        GetForeColor(&oldForeColor);
50:        GetBackColor(&oldBackColor);
51:     }
52:     saveFont = theDialog->txFont;
53:     saveSize = theDialog->txSize;
54:     saveFace = theDialog->txFace;
55:     saveMode = theDialog->txMode;
56:     TextSize(12);
57:     TextFont(systemFont);
58:     TextMode(srcOr);
59:     TextFace(0);
```

Chapter 19 Pop-up Menus

```
60:    PenNormal();
61:    GetMouse(&mouseLoc);
62:    GetDItem(theDialog, itemHit, &theType, &theHdl, &popUpBox);
63:    GetDItem(theDialog, itemHit, &theType, &theHdl,
                &promptBox);
64:    if (hasColor)
65:    {
66:       oldHiliteRGB = HiliteRGB;
67:       pMCEntry = GetMCEntry(popMenuID, 0);
68:       if (pMCEntry != NIL)
69:       {
70:          newHiliteRGB = pMCEntry->mctRGB3;
71:          newForeColor = pMCEntry->mctRGB2;
72:          HiliteRGB = newHiliteRGB;
73:          BitClr(HiliteMode, pHiliteBit);
74:          InvertRect(&promptBox);
75:          HiliteRGB = oldHiliteRGB;
76:          RGBForeColor(&newForeColor);
77:          RGBBackColor(&oldBackColor);
78:          v = promptBox.top + (*(((DialogPeek)
79:              theDialog)->textH))->fontAscent;
80:          h = promptBox.left + 1;
81:          MoveTo(h, v);
82:          DrawString(theString);
83:       }
84:       else
85:       {
86:          BitClr(HiliteMode, pHiliteBit);
87:          InvertRect(&promptBox);
88:       }
89:    }
90:    else
91:    {
92:       InvertRect(&promptBox);
93:    }
94:    InsertMenu(popMenu, -1);
95:    popLoc.v = popUpBox.top;
96:    popLoc.h = popUpBox.left;
97:    LocalToGlobal(&popLoc);
98:    CalcMenuSize(popMenu);          /* Work around Menu Mgr bug */
99:    v = popLoc.v;
100:   h = popLoc.h;
101:   chosen = PopUpMenuSelect(popMenu, v, h, choice);
102:   if (hasColor)
103:   {
104:      oldHiliteRGB = HiliteRGB;
```

```
105:        pMCEntry = GetMCEntry(popMenuID, 0);
106:        if (pMCEntry != NIL)
107:        {
108:           newHiliteRGB = pMCEntry->mctRGB3;
109:           newForeColor = pMCEntry->mctRGB3;
110:           HiliteRGB = newHiliteRGB;
111:           BitClr(HiliteMode, pHiliteBit);
112:           InvertRect(&promptBox);
113:           HiliteRGB = oldHiliteRGB;
114:           RGBForeColor(&newForeColor);
115:           RGBBackColor(&oldBackColor);
116:           v = promptBox.top + (*(((DialogPeek)
117:                  theDialog)->textH))->fontAscent;
118:           h = promptBox.left + 1;
119:           MoveTo(h, v);
120:           DrawString(theString);
121:        }
122:        else
123:        {
124:           BitClr(HiliteMode, pHiliteBit);
125:           InvertRect(&promptBox);
126:        }
127:     }
128:     else
129:     {
130:        InvertRect(&promptBox);
131:     }
132:     DeleteMenu(popMenuID);
133:     if (chosen != 0)
134:     {
135:        newChoice = LoWord(chosen);
136:        if (newChoice != choice)
137:        {
138:           CheckItem(popMenu, choice, false);
139:           CheckItem(popMenu, newChoice, true);
140:           choice = newChoice;
141:           GetItem(popMenu, choice, theString);
142:           InsetRect(&popUpBox, -1, -1);
143:           FitString(theString, popUpBox.right - popUpBox.left);
144:           if (hasColor)
145:           {
146:              SetRGBColor(&newForeColor, 0x0000, 0x0000, 0x0000);
147:              SetRGBColor(&newBackColor, 0xFFFF, 0xFFFF, 0xFFFF);
148:              RGBForeColor(&newForeColor);
149:              RGBBackColor(&newBackColor);
150:           }
```

284 ▶ Chapter 19 Pop-up Menus

```
151:        ShadowFrame(theDialog, itemHit);
152:        if (hasColor)
153:        {
154:          pMCEntry = GetMCEntry(popMenuID, 0);
155:          if (pMCEntry != NIL)
156:          {
157:            newBackColor = pMCEntry->mctRGB4;
158:            newForeColor = pMCEntry->mctRGB1;
159:            RGBForeColor(&newForeColor);
160:            RGBBackColor(&newBackColor);
161:          }
162:        }
163:        InsetRect(&popUpBox, 1, 1);
164:        EraseRect(&popUpBox);
165:        v = popUpBox.left + leftSlop;
166:        h = popUpBox.bottom - bottomSlop;
167:        MoveTo(v, h);
168:        DrawString(theString);
169:      }
170:    }
171:    TextFont(saveFont);                  /* Return old settings */
172:    TextSize(saveSize);
173:    TextFace(saveFace);
174:    TextMode(saveMode);
175:    SetPenState(&penStuff);
176:    if (hasColor)
177:    {
178:      RGBForeColor(&oldForeColor);
179:      RGBBackColor(&oldBackColor);
180:    }
181:    SetPort(savePort);
182:  }
183:
184:  extern  RGBColor HiliteRGB : 0xDA0;
```

Important ▶ Lines 33 and 34 contain a macro. Because of its length, we have put it on two lines in this book. However, when you use this routine in your application, be sure to put all of the macro on one line only; C will not tolerate a carriage return inside of a macro.

The first part of this routine is very similar to DrawPopUp.c. See the review of DrawPopUp.c earlier in this chapter for a detailed discussion of the code.

The notable difference between the two routines starts at line 61 of DoPopUp.c, where the call gets the location of the mouse. Then lines 62 and 63 get the pop-up and prompt boxes.

The code on lines 64–93 highlights the pop-up and prompt boxes in color, if it is available, or in black-and-white. See the review of DrawPopUp.c for a discussion of foreground and background colors. Here, when an item is highlighted, the colors switch. Note the statements on lines 86 and 87. Assuming that color is available, you call the Toolbox routine BitClr and pass it the global variable *HiliteMode* (defined in a THINK C Include file) and the constant pHiliteBit. With this call you say, "If I clear a bit inside of the *HiliteMode* variable, then the next time I say 'Invert the rectangle,' I don't really invert the colors; instead I switch the foreground and background colors."

However, if the routine is not running on a color machine, the statement on line 92 will invert the black and the white values.

Up to this point, you have determined that a mouse button has been pressed, and you have highlighted the static text in the pop-up box and in the prompt box. Now, on line 94, you bring up the pop-up menu with the Toolbox call InsertMenu. Pass it the handle to the pop-up menu and a negative 1.

Lines 95 and 96 compute the location for the pop-up menu by getting the point at which the top left-hand corner of the menu box will appear.

Line 97 converts that location to global coordinates.

On line 98 you work around a bug in the Menu Manager by calling CalcMenuSize and passing it the handle to the pop-up menu. (This is recommended by the Macintosh Development Technical Services at Apple.) The call doesn't have any visual effect, but it takes care of some internal problem that you will definitely notice if you leave the call out.

Lines 99 and 100 break out the pop-up location point into separate vertical and horizontal numbers.

Line 101 contains the meat of this routine by bringing the pop-up menu to the screen. You call PopUpMenuSelect, pass it the handle to the menu, and the vertical and horizontal coordinates of where you want the menu to be drawn. PopUpMenuSelect returns the choice (the item selected) and takes over. It handles the dragging up and down of the menu as the item selected changes.

Lines 102–131 do the reverse of the procedure for highlighting the prompt box and the selected item in the pop-up menu.

Now that the menu item has been selected and checkmarked, you delete the pop-up menu with the statement on line 132.

The code on lines 133–170 redraws the pop-up box and the string in the box. See the review of DrawPopUp.c earlier in this chapter (lines 60–91) for details of the drawing procedure.

Lines 171–182 return the font, pen, colors, and port back to their original states.

The statement on line 184 is a C command that externalizes *HiliteRGB*. That is a low-memory global variable that was not set up by THINK C, but was set up by hand for this routine. The command sets it outside of the program space.

▶ Updating a Pop-up Menu

After a mouse-down event inside of the pop-up menu, you need to update and redraw the shadow-frame pop-up box and redraw the prompt box.

▶ UpPopUp.c

This routine updates and redraws the pop-up menu on the screen, then, once the pop-up menu has left the screen, redraws the prompt box and the pop-up box.

Listing 19-3. Updating the pop-up menu

```
PROCEDURE UpPopUp(theDialog: DialogPtr, itemHit: INTEGER, popMenuID:
    INTEGER, popMenu: MenuHandle, choice: INTEGER);

 1: /*****************************************************************/
 2: void UpPopUp(DialogPtr theDialog, short itemHit, short
 3:              popMenuID, MenuHandle popMenu, short choice)
 4: /*****************************************************************/
 5: {
 6:     SysEnvRec     sysEnv;
 7:     char          hasColor;
 8:     GrafPtr       savePort;                   /* Old grafPort */
 9:     PenState      penStuff;
10:     RGBColor      oldBackColor;               /* Old and new colors */
11:     RGBColor      oldForeColor;
12:     RGBColor      newBackColor;
13:     RGBColor      newForeColor;
14:     short         saveFont;                   /* Font stuff */
15:     short         saveSize;
16:     Style         saveFace;
17:     short         saveMode;
18:     short         theType;                    /* Not used */
19:     Rect          promptBox;                  /* Size of user item */
20:     Rect          popUpBox;
21:     Handle        theHdl;                     /* Not used */
22:     short         i;                          /* Loop index */
```

```
23:        Str255          theString;                /* Temporary strings */
24:        short           h, v;                                /* Offsets */
25:        MCEntryPtr      pMCEntry;
26:        #define         SysEnvironsTrap 0xA090    /* Toolbox traps */
27:        #define         UnknownTrap     0xA89F
28:        #define         SetRGBColor(rgb,r,g,b) {(rgb)->red = (r);
29:           (rgb)->green = (g); (rgb)->blue = (b);}
30:        #define         leftSlop        13
31:        #define         bottomSlop      5
32:        hasColor = false;                         /* Test for color */
33:        if ((long)NGetTrapAddress(SysEnvironsTrap, OSTrap) !=
34:              (long)NGetTrapAddress(UnknownTrap, ToolTrap))
35:        {
36:           SysEnvirons(1, &sysEnv);
37:           hasColor = sysEnv.hasColorQD;
38:        }
39:        GetPort(&savePort);               /* Init port, pen, font */
40:        SetPort(theDialog);
41:        GetPenState(&penStuff);
42:        if (hasColor)
43:        {
44:           GetForeColor(&oldForeColor);
45:           GetBackColor(&oldBackColor);
46:        }
47:        saveFont = theDialog->txFont;
48:        saveSize = theDialog->txSize;
49:        saveFace = theDialog->txFace;
50:        saveMode = theDialog->txMode;
51:        TextSize(12);
52:        TextFont(systemFont);
53:        TextMode(srcOr);
54:        TextFace(0);
55:        PenNormal();
56:        GetItem(popMenu, choice, theString);  /* Check the choice */
57:        GetDItem(theDialog, itemHit,          /* Draw the popup */
58:                 &theType, &theHdl, &popUpBox);
59:        InsetRect(&promptBox, -1, -1);
60:        FitString(theString, promptBox.right - promptBox.left);
61:        if (hasColor)
62:        {
63:           SetRGBColor(&newForeColor, 0x0000, 0x0000, 0x0000);
64:           SetRGBColor(&newBackColor, 0xFFFF, 0xFFFF, 0xFFFF);
65:           RGBForeColor(&newForeColor);
66:           RGBBackColor(&newBackColor);
67:        }
68:        ShadowFrame(theDialog, itemHit);
69:        if (hasColor)                            /* Draw the title */
70:        {
```

```
 71:      pMCEntry = GetMCEntry(popMenuID, 0);
 72:      if (pMCEntry != NIL)
 73:      {
 74:         newForeColor = pMCEntry->mctRGB3;
 75:         RGBForeColor(&newForeColor);
 76:         RGBBackColor(&oldBackColor);
 77:      }
 78:   }
 79:   GetDItem(theDialog, itemHit + 1,
 80:            &theType, &theHdl, &promptBox);
 81:   GetIText(theHdl, theString);
 82:   v = promptBox.top + (*(((DialogPeek)
 83:            theDialog)->textH))->fontAscent;
 84:   h = promptBox.left + 1;
 85:   MoveTo(h, v);
 86:   DrawString(theString);
 87:   if (hasColor)
 88:   {
 89:      pMCEntry = GetMCEntry(popMenuID, 0);
 90:      if (pMCEntry != NIL)
 91:      {
 92:         newBackColor = pMCEntry->mctRGB4;
 93:         newForeColor = pMCEntry->mctRGB1;
 94:         RGBForeColor(&newForeColor);
 95:         RGBBackColor(&newBackColor);
 96:      }
 97:   }
 98:   InsetRect(&popUpBox, 1, 1);
 99:   EraseRect(&popUpBox);
100:   v = popUpBox.left + leftSlop;
101:   h = popUpBox.bottom - bottomSlop;
102:   MoveTo(v, h);
103:   DrawString(theString);
104:   TextFont(saveFont);              /* Return old settings */
105:   TextSize(saveSize);
106:   TextFace(saveFace);
107:   TextMode(saveMode);
108:   SetPenState(&penStuff);
109:   if (hasColor)
110:   {
111:      RGBForeColor(&oldForeColor);
112:      RGBBackColor(&oldBackColor);
113:   }
114:   SetPort(savePort);
115: }
```

This routine closely resembles DrawPopUp.c, discussed at the beginning of this chapter. See the review of that routine for details of the code.

▶ A Simple Pop-up Menu Example

The following source code and RMaker resource file together create a simple pop-up menu example, complete with static text, prompt box, shadow-frame pop-up box, menu items, and Quit button. The .c and .R files always go together to make up an application.

▶ PopUpExample.c

This listing contains the source code for the pop-up menu example. See Figure 19-1 for a picture of the pop-up menu created with this file.

Listing 19-4. Example of a pop-up menu

```c
/********************************************************************/
void    main()                              /* Routine to test Popups */
/********************************************************************/
{
    DialogPtr           theDialog;
    short               itemHit;
    short               choice;
    MenuHandle          hMenu;
    InitToolBox();
     OpenResources("\pPopUpExample.rsrc");          /* For devel purposes */
    CenterDialog(300);
    OpenDialog(&theDialog, 300);
    FrmDefItem(theDialog);
    choice = 2;
    DrawPopUp(theDialog, 2, 128, &hMenu, choice);
    for(;;)
    {
       MyModalDialog(&itemHit)
       switch (itemHit)
       {
         case (1):
           break;
         case (2):
         case (3):
            DoPopUp(theDialog, 2, 128, hMenu, choice);
            continue;
         case (-updateEvt):
            BeginUpdate(theDialog);
              UpDialog(theDialog);
              UpPopUp(theDialog, 2, hMenu, choice);
              FrmDefItem(theDialog);
```

290 ▶ Chapter 19   Pop-up Menus

```
            EndUpdate(theDialog);
          continue;
       default:
          continue;
     }
     break;
  }
  DisposeDialog(theDialog);
}
```

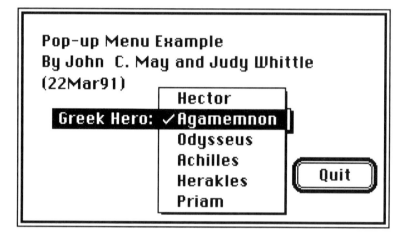

Figure 19-1. Dialog box showing a pop-up menu created with PopUpExample.c

▶ PopUpExample.R

PopUpExample.R is the resource file that forms a pair with PopUpExample.c in a demonstration application that draws a pop-up menu on the screen.

Listing 19-5. Resource file for example of a pop-up menu

```
PopupExample.rsrc
rsrcRSED

Type DLOG
,300
Pop-up Test
50 50 204 332
Visible NoGoAway
1
1
300

Type DITL
,300
4

* 1
Button
110 210 130 270
Quit

* 2
UserItem
70 106 86 210

* 3
StaticText
70 20 86 105
 Greek Hero:

* 4
StaticText Disabled
10 10 60 280
Pop-up Menu Example\0Dby John C. May and Judy Whittle\0D(22Mar91)

Type MENU
,128
Greeks
Hector
Agamemnon
Odysseus
Achilles
Herakles
Priam
```

▶ Summary

This chapter presented three routines to handle pop-up menus.

- The first draws a pop-up menu in a dialog box
- The second handles a mouse-down event when a user clicks on an item in the pop-up menu
- The third redraws the dialog box when the mouse button is released

The chapter also provided a pop-up menu example along with the source code and resource file used to create the example.

20 ▶ Putting It All Together

▶ A Comprehensive Example

As mentioned in the Introduction, the routines in this book are immediately workable. You can incorporate any of them into your application, and they will do the job. To give you an idea of how to combine them, we've created the following example, which is, as shown in Figure 20-1, a control panel at the helm of an intergalactic space ship.

▶ Kit and Caboodle.c

Kit and Caboodle combines nineteen of our routines, which in turn incorporate dozens of Toolbox routines. The nineteen routines are as follows.

InitToolbox.c	Chapter 3
CenterDialog.c	Chapter 6
DispToggleIcon.c	Chapter 12
DoPopUp.c	Chapter 19
DoToggleIcon.c	Chapter 12
DrawDottedLine.c	Chapter 16
DrawPopUp.c	Chapter 19
DrawScrollList.c	Chapter 18
FrmDefItem.c	Chapter 9
GetListString.c	Chapter 18
GetStringList.c	Chapter 18
GetToggleIcon.c	Chapter 12

MyModalDialog.c   Chapter 6
OpenDialog.c   Chapter 6
PushRadioButton.c   Chapter 11
ShadowFrame.c   Chapter 17
UpDialog.c   Chapter 6
UpPopUp.c   Chapter 19
UpScrollList.c   Chapter 18

Listing 20-1. A comprehensive example

```
 1:  /***************************************************************/
 2:  void    main()                          /* Kit and Caboodle example */
 3:  /***************************************************************/
 4:  {
 5:    DialogPtr       theDialog;
 6:    short           itemHit;
 7:    short           choice;
 8:    MenuHandle      hMenu;
 9:    ListHandle      theListHandle;
10:    Str255          theString;
11:    iconTog         theSwitch1, **hSwitch1;
12:    iconTog         theSwitch2, **hSwitch2;
13:    iconTog         theSwitch3, **hSwitch3;
14:    InitToolBox();
15:    CenterDialog(128);
16:    OpenDialog(&theDialog,128);
17:    FrmDefItem(theDialog);
18:    choice = 3;
19:    DrawPopUp(theDialog, 3, 128, &hMenu, choice);
20:    DrawSList(theDialog, 6, &theListHandle);
21:    GetStringList(128, theListHandle);
22:    ShadowFrame(theDialog, 6);
23:    PushRadioButton(theDialog, 7, 7, 10);
24:    DrawDottedLine(theDialog, 23);
25:    DrawDottedLine(theDialog, 24);
26:    hSwitch1 = (hIconTog)GetTogIcon(theDialog, 16, 2000, 2001)
27:    hSwitch2 = (hIconTog)GetTogIcon(theDialog, 17, 2030, 2031)
28:    hSwitch3 = (hIconTog)GetTogIcon(theDialog, 18, 2020, 2021)
29:     for(;;)
30:    {
31:      MyModalDialog(&itemHit)
32:      switch (itemHit)
33:       {
34:        case (1):                                        /* OK */
35:          break;
```

```
36:        case (2):                               /* Cancel */
37:          break;
38:        case (3):                     /* Planets popup prompt */
39:        case (4):                       /* Planets popup menu */
40:          DoPopUp(theDialog, 3, 128, hMenu, choice);
41:          continue;
42:        case (6):                         /* Constellations list */
43:          if (GetListString(theString, theListHandle))
44:          {
45:          }
46:          continue;
47:        case (7):                         /* Horizon radio button */
48:        case (8):                         /* Equator radio button */
49:        case (9):                         /* Ecliptic radio button */
50:        case (10):                        /* Galactic radio button */
51:          PushRadioButton(theDialog, itemHit, 7, 10);
52:          continue;
53:        case (11):                              /* Right Ascension */
54:          continue;
55:        case (12):                                 /* Declination */
56:          continue;
57:        case (13):                                    /* Distance */
58:          continue;
59:        case (14):                               /* Proper Motion */
60:          continue;
61:        case (16):                                  /* Red switch */
62:          DoTogIcon(hSwitch1);
63:          continue;
64:        case (17):                                /* Green switch */
65:          DoTogIcon(hSwitch2);
66:          continue;
67:        case (18):                                 /* Blue switch */
68:          DoTogIcon(hSwitch3);
69:          continue;
70:        case (-updateEvt):                         /* Update event */
71:          BeginUpdate(theDialog);
72:            UpDialog(theDialog);
73:            UpPopUp(theDialog, 3, hMenu, choice);
74:            UpSList(theDialog, theListHandle);
75:            FrmDefItem(theDialog);
76:            ShadowFrame(theDialog, 6);
77:            DrawDottedLine(theDialog, 23);
78:            DrawDottedLine(theDialog, 24);
79:          EndUpdate(theDialog);
80:          continue;
81:        default:
```

```
82:            continue;
83:         }
84:       break;
85:     }
86:     DispTogIcon(hSwitch1);
87:     DispTogIcon(hSwitch2);
88:     DispTogIcon(hSwitch3);
89:     DisposeDialog(theDialog);
90: }
```

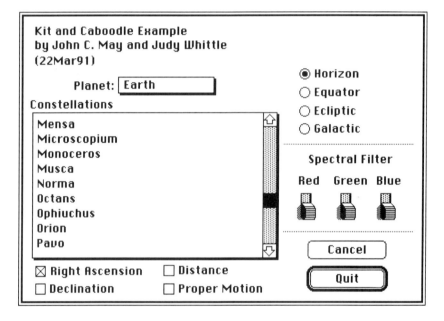

Figure 20-1. Comprehensive example created with Kit and Caboodle.c

Given that the example is utter nonsense, it still looks credible. The radio buttons, check boxes, toggle icons, default button, scrolling list, and pop-up menu are all drawn to conform with Apple's Human Interface Guidelines.

A quick walk through the code shows that after several lines of declarations and the initialization of the Toolbox, the first active code on line 15 centers the dialog box. The statements on lines 16 and 17 open the dialog box and frame the default item (Quit button).

On line 19 you draw the pop-up menu, which contains the names of the nine solar system planets and the asteroid Ceres. On line 20 you draw the scrolling list.

Line 21 gets the string list for the scrolling list. This list contains the names of eighty-seven constellations.

The statement on line 22 draws the shadow frame for the pop-up box. Line 23 selects the radio button.

Now, looking at the right-hand side of Figure 20-1, you can see that the code on lines 24–28 draws the two dotted lines and the three toggle icons.

The for-loop incorporating MyModalDialog on lines 29–69 draws all of the static text on the dialog box. Then, on lines 70–85, all of the update events take place.

Lines 86–90 dispose of the three toggle icons and the dialog box.

▶ Kit and Caboodle.R

Kit and Caboodle.R is the resource file that forms a pair with the file Kit and Caboodle.c to bring up Figure 20-1 on the screen.

Listing 20-2. Resource file for comprehensive example

```
Kit and Caboodle.rsrc
rsrcRSED

Type DLOG
Kit and Caboodle,128
Pop-up Test                 ;; Message (Title)
30 18 329 453               ;; Rect (T,L,B,R)
Visible NoGoAway            ;; Flags
1                           ;; Proc ID
1                           ;; RefCon
128                         ;; Resource ID of DITL list


Type DITL
Kit and Caboodle,128
24

* 1
Button      Enabled
273 316 293 401             ;; Rect (T,L,B,R)
Quit                        ;; Message
```

```
* 2
Button      Enabled
243 316 263 401              ;; Rect (T,L,B,R)
Cancel                       ;; Message

* 3
UserItem    Enabled
63 137 79 241                ;; Rect (T,L,B,R)

* 4
StaticText  Enabled
63 51 79 137                 ;; Rect (T,L,B,R)
 Planet:                     ;; Message

* 5
StaticText  Disabled
5 10 55 280                  ;; Rect (T,L,B,R)
Kit and Caboodle Example     ;; Message
by John C. May and Judy Whittle
(22Mar91)

* 6
UserItem    Disabled
100 13 255 283               ;; Rect (T,L,B,R)

* 7
RadioButton Enabled
50 303 68 409                ;; Rect (T,L,B,R)
Horizon                      ;; Message

* 8
RadioButton Enabled
70 303 88 409                ;; Rect (T,L,B,R)
Equator                      ;; Message

* 9
RadioButton Enabled
90 303 108 409               ;; Rect (T,L,B,R)
Ecliptic                     ;; Message

* 10
RadioButton Enabled
109 303 127 409              ;; Rect (T,L,B,R)
Galactic                     ;; Message
```

```
* 11
CheckBox    Enabled
260 13 279 147              ;; Rect (T,L,B,R)
Right Ascension             ;; Message

* 12
CheckBox    Enabled
280 12 298 146              ;; Rect (T,L,B,R)
Declination                 ;; Message

* 13
CheckBox    Enabled
260 155 278 277             ;; Rect (T,L,B,R)
Distance                    ;; Message

* 14
CheckBox    Enabled
279 155 298 277             ;; Rect (T,L,B,R)
Proper Motion               ;; Message

* 15
StaticText  Disabled
83 8 99 102                 ;; Rect (T,L,B,R)
Constellations              ;; Message

* 16
IconItem    Disabled
184 302 216 334             ;; Rect (T,L,B,R)
2000                        ;; ID

* 17
IconItem    Disabled
184 346 216 378             ;; Rect (T,L,B,R)
2030                        ;; ID

* 18
IconItem    Disabled
184 390 216 422             ;; Rect (T,L,B,R)
2020                        ;; ID

* 19
StaticText  Disabled
165 304 181 332             ;; Rect (T,L,B,R)
Red                         ;; Message
```

```
* 20
StaticText   Disabled
165 343 181 383              ;; Rect  (T,L,B,R)
Green                        ;; Message

* 21
StaticText   Disabled
165 390 181 422              ;; Rect  (T,L,B,R)
Blue                         ;; Message

* 22
StaticText   Disabled
142 315 157 413              ;; Rect  (T,L,B,R)
Spectral Filter              ;; Message

* 23
UserItem     Disabled
132 288 137 431              ;; Rect  (T,L,B,R)

* 24
UserItem     Disabled
226 287 231 430              ;; Rect  (T,L,B,R)

Type MENU
Planets,128
Planets
Mercury
Venus
Earth
Mars
(Ceres)
Jupiter
Saturn
Uranus
Neptune
Pluto


Type STR#
Constellations,128
87                           ;; Number of strings
Andromeda
Antlia
Apus
Aquarius
```

```
Aquila
Ara
Aries
Auriga
Bootes
Caelum
Camelopardus
Cancer
Canes Venatici
Canis Major
Canis Minor
Capricornus
Carina
Cassiopeia
Centaurus
Cephus
Cetus
Chamaeleon
Circinus
Columba
Coma Berenices
Corona Australis
Corona Borealis
Corvus
Crater
Crux
Cygnus
Delphinus
Dorado
Draco
Equuleus
Eridanus
Fornax
Gemini
Grus
Hercules
Horologium
Hydra
Hydrus
Indus
Lacerta
Leo
Leo Minor
Lepus
Libra
```

Lupus
Lynx
Mensa
Microscopium
Monoceros
Musca
Norma
Octans
Ophiuchus
Orion
Pavo
Pegasus
Perseus
Phoenix
Pictor
Pisces
Piscis Austrinus
Puppis
Pyxis
Reticulum
Sagitta
Sagittarius
Scorpius
Sculptor
Scutum
Serpens
Sextans
Taurus
Telescopium
Triangulum
Triangulum Australe
Tucana
Ursa Major
Ursa Minor
Vela
Virgo
Volans
Vulpecula

* These ICONs can be replaced with cicn's for color machines.

A Comprehensive Example

```
Type ICON=GNRL
,2000
00000000  00000000  03FFC000  0244C000  0311C000  0244C000  0311C000  0244C000

0311C000  0244C000  0311C000  0244C000  03FFC000  03002000  03801000  07C00800

0BFFFC00  17E00400  2BFFFE00  17F00200  2BFFFE00  17F00200  2BFFFE00  17F00200

2BFFFE00  17F00200  2BFFFE00  17F00200  2BFFFE00  15E00400  0AFFFC00  00000000


Type ICON=GNRL
,2001
00000000  00000000  03FFC000  03002000  07801000  0BC00800  17FFFC00  2BE00400

17FFFE00  2BF00200  17FFFE00  2BF00200  17FFFE00  2BF00200  17FFFE00  2BF00200

17FFFE00  2BF00200  17FFFE00  2AE00400  057FFC00  0244C000  0311C000  0244C000

0311C000  0244C000  0311C000  03FFC000  03FFC000  00000000  00000000  00000000


Type ICON=GNRL
,2020
00000000  00000000  03FFC000  0244C000  0311C000  0244C000  0311C000  0244C000

0311C000  0244C000  0311C000  0244C000  03FFC000  03002000  03801000  07C00800

0BFFFC00  17E00400  2BFFFE00  17F00200  2BFFFE00  17F00200  2BFFFE00  17F00200

2BFFFE00  17F00200  2BFFFE00  17F00200  2BFFFE00  15E00400  0AFFFC00  00000000


Type ICON=GNRL
,2021
00000000  00000000  03FFC000  03002000  07801000  0BC00800  17FFFC00  2BE00400

17FFFE00  2BF00200  17FFFE00  2BF00200  17FFFE00  2BF00200  17FFFE00  2BF00200

17FFFE00  2BF00200  17FFFE00  2AE00400  057FFC00  0244C000  0311C000  0244C000

0311C000  0244C000  0311C000  03FFC000  03FFC000  00000000  00000000  00000000
```

```
Type ICON=GNRL
,2030
00000000 00000000 03FFC000 0244C000 0311C000 0244C000 0311C000 0244C000

0311C000 0244C000 0311C000 0244C000 03FFC000 03002000 03801000 07C00800

0BFFFC00 17E00400 2BFFFE00 17F00200 2BFFFE00 17F00200 2BFFFE00 17F00200

2BFFFE00 17F00200 2BFFFE00 17F00200 2BFFFE00 15E00400 0AFFFC00 00000000


Type ICON=GNRL
,2031
00000000 00000000 03FFC000 03002000 07801000 0BC00800 17FFFC00 2BE00400

17FFFE00 2BF00200 17FFFE00 2BF00200 17FFFE00 2BF00200 17FFFE00 2BF00200

17FFFE00 2BF00200 17FFFE00 2AE00400 057FFC00 0244C000 0311C000 0244C000

0311C000 0244C000 0311C000 03FFC000 03FFC000 00000000 00000000 00000000
```

Appendix A
Glossary

ampersand &   Character in C that denotes a var and must precede it in the code.

active window   The window that is in front of all other windows on the desktop.

argument   Roughly equivalent to an operand; defines the scope of an activity.

bit map   A set of bits representing a corresponding set of items. In QuickDraw, a bit map is a pointer to a bit image, its row width, and its boundary rectangle.

brackets [ ]   Used for subscripting an array.

branch   Instruction telling the Mac to jump to another place in the program instead of following the normal sequence by executing the next instruction.

call   Instruction that passes control to a different part of the program or subroutine. A call executes other programs or parts of programs as though they were written in at the point where the call occurs.

compiler   Utility that translates the source code from a high-level programming language, C, into the object code used in running the machine. See **linker**.

curly braces { }	Also called braces, used in C to enclose executable statements.
declaration	Statement of values and data types having a global influence on a program.
dialog	"Conversation" between you and the Mac when the Mac asks for, and receives, information it needs to obey your instructions.
dialog box	Window through which you interface with the Mac in a dialog.
event loop	A loop that repeatedly calls the Toolbox Event Manager to get events and act upon them.
executable statement	Statement that will perform a machine language instruction.
function	Equivalent to a subroutine or function in FORTRAN or a procedure in Pascal, a function is a basic operational entity of any C program. A function encapsulates a series of computations in a black box, which you can then use without worrying about what is inside. With properly designed functions, you can ignore how a job is done and concentrate on what is done.
handle	Pointer to a master pointer.
heap	Area of memory where space is allocated and released on demand via the Memory Manager.
highlight	To display an object on a screen in a uniquely distinctive way.
initialize	To set each variable to its starting value in a program. Essential first step in every program.
integer	Whole number; that is, containing no fractions or decimal points.
invert	To highlight by changing white pixels to black pixels and vice versa, a foreground color to a background color and vice versa, or a foreground color to a highlight color.

linker	Utility that links individual object-coded modules produced by a compiler into a complete machine language program ready for execution.
lock	To temporarily prevent a movable block of memory from being moved during a heap operation.
long	Variable with a data length of 4 bytes.
master pointer	Pointer to a pointer. Master pointers enable the Memory Manager to keep track of memory locations that it has relocated.
object code	Machine language produced by compilation of the source code.
operand	In an instruction, the part that is acted on; for instance, "hair cut" in "Get your hair cut."
operator	In an instruction, the part that acts; for instance, "Get" in "Get your hair cut."
parameter	Item of information needed to control a program.
parenthesis ( )	In C, a pair of parentheses encloses a variable in a statement. If no variable is to be passed in, nothing goes between the parentheses, but they are still required by C syntax.
pattern	An eight-by-eight bit image that is used to repeat a design or tone, such as a plaid or a value of gray.
picture	The format of a picture is defined by QuickDraw as a record of the series of operations necessary to regenerate the image on the screen.
pixel	Short for picture element, it is a dot on a display screen.
pointer	Memory address containing a data item used in running a program.
ResEdit	Popular resource editor provided free of charge by Apple and commonly available through bulletin boards.

Resource	Data unit representing a dialog box, menu, alert, icon or other element of the Apple graphical interface.
returned value	A value that is returned by a function.
Rez	Resource editor more recent than ResEdit, incorporating certain enhancements, but available only within the Macintosh Programmer's Workshop environment.
RMaker	Apple program that creates resources.
short	Variable with the default length of 2 bytes in C.
source code	Statements in a programming language.
structure	Logical arrangement of a program.
system font	The font (Chicago) that the system uses in menus, dialog boxes, window title bars, and other desktop interfaces.
system font size	The size of text drawn in the system font (Chicago), normally 12 points.
trap	A call to the Macintosh Toolbox or Operating System.
var	Var is Pascal terminology for a variable to which you have to pass a pointer.
variable	Value that changes with program dynamics and is written to or read from memory as required.
void function	Indicates to the Mac that there is no value to return for a particular function.

Appendix B
Modules Developed in This Book

The functions in this appendix appear in routines in the book. However, they are not reviewed or described in the text. We include them here so that you can keyboard them for inclusion in your own programs.

▶ FitString.c

FitString.c determines whether the string of the checkmarked menu item will fit in the rectangle in a dialog box. If it is too long, the routine automatically shortens it and adds a elipsis to indicate that there is more to the item.

```
/****************************************************************/
void            FitString(Str255 theString, short spaceForString)
/****************************************************************/
{
  short             strPixels;
  short             strLenth;

  if (spaceForString <= 0)                   /* Space for string? */
  {
    spaceForString = 0;                                  /* No. */
    theString[0] = '\0';              /* Make string an empty */
  }
  strPixels = StringWidth(theString);
  if (strPixels > spaceForString)
  {
```

309

```
      strLenth = theString[0];
      spaceForString = spaceForString - CharWidth('…');
      if (spaceForString <= 0)
      {
        spaceForString = 0;
        theString[0] = '\0';
      }
      else
      {
        for (strLenth = theString[0];
              strLenth && strPixels >= spaceForString; —strLenth)
        {
          strPixels = strPixels - CharWidth(theString[strLenth]);
        }
        strLenth = strLenth + 1;
        theString[strLenth] = '…';
        theString[0] = (unsigned char)strLenth;
      }
    }
  }
}
```

▶ GetStrNum.c

GetStrNum.c gets a particular string out of a STR# resource.

```
/******************************************************************/
void GetStrNum(short theID,short theStringNum,Str255 theString)
/******************************************************************/
{
  typedef   struct
  {
    short           numStrings;
    char            theStrings[];
  } StrList, *StrListPtr, **StrListHandle;
  StrListHandle     TheHandle;
  short             theIndex;
  short             i, j;
  short             numStrings;
  short             stringLen;
  theHandle = (StrListHandle)GetResource("STR#", theID);
  theIndex = 1;
  for (i = 1; i <= (*theHandle)->numStrings; i++)
  {
    stringLen = theStrings[theIndex];
    if (i == theStringNum)
```

```
      {
        if (stringLen > 0)
        {
          for (j = 1; j <= stringLen; j++)
          {
             theString[j] = theStrings[theIndex];
             theIndex = theIndex + 1;
          }
        }
        break;
      }
      else
      {
        theIndex = theindex + stringLen + 1;
        continue;
      }
    }
  }
}
```

▶ OpenResources.c

OpenResources.c is a routine a programmer can use during the development stage of an application to separate code resources from all other resources.

```
/****************************************************************/
void OpenResources(Str255 file)
/****************************************************************/
{
  short   fRefNum;

  fRefNum = OpenResFile(file);
  if (fRefNum < 0)
  {
    SysBeep(20);
    Stop;
  }
}
```

Bibliography

1. Allen, Daniel K. *On Macintosh Programming: Advanced Techniques.* Reading, MA: Addison-Wesley, 1990.
2. Beekman, George and Michael Johnson. *Oh! Macintosh Pascal.* New York, NY: W. W. Norton and Company, 1986.
3. Chernicoff, Stephen. *Macintosh Revealed, Volume I—Unlocking The Toolbox.* Hasbrouck Heights, NJ: Hayden, 1985.
4. Chernicoff, Stephen. *Macintosh Revealed, Volume II—Programming with the Toolbox.* Hasbrouck Heights, NJ: Hayden, 1985.
5. Chernicoff, Stephen. *Macintosh Revealed, Volume III—Mastering the Toolbox.* Indianapolis, IN: Hayden, 1989.
6. Chernicoff, Stephen. *Macintosh Revealed, Volume IV—Expanding the Toolbox.* Carmel, IN: Hayden, 1990.
7. Coan, James S. and Louisa Coan. *Basic Microsoft Basic for the Macintosh.* Hasbrouck Heights, NJ: Hayden, 1985.
8. Crandall, Richard E. and Marianne M. Colgrove. *Scientific Programming with Macintosh Pascal.* New York, NY: John Wiley & Sons, 1986.
9. DeFuria, Steve and Joe Scacciaferro. *MIDI Programming for the Macintosh.* Redwood City, CA: M & T Books, 1988.
10. Hogan, Thom. *The Programmer's Apple Mac Sourcebook.* Redmond, WA: Microsoft Press, 1989.
11. *Human Interface Guidelines: The Apple Desktop Interface.* Reading, MA: Addison-Wesley, 1987.

12. Huxham, Fred A., David Burnard and Jim Takatsuka. *Using the Macintosh Toolbox with C (Second Edition)*. San Francisco, CA: Sybex, 1989.
13. *Inside Macintosh,* volumes 1, 2, and 3. Apple Technical Series. Reading, MA: Addison-Wesley, 1985.
14. *Inside Macintosh,* volume 4. Apple Technical Series. Reading, MA: Addison-Wesley, 1986.
15. *Inside Macintosh,* volume 5. Apple Technical Series. Reading, MA: Addison-Wesley, 1988.
16. *Inside Macintosh X-Ref.* Apple Technical Series. Reading, MA: Addison-Wesley, 1988.
17. Kernighan, Brian W. and Dennis M. Ritchie. *The C Programming Language*. Englewood Cliffs, NJ: Prentice-Hall, Inc., 1978.
18. Knaster, Scott. *How to Write Macintosh Software*. Indianapolis, IN: Hayden Books, 1986.
19. Knaster, Scott. *Macintosh Programming Secrets*. Reading, MA: Addison-Wesley, 1988.
20. Krantz, Donald and James Stanley. *68000 Assembly Language*. Reading, MA: Addison-Wesley, 1986.
21. Lewis, Greg A. *One Flew Over the Quickdraw's Nest*. Montreal, Que.: Valuable Information Press, 1985.
22. *MC68020, 32-Bit Microprocessor User's Manual, Second Edition*. Englewood Cliffs, NJ: Prentice-Hall,1985.
23. *M68000, 8-/16-/32-Bit Microprocessor Programmer's Reference Manual, Fifth Edition*. Englewood Cliffs, NJ: Prentice-Hall,1986.
24. Mark, Dave and Cartwright Reed. *Macintosh C Programming Primer,* volume I. Reading, MA: Addison-Wesley, 1989.
25. Mark, Dave. *Macintosh C Programming Primer,* volume II. Reading, MA: Addison-Wesley, 1990.
26. Mark, Dave and Cartwright Reed. *Macintosh Pascal Programming Primer,* volume I. Reading, MA: Addison-Wesley, 1991.
27. Mathews, Keith. *Assembly Language Primer for the Macintosh*. New York, NY: The Waite Group, 1985.
28. Mathews, Keith and Jay Friedland. *Encyclopedia MAC® ROM*. New York, NY: Brady, 1988.
29. Mednieks, Zigurd R. and Terry M. Schilke. *C Programming Techniques for the Macintosh*. Indianapolis, IN: Howard W. Sams, 1987.

30. Morgan, Christopher L. *Hidden Powers of the Macintosh.* New York, NY: The Waite Group, 1985.
31. Peatroy, David B. and DATATECH Publications. *Mastering the Macintosh Toolbox.* Berkeley, CA: Osborne McGraw-Hill, 1986.
32. *Programmers Introduction to the Macintosh Family.* Apple Technical Series. Reading, MA: Addison-Wesley, 1988.
33. *ResEdit Reference.* Reading, MA: Addison-Wesley, 1990. (An Apple® development document.)
34. Rosenzweig, Edwin and Harland Harrison. *Programming the 68000 — Macintosh Assembly Language.* Hasbrouck Heights, NJ: Hayden, 1986.
35. Shafer, Dan. *Games and Utilities for the Macintosh.* New York, NY: The Waite Group, 1985.
36. Simonoff, Jonathan D. *Introduction to Macintosh Pascal.* Hasbrouck Heights, NJ: Hayden, 1985.
37. Smith, David E., ed. *The Best of MacTutor—The Macintosh Programming Journal,* volume I. Anaheim, CA: MacTutor, 1986.
38. Smith, David E., ed. *The Complete MacTutor—The Macintosh Programming Journal,* volume II. Anaheim, CA: MacTutor, 1987.
39. Smith, David E., ed. *The Essential MacTutor—The Macintosh Programming Journal,* volume III. Anaheim, CA: MacTutor, 1988.
40. Smith, David E., ed. *The Definitive MacTutor—The Macintosh Programming Journal,* volume IV. Anaheim, CA: MacTutor, 1989.
41. Smith, David E. and Kirk Chase, eds. *The Best of MacTutor—The Macintosh Programming Journal,* volume V. Anaheim, CA: MacTutor, 1990.
42. Smith, David E. and Kirk Chase, eds. *The Best of MacTutor—The Macintosh Programming Journal,* volume VI. Anaheim, CA: MacTutor, 1991.
43. *Technical Introduction to the Macintosh Family.* Apple Technical Series. Reading, MA: Addison-Wesley, 1987.
44. *THINK C User's Manual.* Cupertino, CA: Symantec, 1989.
45. Traister, Robert J. *Mastering C Pointers.* San Diego, CA: Academic Press, 1990.
46. Twitty, William B. *The Magic of Macintosh, Programming Graphics and Sound.* Glenview, IL: Scott, Foresman and Company, 1986.
47. Twitty, William B. *Programming the Macintosh, an Advanced Guide.* Glenview, IL: Scott, Foresman and Company, 1986.

48. West, Joel. *Programming with Macintosh Programmer's Workshop*. Ont.: Canada: Bantam Books, 1988.
49. Weston, Dan. *The Complete Book of Macintosh Assembly Language Programming*, Glenview, IL: Scott, Foresman and Company, 1986.
50. Weston, Dan. *The Complete Book of Macintosh Assembly Language Programming,* volume 2. Glenview, IL: Scott, Foresman and Company, 1987.
51. Wilson, David A. *Programming the Macintosh II*. Palo Alto, CA: Personal Concepts, 1987.
52. Wilson, David A. *Macintosh Programming—An Introduction*. Palo Alto, CA: Personal Concepts, 1988.
53. Wilson, David A., Larry S. Rosenstein and Dan Shafer. *Programming with MacApp*. Addison-Wesley, 1990.

Index

; (semicolon), 2, 8, 10, 16, 93, 98
! (exclamation point), 98
"" (quotation marks), 83
+ (plus sign), 9
* (asterisk), 9, 93
* (star), 16, 93
\ (backward slash), 93
/ (forward slash), 16, 93
"#define" statements, 11
& (ampersand), 17, 53, 259, 305
&cSize variable, 259
&DataBounds variable, 259
&ItemRect variable, 259

A

Abort command, 65
AboutDialog.c routine, 67-70, 73
AboutExample.c routine, 70-71
AboutExample.R routine, 72-73
ActiveStatic.c routine, 163-64, 165, 166
AddCell.c routine, 262-63
AddResMenu routine, 23, 34
AddResourceMenu routine, 33
AlertExample.c routine, 83-84, 85
AlertExample.R routine, 84, 85-86
Alerts, 77-86

All Caps command, 65
ALRT resource, 94
Apple Desktop Interface, 101, 129
Argument, definition of, 305
Arithmetic Operators Rule, 9
Array, keymap, 30
Arrow cursor, 37, 38, 40, 41
ASCII, 87, 89, 173, 176, 181, 184-85, 188, 196, 221
    and scrolling lists, 270
    strings, of numbers, 213-15
Auto-key events, 65

B

BitClr routine, 285
Bit map, definition of, 305
BitTst routine, 29
Black-and-white
    cursors, 37-38, 39, 40, 41
    icons, 132, 135
    menus, 285
    pictures, 150
BNDL resource, 94
Booleans, 29
Brace Rule I (separate lines), 6-7
Brace Rule 2 (if and else), 7-8
Brackets, definition of, 305

317

Branch, definition of, 305
Builders, 93
Button(s), 101-8
    control, use of icons as, 130-36
    default, 238, 196
    and dialog records, 169
    radio, 119-28, 169, 173, 296
    real-world, 129
ButtonExample.c routine, 106-7
ButtonExample.R routine, 107-8

C

CalcMenuSize call, 285
Call, definition of, 305
Capitalization, 2, 10-11, 16, 97, 220-24
CapsLockIsDown.c routine, 28, 30-31
Case statements, 5-6, 65
CautionAlert.c routine, 78, 79-80
CenterDialog function, 2, 293
CenterDialog.c routine, 52-54, 55
CenterWindow.c routine, 54-56
Change Case command, 65, 220
CharCodeMask variable, 65
Check boxes, 109-17, 169, 296
CheckBoxExample.c routine, 113-15
CheckBoxExample.R routine, 115-16
Chooser, 34
Clipboard, 17, 215, 217-19, 228
CNTL resource, 94
Color, 11, 50
    cursors, 37-38, 39, 40-41, 48
    default, 104-5
    icons, 132, 133, 135
    and menus, 275, 279, 280, 285, 286
    pictures, 150
    programs, and memory consumption, 18-19
    QuickDraw, 40
CommandISDown.c routine, 28, 29-30, 32
Command key, 28, 29, 65, 261
Command-P, 49
Commas Rule, 9
Comments, 93
Compiler, 92, 208, 251, 305
Confirmation.c routine, 81-83
Constants, 285
ControlIsDown.c routine, 28, 31
Control Panel, 34
Copying, 65, 66-67, 216, 217
CopyrightDialog.c routine, 73-76
Copyright routine, 73-76
CountMItems routine, 26
C programming, 3, 208
    and edit text fields, 176, 184
    and enumeration-statements, 204
    and floating-point numbers, 191
    global declarations in, 130
    and macros, 284
    and menus, 286
    and Rez, 92
    and RMaker, 93
    standards, 1, 5-11
    and TECopy.c, 216
Crosshairs cursor, 37
Curly braces, 5, 306
CursorExample.c routine, 41-43
CursorExample.R routine, 43-47
Cursors, 1, 37-47
    arrow, 37, 38, 40, 41
    black-and-white, 37-38, 39, 40, 41
    color, 37-38, 39, 40-41, 48
    crosshairs, 37

Index   319

ID numbers of, 38, 39, 40, 41
plus sign, 37
positioning of, and Edit text fields, 172-73
wristwatch, 37-38
Cutting, 65, 216

D

DablMenuItems.c routine, 24-25
DAllMenuItems.c routine, 25-26, 27
Declarations
    definition of, 306
    global, 130
Desk accessories, 34
Device driver event, 65
Dialog(s), 1, 49-77
    creation of, 51-52
    Creator, 93
    default, font, 66-67
    definition of, 306
    Event routine, 64
    modal, 57-65. *See also* Alerts
    Peek, 67
    position, 52-54
    Print, 206
    records, 12, 50-51, 169
    Select routine, 63, 64, 65
    and resources, 90. *See also* Dialog box(es); Dialog Manager
Dialog box(es), 89, 296-97
    and buttons, 102-5
    and check boxes, 109
    definition of, 306
    and edit text fields, 169. *See also* Edit text fields
    and resources, 91-92
Dialog Manager, 50, 103, 242
    and initialization, 17-18
    and modal dialogs, 57
    routines, 280
Digit variable, 205

Disk-inserted events, 65
DisposCursor routine, 41
DisposHandle routine, 136, 140, 143
DispToggleIcon.c routine, 140, 293
DITL resource, 72, 86, 94, 149, 241, 252
DLOG resource, 88, 91-94, 98-99, 236, 240, 252
DoAppleMenu.c routine, 23-24
DoButtonIcon.c routine, 133-36
DoPopUp.c routine, 280-86, 293
DoScrollList.c routine, 260-61
DoToggleIcon.c routine, 138-40, 142, 143, 293
DoubleFrame.c routine, 247
Double precision number, 190
DrawControls routine, 262
DrawDottedLine.c routine, 231-33, 234, 293
DrawIt variable, 259
DrawLine.c routine, 233-34, 244
DrawMBar.c routine, 21, 33-34
DrawMenuBar routine, 23, 32
DrawPict.c routine, 150-51, 152-54
DrawPop.c routine, 276-80
DrawPopUp.c routine, 284, 285, 289, 293
DrawScollList.c routine, 257-59, 267, 293
DrawString routine, 67
DRVR resource, 23
DRVR string, 34
DStorage variable, 51
Dummy variable, 217

E

EablMenuItem.c routine, 25
EAllMenuItems.c routine, 26-27
EditOpen variable, 51
Editors, 92, 93

EditText, 58-59
EditTextExample.c routine, 224-26
EditTextExample.c routine, 226-28
Edit text fields, 169-229
    active, 170-73
    and displaying strings, 213-15
    and floating-point numbers, 190-206
    get and put routines for, 206-13
    and text edit routines, 215-20
Errors, 12, 16, 237
Event loop, definition of, 306
Event Manager, 70
Event variable, 70
EveryEvent variable, 19
Excel, 256
Executable statement, definition of, 306
Exponent, 190
ExponentBuffer variable, 206

F

FetchCursor.c routine, 38-41
FieldLength variable, 213
File extensions, 83, 89, 105, 113, 151, 165, 270
File Manager, 81
File menu, 255, 256
Finder, 17, 89, 92
Find function, 129
FindWindow routine, 64
FitString.c routine, 279, 309-10
FlushEvents, 19
Font
    Chicago, 28, 66, 67
    Courier, 3, 89
    default dialog, 66-67
    Helvetica, 90
    Manager, 17
    and menus, 286
    and monochrome monitors, 50
    monospace, 3
    size, definition of, 308
    system, 17, 308
Forks, 87, 88
FORTRAN, 93, 190
FoundDigit variable, 177
FoundInteger variable, 177
FoundNumber variable, 197, 198
FractionLength variable, 204
FrameRoundRect routine, 105
FREF resource, 94
FrmDefItem.c routine, 3, 101, 102-5, 106, 244
FrmDefItem function, 3, 293
Function(s)
    CenterDialog, 2, 293
    definition of, 306, 308
    Find, 129
    FrmDefItem, 3, 293
    names of, and capital letters, 2
    PutScrap, 217
    Spelling, 163

G

GetActiveEditText.c routine, 170-71, 172
GetButtonIcon. c routine, 130-33
GetCell.c routine, 264-65
GetCheckBox.c routine, 111-12, 113
GetCIcon routine, 132
GetCtlValue routine, 112
GetCursor routine, 41
GetDefItem call, 69
GetDItem routine, 64, 112, 124, 133, 165, 232, 280
Get-Do-Dispose sequence, 136
GetEditFloat.c routine, 211-12

Index

GetEditLong.c routine, 210, 213
GetEditShort.c routine, 111, 207-8, 210, 213
GetEditString.c routine, 213-14
Get Information dialog box, 91
GetItem routine, 279
GetIText routine, 164, 208
GetKeys routine, 29
GetListString.c routine, 265-66, 293
GetMenu routine, 22, 24, 25
GetMouse routine, 260
GetNewDialog routine, 51
GetNExtEvent, 64
GetRadioButton.c routine, 120-21, 122
GetResource routine, 53, 151
GetStringList.c routine, 267-70, 293
GetStrNum.c routine, 154, 310-11
GetToggleIcon.c routine, 137-38, 143, 293
Global
    code, and toggle icon routines, 136-37
    declarations, 130
    locations, 91
    variables, 12, 17, 216-17, 285, 286
GNRL resource, 72, 94
GrafPort, 67, 104-5, 112-13, 170, 232, 245, 262

H

Handles, definition of, 306
HasColor variable, 40
HasGrow variable, 259
Heap, definition of, 306
Highlight, definition of, 306
HiliteMode variable, 285
Human Interface Guidelines, 1, 101, 123, 171, 296

I

Icon(s), 81, 85, 129-47
    Builder, 93
    Designer, 93
    resource, 88
    toggle, 136-43, 296
    use of, as control buttons, 130-36
IconBut variable, 130
IconExample.c routine, 143-47
IconExample.R routine, 145-47
IconOff.c routine, 141-42, 143
IconOn.c routine, 142-43
IconTog variable, 137
Ictb resources, 50
ID numbers, 88, 91-92, 97-98, 149, 150-51, 240-41, 255
    for alerts, 79, 82, 86
    for cursors, 38, 39, 40, 41
    for dialogs, 51, 72, 73, 252
    and drawing rectangles, 244
    and edit text fields, 207
    and menus, 22, 23, 24, 26, 27, 33
    and pictures, 149, 154
    and pop-up menus, 279
    procedure (ProcID), 91
    for radio buttons, 120, 121
    and string lists, 269
IdspButtonIcon.c routine, 136
IGoof, 173, 175, 176, 177, 184, 196-98, 209
ImageWriter, 49
InactiveStatic.c routine, 164-65, 166
Inch variable, 196, 197, 198, 208
Include statements, 3
INFO resource, 150
InitCursor routine, 40, 41
Initialization, 15-19, 77, 217, 296
    definition of, 306
    and pop-up menus, 279

and scrolling lists, 256, 257-59
InitMenu.c routine, 21, 22-23
InitToolBox routine, 2-3, 15-19, 28, 70, 216, 293
InputFloat.c routine, 191, 192-96
InputHexLong.c routine, 181-83
InputHexShort.c routine, 179-81, 183
InputLong c. routine, 178-79
InputShort.c routine, 173, 174-77
InsertMenu routine, 22, 285
Inside Macintosh, 174, 255
Integers
    definition of, 306
    input and output regimes for, 173-206
IntegerLength variable, 205
Invert, definition of, 306
IsDialogEvent routine, 63
ItemHandle variable, 208
ItemHit variable, 64, 69, 172

K

Keyboard, testing of, 28-32, 36
Kit and Caboodle.c routine, 293-97
Kit and Caboodle.R routine, 297-304

L

LAddRow routine, 257, 269
LDoDraw routine, 257, 259
LDraw routine, 257, 264
LineExample.c routine, 235-38, 249
LineExample.R routine, 236, 237, 238-42
Lines, 231-42
Linker, definition of, 307
List Manager, 255-57, 259, 262, 264, 267, 269, 273
LNew routine, 257, 259

Lock, definition of, 307
Long, definition of, 307
LongNumber variable, 187
Lowercase, 65, 220-21
LSetCell routine, 257, 264
LSetSelect routine, 267
LUpDate routine, 257, 262

M

Macintosh Programmer's Workshop (MPW), 92
Macros, 11-12, 284
MaintainCursor.c routine, 64
Manager(s)
    Dialog, 17-18, 50, 57, 103, 242, 280
    Event, 70
    File, 81
    Font, 17
    List, 255-57, 259, 262, 264, 267, 269, 273
    Menu, 17, 21, 23, 32, 132, 276, 279, 285
    Resource, 38, 89
    Text Edit, 38, 89
    Window, 17, 37, 241
Mantissa variable, 204-5
Map coordinates, 243
MarkMenuItem.c routine, 27-28
Master pointers, 18-19
MBAR resource, 21, 32-34
Memory
    and initialization, 18, 19
    low-, global variables, 12, 216
    menu list area of, 33
    and resources, 88, 89
    as segmented, 18
    and system font, 17
    and Text edit routines, 215, 216
    type definitions stored in, 135

Index

Menu Manager, 21, 23, 32, 279, 285
    and initialization, 17
    resources, 276
    routines, 132
MenuExample.c, 34-35
MenuExample.R, 35-36
MENU resource, 22, 94
Menus, 1, 3, 21-36, 73, 255-56
    building of, 21-23, 93
    and fonts, 17
    items, routines involving, 24-28
    pop-up, 21, 275-92, 296
    testing of, 28-32. *See also* Menu Manager
Microsoft Word, 85, 87, 89, 109, 119, 240, 256
ModalDialog routine, 63, 149, 150, 242, 260
Modifier flag, 28
Modifier variable, 260
Monochrome monitors, 39, 48, 50
MoreMasters() statements, 18-19
Mouse, 19, 28, 70, 260
    -down events, in icons, 130, 133-35, 150, 275, 280-86, 292
    -up events, 64, 138
    and windows, 64
MoveWindow routine, 58
MultiFinder, 17
MyModalDialog.c routine, 32, 49, 59-65, 83, 154, 294, 297

N

Network events, 65
New Dialog dialog box, 91
New Handle routine, 132
NeXT computer, 101
NextTemporary variable, 184-85, 186
NIL macro, 11, 12

Notation, engineering, 191, 199
    fixed, 191, 199
    octal, 228
    standard, 190, 204
    variable, 213
NoteAlert.c routine, 78-79, 80, 81
Numbers
    floating-point, 190-206
    hexadecimal, 179-83, 187-89. *See also* ID numbers

O

OffsetRect routine, 54
Open command, 255, 256
OpenDialog.c routine, 51-52, 294
Open File command, 255
OpenResources.c routine, 311
Operand, definition of, 307
Operator, definition of, 307
OptionIsDown.c routine, 28, 31-32
Outch string, 204, 205-6
OutputFloat.c routine, 12, 199-206, 213
OutputHexLong.c routine, 188-89
OutputHexShort.c routine, 187-88
OutputLong.c routine, 186-87
OutputShort.c routine, 173, 183-85

P

PACK resource, 255
PaintRect routine, 165
Parameter, definition of, 307
Parentheses, 8-9, 307
Pascal, 17, 29, 53, 93, 98. *See also* Pascal strings
Pascal strings, 172, 174, 175, 178, 185, 269
    and scrolling lists, 262, 264, 270
Paste command, 65

PatBic variable, 165
Pattern, definition of, 307
PenSize call, 234
PICT
    data type, 217
    files, 149
    handles, 151
    resource, 72, 149-51, 161
PictExample.c routine, 151-54
PictExample.R routine, 154-60
Pictures, 149-61, 307
Pixels, 91, 104, 105, 150
    definition of, 307
    and lines, 231, 233, 237, 240, 242
    and rectangles, 243, 245, 249
    and scrolling lists, 258, 262
PlainFrame.c routine, 244-45, 246
PlotCIcon routine, 133
PlotIcon routine, 133
Plus sign cursor, 37
Pointers, 41, 132
    definition of, 307
    and dialogs, 53, 213-14
    and lines, 232-33
    master, 18-19, 307
    and string lists, 269
    window, 57
PopUpExample.c routine, 289-90
PopUpExample.R routine, 290-92
PopUpMenuSelect call, 285
Preferences Item, 109
Print dialog, 173, 206
Printing, 49-50
Private scrap, 215
PROC resource, 94
PushRadioButton.c routine, 123-24, 125, 128, 294
PutCheckBox.c routine, 109-11, 113
PutEditFloat.c routine, 212-13
PutEditLong.c routine, 210-11
PutEditShort.c routine, 208-9, 211, 212, 213
PutEditString.c routine, 214-15
PutRadioButton.c routine, 121-22
PutScrap function, 217

Q

QuickDraw, 104, 149
    color, 40
    and dialog boxes, 52
    Draw Picture routine, 151
    and edit text fields, 171
    and lines, 233, 234
    and the menu bar, 33
    and rectangles, 243
    routines, 16-17, 67

R

RadioButtonExample.c routine, 125-26
RadioButtonExample.R routine, 126-27
RealNumber variable, 196, 198
Rectangles, 243-53, 256, 258, 279
RectExample.c routine, 249-51
RectExample.R routine, 251-53
REdit, 93
RefCon, 92
ResEdit, 86, 93
    definition of, 307
    drawing sequence in, 150
    and lines, 240
    and resources, 88, 89, 91, 97
    and scrolling lists, 258
Resource(s), 1, 87-99
    definition of, 87, 308
    editors, 92
    Manager, 38, 89
    maps, 87-88. *See also* specific resources
Rez, 89, 92, 93, 308

RMaker, 3, 85-86, 89, 92, 98, 99
    definition of, 308
    and lines, 240
    and menus, 289
    program syntax, 93-98
    and resources, 108
RoundedDigit variable, 205
Routines
    and default buttons, 101-5
    five is-down, 28-32. *See also* specific routines
RSED resource, 98

S

Save As command, 81
Save command, 255, 256
Scrapbook, 17
ScreenRect variable, 2, 53
ScrollHoriz variable, 259
ScrollingListExample.c routine, 270-71
ScrollingListExample.R routine, 272-73
Scrolling lists, 91, 255-74, 275, 296
ScrollVert variable, 259
Select All command, 65
SelectCell.c routine, 266-67
SetActiveEditText.c routine, 171-73
SetCell.c routine, 263-64, 269
SetCtlValue routine, 64, 122, 124
SetCursor routine, 41
SetDFont.c routine, 66-67
SetItemMark routine, 28
SetIText routine, 164
ShadowFrame.c routine, 248-49, 279, 294
ShiftIsDown.c routine, 28, 32
Short, definition of, 308
ShortNumber variable, 175, 176, 177, 181, 185, 187
Short variable, 175
ShowWindow routine, 52

Single precision number, 190
Slop, 57, 58
Spelling function, 163
StackWindow.c routine, 56-58
Standard float number, 190
Statements
    case, 5-6, 65
    enumeration-statements, 204
    executable, 306
    include, 3
    MoreMasters(), 18-19
    void, 16
Static text, 163-68, 169
StaticTextExample.c routine, 166-67
StaticTextExample.R routine, 167-68
StopAlert.c routine, 78, 80-81
STR# resource, 94, 269, 310
String(s)
    ASCII, 213-15
    display of, 213-15
    DRVR, 34
    and edit text fields, 213-15
    inch, 208-9
    lists, 256, 267-73
    outch, 204, 205-6. *See also* Pascal strings
Structure, definition of, 308
SysEnvirons, 40, 104, 132
System file, 255

T

TECapitalize.c routine, 222-23
TEChgCase.c routine, 223-24
TECopy.c routine, 216-18
TECut.c routine, 218
TEGetText routine, 221
TEInit routine, 216, 219
TeLower.c routine, 220-21, 223, 224
Template handles, 53-54

TemporaryInteger variable, 184-85, 186, 188
TempW variable, 58
TEPaste.c routine, 218-19
TERecord routine, 50
TEScrap routine, 17, 215
TESelectAll.c routine, 219-20
TEUpper.c routine, 221-22
TEXT data type, 217
TextEdit, 67, 215, 216, 221
    Manager, 17
    record, limit, 220
    routines, 215-20
    scrap, and initialization, 17
Text fields, 169
TheDialog variable, 52, 67, 171, 172
TheHandle variable, 53
ThePattern variable, 233
ThePort variable, 17
TheRect variable, 54
TheString variable, 82, 269
ThickFrame.c routine, 246
THINK C, 1, 3, 11, 92, 256, 286
TickCount routine, 75
To box, 173
Toggle
    icons, 136-43, 296
    switches, 109, 112-13, 117, 136-43
ToggleCheckBox.c routine, 112-13
ToolboxSysEnvirons routine, 40
Trap
    definition of, 308
    dispatchers, 11
TRUE/FALSE status, 29, 64, 83, 260, 266

U
Undo command, 65
Update events, 65
Uppercase, 65, 220, 221-22

UpPopUp.c routine, 286-89, 294
UpScrollList.c routine, 257, 261-62, 294

V
Values, 12-13, 308
Value variable, 212, 213
Var, definition of, 308
Var variable, 175
Variables, 1, 17
    definition of, 308
    global, 12, 17, 216, 217, 285, 286. *See also* specific variables
Viruses, 90
"Void" statements, 16

W
WDEF virus, 90
Where variable, 260
WIND resource, 94
Window(s) 49-77
    active, definition of, 305
    Color Table resource ('wctb'), 37
    and lines, 241
    Manager, 17, 37, 241
    positioning, 54-56
    specification of, 91
    stacking, 56-58
    titles, 17
WindowKind variable, 171
WindowList, 57
Word Perfect, 89
Wristwatch cursor, 37, 38

X, Y, Z
Yes-or-no question, 81, 82

Extending the Macintosh® Toolbox Programming Menus, Windows, Dialogs, and More: The Disk!

The disk contains the 104 routines and examples in this book, plus additional routines, updates, enhancements, and debugs. The routines can be copied into and used immediately for the applications you are writing. If you would like a complete set of source codes, projects, and resources from *Extending the Macintosh Toolbox:*

1. Fill out the coupon. Print clearly.
2. Attach a check or money order for $35. If you want the disk C.O.D., add $5.50. Make the check out to **Extending the Toolbox**. Make sure that the check is in **U.S. dollars**, drawn on a U.S. or Canadian bank. If you would like the disk shipped outside the United States, please add $5.
3. Send the check (or money order) and the coupon to:

   Extending the Toolbox
   822 Hartz Way, Suite 392
   Danville, CA 94526

Here's my $35!
Send me Extending the Macintosh Toolbox Disk 1 right away! Mail the disk to:

Name _____

Company _____

Address _____

City _____ State _____ Zip _____

California residents, add 7% sales tax.
No credit cards, please.

Titles in the Macintosh Inside Out Series

▶ **Extending the Macintosh® Toolbox**
Programming Menus, Windows, Dialogs, and More
John C. May and Judy B. Whittle
A complete guide to programming the Macintosh interface.
352 pages, $24.95, paperback, order #57722

▶ **Programming QuickDraw™**
Includes Color QuickDraw and 32-Bit QuickDraw
David A. Surovell, Fred M. Hall, and Konstantin Othmer
The first in-depth reference to the Macintosh graphics system.
352 pages, $24.95, paperback, order #57019

▶ **Programming for System 7**
Gary Little and Tim Swihart
A complete programmer's handbook to the newest version of the Macintosh system software.
400 pages, $26.95, paperback, order #56770

▶ **Programming with AppleTalk®**
Michael Peirce
An accessible guide to creating applications that run with AppleTalk.
352 pages, $24.95, paperback, order #57780

▶ **The A/UX® 2.0 Handbook**
Jan L. Harrington
A complete and up-to-date introduction to UNIX on the Macintosh.
448 pages, $26.95, paperback, order #56784

▶ **System 7 Revealed**
Anthony Meadow
A first look inside the important new Macintosh system software from Apple.
368 pages, $22.95, paperback, order #55040

▶ **ResEdit™ Complete**
Peter Alley and Carolyn Strange
Contains the popular ResEdit software and complete information on how to use it.
576 pages, $29.95, book/disk, order #55075

▶ **The Complete Book of HyperTalk® 2**
Dan Shafer
Practical guide to HyperTalk 2.0 commands, operators, and functions.
480 pages, $24.95, paperback, order #57082

▶ **Programming the LaserWriter®**
David A. Holzgang
Now Macintosh programmers can unlock the full power of the LaserWriter.
480 pages, $24.95, paperback, order #57068

▶ **Debugging Macintosh® Software with MacsBug**
Includes MacsBug 6.2
Konstantin Othmer and Jim Straus
Everything a programmer needs to start debugging Macintosh software.
576 pages, $34.95, book/disk, order #57049

▶ **Developing Object-Oriented Software for the Macintosh®**
  Analysis, Design, and Programming
  Neal Goldstein and Jeff Alger
  An in-depth look at object-oriented programming on the Macintosh.
  352 pages, $24.95, paperback, order #57065

▶ **Writing Localizable Software for the Macintosh®**
  Daniel R. Carter
  A step-by-step guide which opens up international markets to Macintosh software developers.
  352 pages, $24.95, paperback, order #57013

▶ **Programmer's Guide to MPW®, Volume I**
  Exploring the Macintosh® Programmer's Workshop
  Mark Andrews
  Essential guide and reference to the standard Macintosh software development system, MPW.
  608 pages, $26.95, paperback, order #57011

▶ **Elements of C++ Macintosh® Programming**
  Dan Weston
  Teaches the basic elements of C++ programming, concentrating on object-oriented style and syntax.
  512 pages, $22.95, paperback, order #55025

▶ **Programming with MacApp®**
  David A. Wilson, Larry S. Rosenstein, and Dan Shafer
  Hands-on tutorial on everything you need to know about MacApp.
  576 pages, $24.95, paperback, order #09784
  576 pages, $34.95, book/disk, order #55062

▶ **C++ Programming with MacApp®**
  David A. Wilson, Larry S. Rosenstein, and Dan Shafer
  Learn the secrets to unlocking the power of MacApp and C++.
  624 pages, $24.95, paperback, order #57020
  624 pages, $34.95, book/disk, order #57021

Order Number	Quantity	Price	Total

Name _____

Address _____

_____

City/State/Zip _____

Signature (required) _____

TOTAL ORDER _____

___Visa   ___MasterCard   ___AmEx

Account # _____ Exp. Date _____

Shipping and state sales tax will be added automatically.

Credit card orders only please.

Offer good in USA only. Prices and availability subject to change without notice.

Addison-Wesley Publishing Company
Order Department
Route 128
Reading, MA 01867
To order by phone, call (617) 944-3700